Research in Education

Evidence-Based Inquiry

Custom Edition

Taken from:
Research in Education: Evidence-Based Inquiry, Sixth Edition
by James H. McMillan and Sally Schumacher

Cover Art: Courtesy of Photodisc/Getty Images

Taken from:

Research in Education: Evidence-Based Inquiry, Sixth Edition
by James H. McMillan and Sally Schumacher

Published by Allyn & Bacon
Boston, Massachusetts 02116

This special edition published in cooperation with Pearson Custom Publishing.

Printed in the United States of America

10 9 8 7 6 5 4 3 2 1

ISBN 0-536-56747-6

2008220018

SB

Please visit our web site at *www.pearsoncustom.com*

PEARSON CUSTOM PUBLISHING
501 Boylston Street, Suite 900, Boston, MA 02116
A Pearson Education Company

Brief Contents

Contents

Preface

In the last few years, there have been major developments in the field of educational research and evaluation. Most important, empirical research has become essential for making decisions and for forming and changing policies (e.g., data-driven decision making). Educators are now expected to understand and critique studies that can be used as evidence for changing curriculum, instruction, counseling, assessment, and other educational practices. Researchers have more stringent standards for conducting quality research that must be met. At the federal level, legislation related to the 2001 law, No Child Left Behind, and the Education Sciences Reform Act of 2002, has resulted in a new definition of *scientifically based education research*, which is being used pervasively to evaluate and synthesize research and to provide the basis for program evaluation. The sixth edition of *Research in Education: Evidence-Based Inquiry* has been revised to respond to these changes and, at the same time, maintain a balanced emphasis on both quantitative and qualitative methods. Our goal is to provide a comprehensive yet relatively nontechnical introduction to the principles, concepts, and methods currently used in educational research and evaluation.

Students enrolled in their first educational research course typically have two instructional needs. Some plan to do additional work in statistics, research design, qualitative methodologies, and evaluation. In addition to mastering the fundamental principles of research, these students need to develop both an awareness of the breadth of educational research and a broad conceptual base for understanding more technical and advanced aspects of research. Other students, whose immediate career goals lie more in educational practice than in conducting research, need to understand key research terms, gain practice in reading studies critically, know how research designs and procedures may affect empirical findings, and understand applied and evaluation research. *Research in Education* is designed to meet both of these instructional needs.

RATIONALE FOR THE TEXT

Educational research has become more diverse during the past few decades. It is now well established that quantitative, qualitative, and mixed-method inquiry contribute significantly to the field of knowledge in education. Our experience is that by learning about both quantitative and qualitative research and by changing "lenses" when viewing education, students gain a deeper understanding, knowledge, and appreciation for each of these traditions in educational research as well as for mixed-method designs.

NEW AND IMPROVED FEATURES

There are several significant changes in the sixth edition that improve student learning:

- All chapters have undergone substantial revision.
- Four new complete published research articles have been added.
- The number of excerpts from published articles has been increased to 166, from 78 different journals.
- A new chapter has been added on mixed-method designs, secondary data analysis, and action research.
- "Alerts" have been added to emphasize key points.
- "Misconceptions versus Evidence" boxes have been added to show the importance of accurate interpretations of research findings.
- The book's Companion Website has been expanded.
- The design of the book has been improved, including the use of boxes and color.

ORGANIZATION OF THE SIXTH EDITION

The sixth edition is divided into four parts. Part I (Chapters 1 through 4) defines *research* as scientific, evidence-based inquiry that is designed to produce knowledge and to improve educational practice. We briefly introduce quantitative and qualitative research; delineate the functions of basic, applied, and evaluation research; and then describe the limitations of educational research. We present an overview of research designs, techniques, and formats. Selection, formulation, and statements of both quantitative and qualitative problems are discussed and illustrated. The literature review chapter (Chapter 4) includes updated techniques for computer searches, presented in easy-to-follow steps, as well as guidelines for writing literature reviews in quantitative and qualitative research.

Part II (Chapter 5) introduces quantitative designs by presenting fundamental principles of sampling, measurement, and experimental validity. Descriptive statistics are presented to provide a foundation for understanding the more detailed coverage of measurement. Computations are reserved for Appendix B.

Part III (Chapter 6) is an introduction to designing qualitative research, which emphasizes research questions and significance, design, purposeful sampling, and strategies to enhance validity, usefulness, reflexivity, and field work ethics.

Three emerging methodologies are identified in Part IV (Chapter 7): mixed-method designs, secondary data analysis, and action research. These contemporary approaches represent new directions and possibilities.

INSTRUCTIONAL AIDS

In each chapter, we have retained a number of instructional aids to assist students: a concept map at the beginning, a list of key terms, application problems, and criteria for evaluating studies conducted by different methodologies. We believe the instructor, rather than the book, should determine the course objectives and level of student competency. Given that, the book has been organized so that the instructor can emphasize general knowledge, certain methodologies, or specific skills, such as making an annotated bibliography on a topic, writing a critical literature review, developing a preliminary proposal with a problem statement and design, or conducting a small-scale study. We have used numerous approaches to meet different student and programming needs.

The book's Companion Website has been continued in this sixth edition and can be accessed by students at www.ablongman.com/mcmillanschumacher6e. It includes chapter objectives and outlines, application exercises, web links to additional resources, and multiple-choice questions on chapter content. The Instructor's Manual provides course objectives, alternative course organizations, teaching techniques, PowerPoint presentations, and test items for each chapter.

A major instructional aid in this book is the use of excerpts from published studies in all chapters except 1. Excerpts were chosen to represent different disciplines and to be applicable to the practices in a variety of education areas, such as administration, supervision, instruction, special education, early childhood, counseling, adult education, and programs in noneducational agencies. Most of the excerpts have been updated for this edition. The excerpts are especially helpful in gradually introducing students to the style and format of a published article.

ACKNOWLEDGMENTS

Because this book has resulted from a merging of our specializations as researchers and professors, there is no senior author; each author has contributed equally to the book. Many other people also contributed to this endeavor.

We gratefully acknowledge the support of our colleagues, mentors, and friends, who are too numerous to name. We especially thank our master's degree and doctoral candidates, who challenged us to be more explicit. And we thank those individuals who reviewed this book, whose ideas, criticisms, and suggestions helped shape this new edition. The reviewers for the first edition were H. Parker Blount, Georgia State University; Alice Boberg, University of Calgary; David J. Cowden, Western Michigan University; Jane A. Goldman, University of Connecticut; Harry Hsu, University of Pittsburgh; Sylvia T. Johnson, Howard University; Stephen Olejnick, University of Florida; and Robert J. Yonker, Bowling Green State University. The reviewers for the second edition were Gerald W. Bracey, Cherry Creek Schools, Colorado; Jane A. Goldman, University of Connecticut; Harry Hsu, University of Pittsburgh; and Herman W. Meyers, University of Vermont. The reviewers for the third edition were Jane A. Goldman, University of Connecticut; Laura Goodwin, University of Colorado at Denver; James McNamara, Texas A & M University; Bud Meyers, University of Vermont; Anton Netusil, Iowa State University; Ellen Weissinger, University of Nebraska; and Wen-Ke Wang, National Changhua Normal University in Taiwan. Reviewers for the fourth edition included Laura Goodwin, University of Colorado at Denver; Judith A. Kennison, Ithaca College; Anton Netusil, Iowa State University; and Ellen Weissinger, University of Nebraska. The fifth edition reviewers included David Anderson, Salisbury State University; Shann Ferch, Gonzaga University; Brian Hinrichs, Illinois State University; Daniel Robinson, University of Louisville; David Tan, University of Oklahoma; and James Webb, Kent State University.

We are indebted to our thoughtful reviewers for the sixth edition: Florence A. Hamrick, Iowa State University; James R. Martindale, University of Virginia Health System; Stephen K. Miller, University of Louisville; and Susan Mulvaney, California State University at Long Beach.

Although some of the chapter reorganization of this edition is new, we hope that it facilitates teaching and learning. We would appreciate receiving comments and suggestions from colleagues and students as we gather material for the seventh edition. Feel free to contact us by e-mail (jmcmillan@vcu.edu).

We especially appreciate the continued guidance and support of our Senior Editor, Arnis Burvikovs, and Senior Development Editor, Virginia Blanford. We also appreciate the special assistance that Donna Simons, Kelly Hopkins, Megan Smallidge, and Audry

Stein, all from Allyn and Bacon, provided during the revision and production phases. Special recognition is given to Donna Jovanovich for revising and expanding the Companion Website, which was done by Jeff Oescher for earlier editions, and to Rich Mohn for proofreading the website content. Finally, our families—Donald F. X. and Marcia Schumacher and Janice McMillan—have provided continued encouragement for this exciting, if at times difficult, undertaking.

James H. McMillan
Sally Schumacher

RESEARCH IN EDUCATION

PART I

FUNDAMENTAL PRINCIPLES OF EDUCATIONAL RESEARCH

What is scientific, evidence-based inquiry? Are there guiding principles for conducting a research study? Educators who are unfamiliar with scientific methods frequently ask these questions. They may also ask, Why are research results considered more useful in making decisions than the experience and advice of others? How does research influence educational practice? What kinds of studies are done in education? Is there a systematic way to evaluate a research article?

Chapters 1 and 2 answer these questions by providing an introduction to the field of educational research, an overview of research designs, and an explanation of the formats of quantitative and qualitative research journal articles. This introduction will familiarize readers with basic terminology and fundamental concepts of research. *All* research begins with a problem statement and requires a literature review. Chapter 3 explains how to recognize, state, and evaluate a research problem. How should a problem be stated in order to be useful in planning a study? What should a problem statement convey to the reader? How are problem statements evaluated? Chapter 4 shows how related literature is used to enhance a study. Why is a literature review important? What sources are available for conducting a literature review? How does one conduct a computer search of the literature, given that much of it is now contained in online databases? How is a literature review organized and evaluated?

Together, these four chapters present basic principles of research that students need to understand to conduct, read, and analyze different types of research and methodologies. Subsequent parts of this text will discuss in greater detail the designs and procedures for specific methodologies.

CHAPTER

1 Introduction to Evidence-Based Inquiry

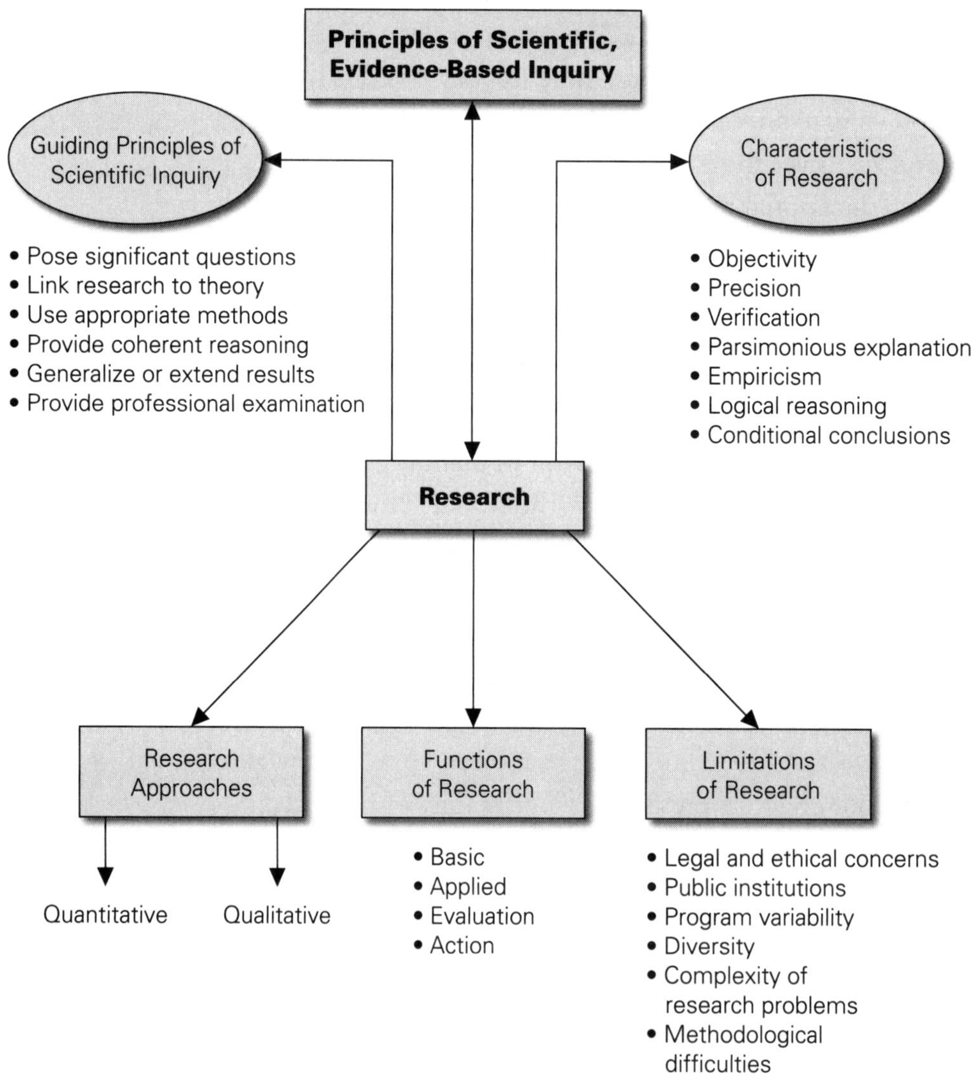

KEY TERMS

replication
evidence-based inquiry
generalization
research
research methods
objectivity
verification
explanation
empirical
data
basic research
theory
applied research
evaluation research
action research

The times we live in are truly amazing in terms of the possibilities for educational research! Powerful tools have been afforded us through the variety of technology and research methods that have been refined throughout the last half century. These tools and methods allow us to address challenging questions and to have greater confidence that our results will be valid and useful. More important, there is a renewed interest at all levels of education for decisions to be data driven and based on hard evidence. This has resulted in a greater need for all educators to understand, conduct, and use research findings.

This chapter introduces educational research by describing the development of knowledge to improve educational practices. Educational research is guided by six principles of scientific, evidence-based inquiry that are applied to both quantitative and qualitative research approaches. Educators and other professionals use basic, applied, evaluation, and action research for different purposes, and some features of education limit scientific studies of educational phenomena.

Most important, Chapter 1 introduces the language and the logic of research used in reading and conducting studies. A brief example of Misconception vs. Evidence appears in most but not all chapters to illuminate how evidence-based knowledge can be misinterpreted or misused.

EDUCATIONAL RESEARCH IN THE TWENTY-FIRST CENTURY

For the foreseeable future, the nature of educational research will be strongly influenced by federal policies. The newly formed Institute of Education Sciences (IES) provides leadership in expanding scientific knowledge and understanding of education from early childhood through postsecondary study. The IES's mission is one of "building evidence-based education" that supports learning and improves academic achievement and access to educational opportunities for all students (see www.ed.gov/about/offices/list/ies/index.html).

Evidence-based studies recently published in professional journals illustrate the variety of topics that interest educators and the public. Consider these examples:

Burko, H., Wolf, S. A., Simmone, S., & Uchiyama, K. P. (2003). Schools in transition: Reform efforts and school capacity in Washington state. *Educational Evaluation and Policy Analysis, 25*(2), 171–201.

Dieker, L. A., McTigue, A., Campbell, G., Rodrequez, J., Savage, M., & Jackson-Tomas, A. (2003). Voices from the field: Teachers from culturally and linguistically diverse backgrounds entering the profession through alternative certification. *Teacher Education and Special Education, 26*(4), 328–340.

Drummond, K. V., & Stipek, D. (2004). Low-income parents' beliefs about their role in children's academic learning. *Elementary School Journal, 104*(3), 197–214.

Farkas, R. D. (2003). Effects of traditional versus learning-styles instructional methods on middle school students. *Journal of Educational Research, 97*(1), 42–51.

Frykholm, J. (2004). Teachers' tolerance for discomfort: Implications for curricular reform in mathematics. *Journal of Curriculum and Supervision, 19*(2), 125–149.

Harrington, T. E., & Pourdavood, R. G. (2002). Exploring the evolving nature of three elementary preservice teachers' beliefs and practices: Three parallel case studies. *Focus on Learning Problems in Mathematics, 24*(1), 45–64.

Honig, M. I. (2003). Building policy from practice: District central office administrator's roles and capacity for implementing collaborative education policy. *Educational Administration Quarterly, 39*(3), 292–338.

Lewis, A. E. (2001). There is not "race" in the school-yard: Color-blind ideology in an (almost) all-white school. *American Educational Research Journal, 38,* 781–811.

Meier, K. J., & Wilkins, V. M. (2002). Gender differences in agency head salaries: The case of public education. *Public Administration Review, 62*(4), 405–412.

Morris, D., Bloodgood, J., & Perney, J. (2003). Kindergarten predictors of first- and second-grade reading achievement. *Elementary School Journal, 104*(2), 93–110.

Preston, J. A. (2003). "He lives as a *Master*"; Seventeenth-century masculinity, gendered teaching, and careers of New England schoolmasters. *History of Education Quarterly, 43*(3), 350–371.

Windschitle, M., & Sahl, K. (2002). Tracing teachers' use of technology in a laptop computer school: The interplay of teacher beliefs, social dynamics, and institutional culture. *American Educational Research Journal, 39,* 165–205.

Why Is Educational Research Important?

Why has educational research become a valuable source of information? We suggest six reasons for the importance of evidence-based inquiry.

First, *educators are constantly trying to understand educational processes and must make professional decisions*. These professional decisions have immediate and long-range effects on others: students, teachers, parents, and, ultimately, our communities and nation. How do educators acquire an understanding to make decisions? Most of us tend to rely on several sources, including personal experience, expert opinion, tradition, intuition, common sense, and beliefs about what is right or wrong. Each of these sources is legitimate in some situations, yet in other situations, each source may be inadequate as the only basis for making decisions.

Second, *noneducational policy groups, such as state and federal legislatures and courts, have increasingly mandated changes in education*. How do policy groups acquire their views of education and obtain their information about schools and instruction? Most policy-makers prefer to have research-based information relevant to the specific policy issue. Many state legislatures mandate state education departments to conduct studies on state educational policies. Both federal and state departments of education also commission funded studies. Researchers are increasingly being asked to work on complex problems in highly politicized environments.

Third, *concerned public, professional, and private groups and foundations have increased their research activities*. Professional educational associations, teacher labor unions, Parent-Teacher Associations, and foundations such as the National Science Foundation have conducted or commissioned studies on topics of special concern to the organization.

Fourth, *reviews of prior research have interpreted accumulated empirical evidence*. For example, studies on retention indicate that retaining a child in a grade serves few educational purposes. Other research reviews have addressed such topics as thinking aloud and reading comprehension; hypermedia and learner comprehension, control, and style; why parents become involved in their children's education; parameters of affirmative action in education; teacher efficacy; the effects of single-sex and co-educational schooling on social, emotional, and academic development; and teacher occupational stress, burnout, and health. Other research reviews identify areas of needed research.

Fifth, *educational research is readily available*. Research about educational practices is found in professional and research journals, funding agencies' published reports, books, library databases, newspapers, television, and the Internet. Although the quality of the research may vary with the specific source, educational research is very accessible.

Sixth, *many educators who are not full-time researchers conduct studies to guide their decisions and to serve as efforts in classroom, school, and system accountability*. Teachers can conduct action research that is relevant for their needs and for the issues about which they feel passionately, such as second-language students, students with disabilities, and teaching approaches in school subjects. Educators often collaborate to conduct research and to form partnerships in projects. Seemingly insignificant findings can add to the current body of evidence in the search for answers to important educational questions. Furthermore, all educators must be able to demonstrate effectiveness in an age of accountability. Educators also need to interpret results accurately and to be responsible in their use of research findings. Evidence-based inquiry provides valid information and knowledge about education that can be used to make informed decisions.

Because research systematically describes or measures phenomena, it is a better source of knowledge than one's own experiences, beliefs, traditions, or intuition alone. Some studies are abstract and provide general information about common educational practices and policies; this type of research influences the way one thinks about education. Other studies provide detailed information about specific practices at particular sites, such as a school, a classroom, or a program; this type of research can be used immediately to improve or justify a specific practice.

Developing Knowledge to Improve Educational Practices

The impact of educational research on schools and policy-makers seeking to improve educational practices may be seen as a process. Figure 1.1 shows the five phases of the process of developing evidence-based knowledge to improve educational practices: (1) identification of research problems, (2) empirical studies, (3) replications, (4) research synthesis and review, and (5) practitioner adoption and evaluation. The [identification of research problems] (Phase 1) begins with determining valued outcomes. Practical fields, like education, are concerned with valued outcomes such as learning. Research questions and problems come from the following sources: common observation, practical wisdom, policy controversies, prior research, and new methods applied in the study of education. Researchers conduct evidenced-based studies (Phase 2), and then they attempt research **replication**[1] (Phase 3) with different subjects and in a variety of settings and circumstances. In research synthesis and review (Phase 4) comparable studies are systematically evaluated and statistically or narratively summarized. Such an analysis helps to organize and make sense of the overall findings of prior research. Thus, the preponderance of evidence from many careful studies, rather than a few exact replications of the original research,

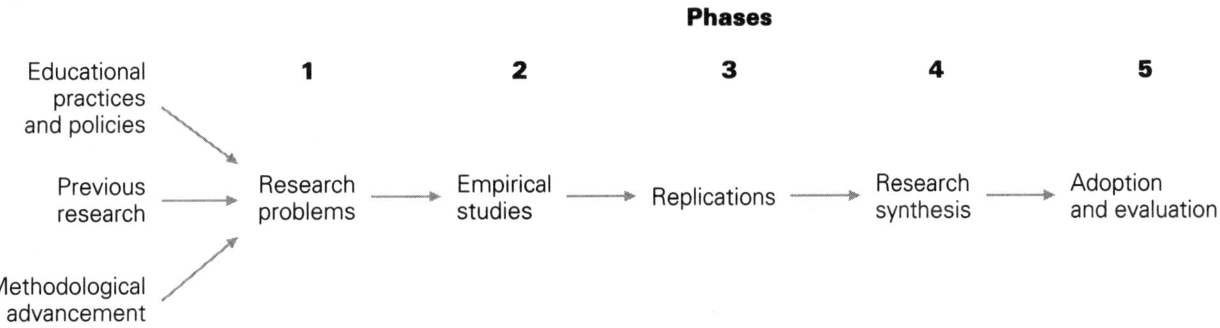

FIGURE 1.1 **Development of Evidence-Based Knowledge to Improve Educational Practice**

builds an evidence-based body of knowledge in education. Practitioners and policy-makers can reasonably accept the implications of research findings that are consistent without harmful side effects. Continuing local evaluation (Phase 5) is the final phase in the process.

To illustrate the potential impact of evidence-based research on educational outcomes, here are some examples of practices that were found to be effective, or "what works" (National Center for Educational Evaluation and Regional Assistance, 2003):

- ***One-on-one tutoring by qualified tutors for at-risk readers in grades 1–3*** The average tutored student read more proficiently than approximately 75 percent of the untutored students in the control group.
- ***Life-skills training for junior high students*** Implementing a low-cost, replicable program reduced smoking by 20 percent and serious level of substance abuse by 30 percent by students' senior year compared to the control group.
- ***Reducing class size in grades K–3*** On average, students in small classes scored higher on the Stanford Achievement Test in reading/math than 60 percent of the students in regular-sized classes.
- ***Instruction for early readers in phonemic awareness and phonics*** The average student in these interventions read more proficiently than approximately 70 percent of the students in the control group.

Clearly, the federal emphasis is on supporting a new generation of rigorous research.

The National Center for Educational Evaluation and Regional Assistance (NCEE) was established as part of the IES's goal to focus on evidence-based program effectiveness and impact questions. The NCEE recently initiated several program effectiveness studies in the following areas: preschool reading, reading instruction in the primary grades, teacher preparation, professional development, educational technology, remedial reading, after-school programs, English-language learning, and charter schools. All of these nationally funded evaluation studies provide either two or three years to address the bottom-line question of causality: Did Program X raise student achievement? The NCEE supports only those studies that can provide credible scientific evidence. The results of these studies will be widely disseminated in scholarly and professional journals.

RESEARCH AS SCIENTIFIC, EVIDENCE-BASED INQU IRY

Conducting research is a relatively new activity in the history of education, just as the concept of providing a free public education for all children is relatively modern in the history of humanity. In the early centuries, before reading and writing were common, individuals developed knowledge of the world around them primarily by two means. The first was through one's own personal experiences along with observation of others' experiences. Collective wisdom was conveyed as a series of detailed stories of people and events. Stories provided an understanding, a repertoire of wisdom from which one could extrapolate or apply known experience to an unknown area and thus form reasonable expectations.

Knowledge was also developed in another manner: by measuring or quantifying human activities using numbers. The early units of measure and scale had very practical purposes: to measure in a reliable manner the length of a day or the distance one walked. A mile was a mile, whether it was on flat, soft sand or on rocky, hard terrain. If these measurements were reliable, one also could measure segments of natural laws that caused events to be orderly and predictable.

Different kinds of evidence-based knowledge are needed in education. Two traditional approaches have been formalized as the quantitative and qualitative modes of inquiry. To the reader, the most obvious distinction between these two research approaches is the form of data presentation. Quantitative research presents statistical results using numbers; qualitative research presents data as a narration with words. These two research methods, however, are distinguished by far more than this obvious difference, which will be explained later in the chapter.

Guiding Principles of Scientific, Evidence-Based Inquiry

Education is a highly contested field of inquiry for two reasons: Values play a central role, and an educational intervention, when extensively investigated, seldom has only one main effect. Both positive and negative unintended consequences are often important. The accumulation of scientific knowledge over time is circuitous and indirect. Making a judgment on the effectiveness of a treatment is complex and requires a myriad of considerations.

The National Research Council (NRC) recently convened a committee of scholars to address two questions of interest to educators: "What constitutes 'scientifically based' research of educational phenomena?" and "Is scientifically based research the only or the best approach to studies which are meaningful in education?" (Eisenhart & Towne, 2003). Although the NRC's report, *Scientific Research in Education* (2002), focused on the first question, much of the subsequent public and academic debate addressed both questions.

To address the first question, some modifications must be made regarding the profound impact of the academic disciplines' standards for research rigor. What comprises rigorous research principles is somewhat different in each of the disciplines. Moreover, among the disciplines, there are variations in designs and methods, both in the process of conducting a study and in the rigor of the criteria. **Evidence-based inquiry** is the search for knowledge using systematically gathered empirical data. Unlike opinion or ideology, evidence-based inquiry is conducted and reported in such a way that the logical reasoning can be painstakingly examined. The term *evidence-based* does not refer to ritualization and using narrow forms of investigation, nor does it necessarily refer to following formal procedures. A study is evidence based when investigators have anticipated the traditional questions that are pertinent and instituted techniques to avoid bias at each step of data collection and reasoning. If the errors or biases cannot be eliminated, investigators discuss the potential effects of these issues in their conclusions.

Scientific inquiry, including educational research, is guided by six principles (National Research Council, 2002). Each is briefly explained in a following section with certain modifications, some of which were reflected in scholarly reviews of the report (Erickson & Gutierrez, 2002; St. Pierre, 2002). It is important to note that these principles are not absolute; they can serve only as guides when applied to education.

Guiding Principle 1: Pose Significant Questions That Can Be Investigated Empirically

The quality of a posed question often determines whether a study will eventually have an impact on the current state of knowledge. A question may be investigated to fill a gap in prior knowledge, to seek new knowledge, to identify the cause or causes of some phenomenon, or to formally test a hypothesis. A good question may reframe a prior research problem in light of newly available methodological or theoretical tools. The significance of a question can be established by citing prior research, relevant theory, and important claims regarding practice or policy. A question may even be articulated at the end of a study, when the researcher has a better understanding of the phenomenon.

Guiding Principle 2: Link Research to a Relevant Theory or Conceptual Framework

Much of scientific inquiry is linked, either explicitly or implicitly, to some overarching theory or conceptual framework that guides the entire research process. Sometimes, the conceptual framework is not formally stated but is easily recognized by the community of scholars working in the particular discipline. For example, the concept of *culture* provides a framework for anthropologists, just as the notion of *group* or *community* often frames the work of sociologists. Theory enters the research process in two important ways. First, scientific research is usually guided by a conceptual framework or theory that suggests possible questions or answers to questions posed. In a second, more subtle way, a conceptual framework influences the research process in the selection of what and how to observe

TABLE 1.1 Guiding Principles of Scientific, Evidence-Based Inquiry

1. Pose significant questions that can be investigated empirically.
2. Link research to a relevant theory or conceptual framework.
3. Use methods that allow direct investigation of the research question.
4. Provide a coherent and explicit chain of reasoning.
5. Replicate/generalize or extend across studies.
6. Disclose research to encourage professional scrutiny and critique.

Adapted from National Research Council (2002). *Scientific research in education.* Committee on Scientific Principles for Education Research. Shavelson, R. J., and Town, L., Eds. Center for Education, Division of Behavioral and Social Sciences and Education. Washington, D.C.: National Academy Press.

(i.e., methodological choice). Thus, the conceptual framework or theory drives the research question, the use of methods, and the interpretation of results (see Table 1.1).

Guiding Principle 3: Use Methods That Allow Direct Investigation of the Research Question A method can only be judged in terms of its appropriateness and effectiveness in undertaking a particular research question. Scientific claims are strengthened when they are tested by multiple methods. Specific research designs and methods are best suited to specific types of questions and can rarely illuminate all the questions and issues in a given line of inquiry. Very different methodological approaches must often be used in different parts of a series of related studies.

Debates about the merits of various methods, especially quantitative versus qualitative, have raged for years. Simply stated, the method used to conduct scientific research must fit the question posed, and the link between question and method must be clearly explained and justified. Fortunately, a wide range of legitimate methods is available.

Guiding Principle 4: Provide a Coherent and Explicit Chain of Reasoning A logical chain of reasoning, which proceeds from evidence to conclusions, is coherent, shareable, and persuasive to the skeptical reader. The validity of inferences made through this process is strengthened by identifying limitations and biases, estimating uncertainty and error, and systematically ruling out other plausible explanations in a rational, convincing way. Detailed descriptions of procedures and analyses are crucial.

Most rigorous research—quantitative and qualitative—embraces the same underlying logic of inference. Nonetheless, the nature of the chain of reasoning will vary depending on the design, which will, in turn, vary depending on the question being investigated.

Guiding Principle 5: Replicate/Generalize or Extend across Studies Scientific inquiry emphasizes checking and validating individual findings. However, the role of contextual factors and the lack of control that exists in social settings make replication difficult. In both social sciences and education, many generalizations are limited to particular times and places. And because the social world changes more rapidly than the physical world, social generalizations usually have shorter life spans than generalizations in the physical world.

Some quantitative research aims at replication and generalization. **Generalization,** in research, is the extent to which the results of one study can be used as knowledge about other populations and situations. For instance, the findings of one quantitative study may also describe the current status of another group and its members' opinions, beliefs, and actions. The goal of most qualitative research, however, is to illuminate what is unique and to understand the particulars of a specific situation (i.e., case) in all its complexity. A body of scientific knowledge is built through the *logical extension* of findings, rather than through the *statistical generalization* of such information. The term *extension of findings* (sometimes used synonymously with *analytical synthesis*, *extrapolation*, *transferability*, or *assertion)* means that others can use the information to understand similar situations and can apply the information in subsequent research. Knowledge is produced not by replication but by the preponderance of evidence found in separate case studies over time.

Guiding Principle 6: Disclose Research to Encourage Professional Scrutiny and Critique Scientific research does not contribute to a larger body of knowledge until its findings have been widely disseminated and undergone professional scrutiny by peers. The intellectual debate at professional meetings, in collaborative projects, and in other situations provides a forum by which scientific knowledge is refined and accepted. A collaborative, public critique is a sign of the health of scientific inquiry.

No single study or series of related studies can satisfy all six of the guiding principles. A single study may adhere to each principle in varying degree, and the extent to which it does assists in gauging its scientific quality. The features of education and of educational research, in combination with the guiding principles of science, set the boundaries for the design of a study. The design per se does not make the study scientific. A wide variety of legitimate scientific designs are available for educational research, ranging from experiments to in-depth qualitative case studies (National Research Council, 2002). To be scientific, the design must allow empirical (i.e., evidence-based) investigation of an important question, suggest appropriate methods for exploring the question, account for the context in which the study occurred, utilize a conceptual framework, demonstrate a chain of logical reasoning, and disclose results to encourage professional examination.

Definition of Research

Briefly defined, **research** is the systematic process of collecting and logically analyzing data for some purpose. This definition is general because many methods are available to investigate a problem or question. While educational research is not limited to the approaches used in the physical and natural sciences, the word *research* should not be used indiscriminately to describe what is actually casual observation and speculation. **Research methods** (sometimes called *methodology*) are the ways in which one collects and analyzes data. These methods have been developed for acquiring knowledge by reliable and valid procedures. Data collection may be done with measurement techniques, extensive interviews and observations, or a set of documents.

Research methodology is systematic and purposeful. Procedures are not haphazard; they are planned to yield data on a particular research problem. In a broader context, the term *methodology* refers to a design whereby the researcher selects data collection and analysis procedures to investigate a specific research problem.

The Characteristics of Educational Research

The following characteristics are common to many types of evidence-based research conducted in education: objective, precise, verifiable, explanatory, empirical, logical, and conditional. Taken together, these characteristics describe the nature of research (see Table 1.2):

1. ***Objectivity*** Objectivity is both a procedure and a characteristic. To the lay person, objectivity means unbiased, open-minded, not subjective. As a procedure, **objectivity** refers to data collection and analysis procedures from which a reasonable interpretation can be made. Objectivity refers to the quality of the data produced by procedures that either control for bias or take into account subjectivity.

2. ***Precision*** Technical language is used in research to convey exact meanings. Expressions such as *validity* and *reliability* in measurement, *research design*, *random sample*, and *statistical significance* convey technical procedures. Other phrases, such as *constant*

TABLE 1.2 Characteristics of Educational Research

Characteristics	Quantitative	Qualitative
Objectivity	Explicit description of data collection and analysis procedures	Explicit description of data collection and analysis procedures
Precision	Measurement and statistics	Detailed description of phenomenon
Verification	Results replicated by others	Extension of understandings by others
Parsimonious explanation	Least complicated explanation preferred	Summary statements
Empiricism	Numerical data	Narrative
Logical reasoning	Primarily deductive	Primarily inductive
Conditional conclusions	Statements of statistical probability	Tentative summary interpretations

comparison and *reflexivity*, refer to strategies in qualitative inquiry. Precise language describes the study accurately so that the study may be replicated or extended and the results may be used correctly.

3. ***Verification*** To develop knowledge, a single study attempts to be designed and presented in such a manner to allow **verification**—that is, the results can be confirmed or revised in subsequent research. Results are verified in different ways, depending on the purpose of the original study. If the research tests a theory, then further testing with other groups or in other settings could confirm or revise the theory. Most qualitative studies, however, provide descriptive interpretations about the selected situation or case. These interpretations are extended but not replicated in subsequent research of other similar situations for revision. Qualitative research is not verified in the same manner nor to the same degree as quantitative research.

4. ***Parsimonious explanation*** Research attempts to explain relationships among phenomena and to reduce the **explanation** to simple statements. The theory "Frustration leads to aggression" is an explanation that predicts, and it can be tested for verification. The summary generalization "Teacher learning and curriculum change cannot be isolated from the social situations in which the curriculum is implemented" (Tobin & LaMaster, 1995) is an explanation that can be investigated further. The ultimate aim of research is thus to reduce complex realities to simple explanations.[2]

5. ***Empiricism*** Research is characterized by a strong empirical attitude and approach. The word *empirical* has both lay and technical meanings. The lay meaning of *empirical* is that which is guided by practical experience, not by research. According to this pragmatic perspective, if it works, it is right; regardless of the reasons, it must be right because it works. To the researcher, **empirical** means guided by evidence obtained from systematic research methods rather than by opinions or authorities. Generally, an empirical attitude requires a temporary suspension of personal experience and beliefs. Critical elements in research are evidence and logical interpretations based on the evidence.

To a researcher, evidence is **data,** that is, results obtained from research from which interpretations or conclusions are drawn. In a general sense, the terms *data, sources,* and *evidence* are used synonymously, to mean information obtained by research methods. Test scores and computer printouts, field notes and interview records, artifacts and historical documents are all called *data*.

6. ***Logical reasoning*** All research requires logical reasoning. Reasoning is a thinking process, using prescribed rules of logic, in which one proceeds from a general statement to the specific conclusion (deduction) or, the reverse, from specific statements to a summary generalization (induction). Both kinds of reasoning are employed in the research process, regardless of the type of design or method being used.

7. ***Conditional conclusions*** One misconception of research is that the results are absolute. This is incorrect. As noted by a leading educational researcher, "Behavioral science and research does not offer certainty. (Neither does natural science!) It does not even offer relative certainty. All it offers is probabilistic knowledge. If A is done, then B will probably occur" (Kerlinger, 1979, p. 28). One way of defining *research* might be to say that it is a method of reducing uncertainty. The social sciences have more uncertainty than the physical sciences.

Drawing conditional conclusions is central to research. All scientific research contains restricted interpretations. Both quantitative and qualitative research statements have implicit or explicit conditional conclusions. Researchers thus often write that their results "tend to indicate" or "are suggestive."

The Research Process

The research process typically involves several phases. These phases are not always sequential nor are they an orderly step-by-step process. Research is more an interactive process between the researcher and the logic of the problem, design, and interpretations. Here is a summary of the process, with variations noted (see Figure 1.2):

1. ***Select a general problem.*** The problem defines the area of education in which research will be conducted, such as instruction, administration, adult education, or special education.

2. ***Review the literature on the problem.*** The most important literature is prior research and theory, but other literature may be useful. In some studies, an exhaustive

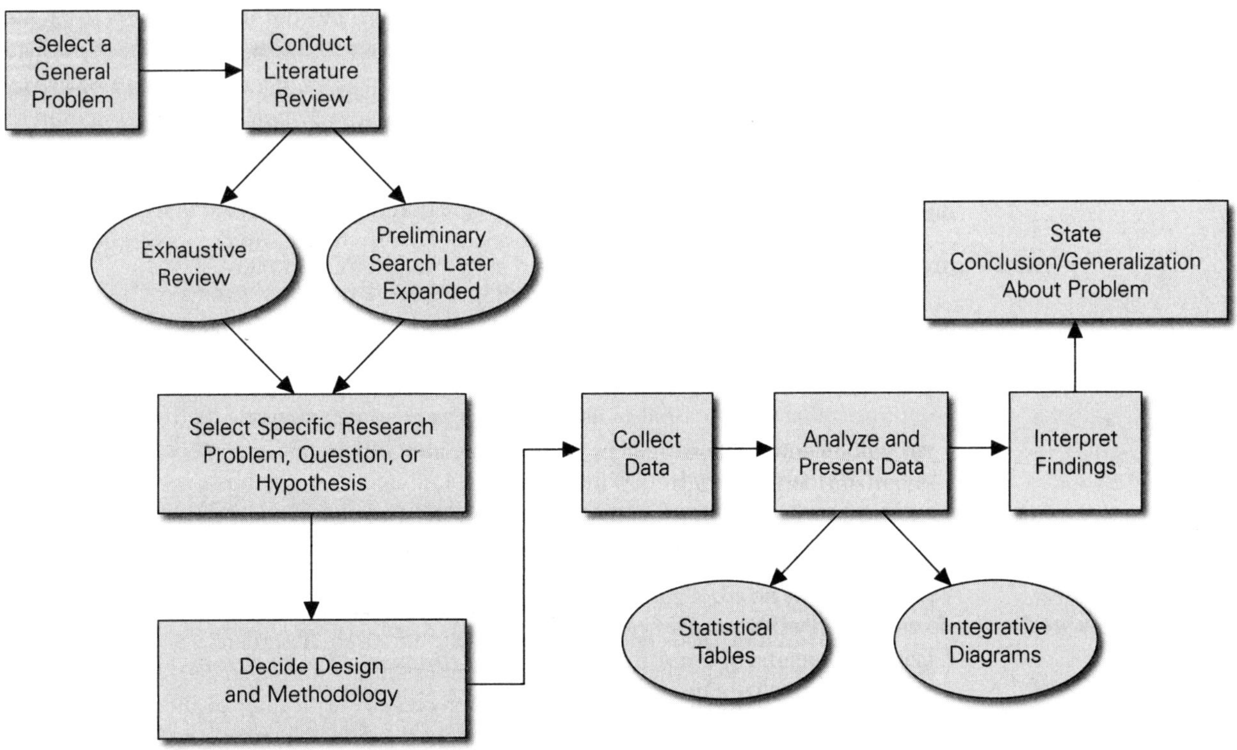

FIGURE 1.2 **The Research Process**

literature review is done before one collects data. In other studies, the literature review is tentative and preliminary before data collection and then expanded as data are collected.

3. ***Decide the specific research problem, question, or hypothesis.*** This requires the investigator to select whether a quantitative or qualitative mode of inquiry is appropriate for the research problem. If a qualitative approach is selected, the research problem or question is a preliminary guide and will become more specific as the research progresses.

4. ***Determine the design and methodology.*** The researcher decides from whom data will be collected, how the subjects will be selected, and how data will be collected.

5. ***Collect data.*** Ethical and legal concerns regarding data collection and analysis must also be resolved.

6. ***Analyze data and present the results.*** Usually, summary visual representations are used, such as statistical tables and integrative diagrams.

7. ***Interpret the findings and state conclusions or a summary regarding the problem.*** Decisions are made about the reporting format appropriate for the purpose of the study and the intended audience or readers. The research process may be relatively short, or it may take several years or longer.

The inquiry process is essentially one of reflection. Each decision made by the researcher is reported explicitly, often with a rationale for the choice. It is an exciting intellectual process, one that uses different skills in the various phases.

QUANTITATIVE AND QUALITATIVE RESEARCH APPROACHES

As noted earlier, the terms *quantitative* and *qualitative* are used frequently to identify different modes of inquiry or approaches to research. The terms can be defined on two levels of discourse. At one level, quantitative and qualitative refer to distinctions about the nature of knowledge: how one understands the world and the ultimate purpose of the research. On another level of discourse, the terms refer to research methods—how data are collected and analyzed—and the types of generalizations and representations derived from the data.

Both quantitative and qualitative research studies are conducted in education. Purists suggest that quantitative and qualitative research methods are based on different assumptions about the world, the research purpose, research methods, prototypical studies, the researcher role, and the importance of context in the study (Denzin & Lincoln, 2000) (see Table 1.3):

1. ***Assumptions about the world*** Quantitative research is usually based on some form of *logical positivism*, which assumes there are stable, social facts with a *single reality*, separated from the feelings and beliefs of individuals. Qualitative research is based more on *constructionism*, which assumes *multiple realities* are socially constructed through individual and collective perceptions or views of the same situation.

2. ***Research purpose*** Quantitative research seeks to establish relationships and explain *causes* of changes in measured social facts. Qualitative research is more concerned with *understanding* the social phenomenon from the participants' perspectives. This occurs through the researcher's participation to some degree in the life of those persons while in a research role.

3. ***Research methods and process*** In quantitative studies, there is an established set of procedures and steps that guide the researcher. In qualitative studies, there is greater flexibility in both the strategies and the research process. Typically, a qualitative researcher uses an *emergent design* and revises decisions about the data collection strategies during the study. In contrast, quantitative researchers choose methods as part of a *pre-established design* before data collection.

TABLE 1.3 Quantitative and Qualitative Research Approaches

Orientation	Quantitative	Qualitative
Assumptions about the world	A single reality, i.e., measured by an instrument	Multiple realities, e.g., interviews of principal, teachers, and students about a social situation
Research purpose	Establish relationships between measured variables	Understanding a social situation from participants' perspectives
Research methods and process	Procedures (sequential steps) are established before study begins	Flexible, changing strategies; design emerges as data are collected
Prototypical study (clearest example)	Experimental design to reduce error and bias	Ethnography using "disciplined subjectivity"
Researcher role	Detached with use of instrument	Prepared person becomes immersed in social situation
Importance of context	Goal of universal context-free generalizations	Goal of detailed context-bound summary statements

4. ***Prototypical studies*** The quantitative researcher employs *experimental* or *correlational* designs to reduce error, bias, and extraneous variables. The prototypical qualitative study of ongoing events is an *ethnography*, which helps readers understand the multiple perspectives of the social scene or system by the persons studied. Whereas quantitative research seeks to control for bias through design, qualitative research seeks to take into account subjectivity in data analysis and interpretation.

5. ***Researcher role*** The ideal quantitative researcher is *detached* from the study to avoid bias. Qualitative researchers become *immersed* in the situation and the phenomenon being studied. For example, qualitative researchers assume interactive social roles in which they record observations and interviews with participants in a range of contexts. Qualitative scholars emphasize the importance of data collected by a skilled, prepared *person* in contrast to an *instrument*. Qualitative research is noted for "disciplined subjectivity" (Erickson, 1973) and "reflexivity" (Mason, 1996), that is, critical self-examination of the researcher's role throughout the entire research process.

6. ***Importance of the context in the study*** Most quantitative research attempts to establish *universal, context-free generalizations*. The qualitative researcher believes that human actions are strongly influenced by the settings in which they occur. The researcher cannot understand human behavior without understanding the framework within which subjects interpret their thoughts, feelings, and actions. This framework or context is noted by the qualitative researcher during data collection and analysis. Qualitative research develops *context-bound* summaries.

Many of these distinctions between quantitative and qualitative research are not absolute when one conducts research or reads a completed study. Experienced researchers can and do combine both quantitative and qualitative research methods in a single study in order to investigate a particular research problem (see Chapter 7). However, combining both approaches in a single study is more difficult than it may appear (Tashakkori & Teddlie, 1998). The distinctions, however, are useful devices in an introduction to research for describing and understanding research methods, a goal of this textbook.

THE FUNCTIONS OF RESEARCH: BASIC, APPLIED, EVALUATION, AND ACTION

The purpose of research is based on the anticipated use of its findings. Basic, applied, evaluation, and action research differ essentially in the degree to which they facilitate decision making.[3] They do not differ, however, in terms of being evidence based. Most studies are designed and judged as adequate for one type of research and as less adequate for other types of research.

Basic Research

The exclusive purpose of **basic research** (sometimes called *pure* or *fundamental research*) is to know and explain through testing specific theories that provide broad generalizations. A **theory** predicts and explains a natural phenomenon. Instead of explaining each specific behavior of adults, for example, the scientist seeks general explanations that link different behaviors. Noted scholar Fred N. Kerlinger (1986) defines a *theory* as a set of interrelated constructs and propositions that specify relations among variables to explain and predict phenomena. By explaining which variables relate to which other variables and how, the scientist can make predictions. For instance, if one can predict from variable A (say, test anxiety) to variable B (test performance), then one can deduce the possibility of control through intervention with, say, instruction on test-taking skills.

A theory may or may not have empirical support. When a theory has considerable empirical support, it is called a *scientific law*. A scientific law such as the law of gravity is generalizable—that is, it explains many individual cases.

Basic research is not designed to solve social problems. The scientist is preoccupied with developing knowledge but is not required to spell out the practical implications of his or her work. Both goals usually cannot be achieved by a single study. Basic research, after considerable time, can indirectly influence the ways people think and perceive phenomena. Much valuable social science research, however, is *not* specifically theory oriented. While having modest, limited, and specific aims is good, formulating and verifying theories is better because theories are more general and explanatory.

Applied Research

Applied research is conducted in a field of common practice and is concerned with the application and development of research-based knowledge about that practice. Medicine, engineering, social work, and education are all applied fields. Applied research (as opposed to basic research) produces knowledge relevant to providing solutions to general problems. In other words, applied studies focus on research problems common to a given field.

In the field of education, applied research usually focuses on problems that need to be solved to improve practice. To the extent that general theories are tested, the results may be generalized to many different educational settings. For example, basic theories of human memory, developed through basic research, could be tested in a new curriculum to discern improved retention of science concepts. Other examples of applied research in education are studies that compare different teaching styles, identify characteristics of effective schools, and examine the effects of lengthening the schoolday on student achievement. Educational research thus focuses on knowledge about *educational* theories and practices, rather than on *universal* knowledge.

Because applied research usually investigates problems that are integral to making decisions, its impact may be immediate. Depending on the topic of study, applied research also may have an indirect effect over time by influencing how practitioners think about and perceive common problems.

Evaluation Research

Evaluation research focuses on a particular practice at a given site. The practice may be a program, a product, or a process, but the site is crucial. Evaluation research assesses the *merit* and *worth* of a particular practice in terms of the values operating at the site. Evaluation determines whether the practice works—that is, Does it do what is intended at the site? Evaluation also determines whether the practice is worth the associated costs of development, implementation, and widespread adoption. Those costs may involve materials, space, staff development, teacher morale, and/or community support.

Evaluation focuses first on the concerns and issues related to the practice at a given site. Such studies can add to existing knowledge about a specific practice and stimulate further research and methodological development. For example, a series of evaluative studies on a particular practice at diverse sites, such as Title IV (Head Start) classrooms, or on the change process within a large organization can add to existing knowledge in the applied field.

Action Research

Action research involves the use of research methods by practitioners to study current problems or issues. Teachers conduct these studies or play important roles in the research process. Action research may focus on three levels: individual teacher research, research by teams in a single school or department, and schoolwide research. Because the focus is on a solution to common issues or everyday concerns in classrooms or a school, the results of action research tend to be localized. Rigorous research control is not essential, and both quantitative and qualitative research approaches may be used.

A more recent variation is *collaborative action research* (Oja & Smulyan, 1989; Stinger, 1996; Stringer, 2004), in which practitioners conduct the inquiry with the help of a consultant. For example, teachers may work with university-based researchers in their classrooms doing participatory research. Collaborative action research usually focuses on both the processes and the outcomes of a change strategy, such as a staff development program.

Many aspects of action research are similar to those of the qualitative approach. Often, both numerical data and qualitative data are used. Important elements of action research include (1) making a time commitment, (2) viewing collaboration as valuing each person's contribution and level of engagement, (3) developing trusting relationships, (4) appraising one's actions, especially professional actions, throughout the process, and (5) accepting change as crucial to remaining an effective teacher.

The *purpose* of research and the *quality* of research are two separate dimensions of inquiry. Researchers use the same kinds of designs and methods for these different types of research. The criteria for determining the quality of a study is related to the design and procedures chosen for the question being investigated. As such, there can be poorly designed basic research and excellent applied studies. Similarly, small-scale action research can be well designed, and large-scale evaluation studies may provide questionable information because of procedural difficulties.

LIMITATIONS OF EDUCATIONAL RESEARCH

Education, as an interdisciplinary field of inquiry, has borrowed concepts and theories from psychology, sociology, anthropology, political science, economics, and other disciplines. Theories based on concepts such as *role*, *status*, *authority*, *self-concept*, and the like have been tested in education, and new educational concepts have emerged. Evidence-based educational research uses methodologies developed originally in the social sciences. Psychology, especially measurement, has traditionally dominated educational research. Other methodologies employed in education are the sociological survey, anthropological participant observation, historical research, and political analysis. While these approaches are often modified for educational research, doing so rarely violates the discipline from which the method was drawn.

The presence of many disciplinary perspectives in education research has at least two implications for evidence-based inquiry. First, since different disciplinary perspectives focus on different parts of the education system, many legitimate research frameworks and methods are available (National Research Council, 2002). But, because most disciplines focus on different parts of the educational system, this also means that contradictory conclusions are possible. Second, advances in educational research often depend on advances in related disciplines and fields.

MISCONCEPTION The recent federal emphasis on scientific inquiry implies that this approach is the *best way* or even the *only way* for educators to make decisions.

EVIDENCE Cognitive studies of administrator decision making suggest that logic, experience, ethical concerns, and legal ramifications are more important than scientific inquiry in making many decisions.

The field of education is often compared to that of medicine, where scientific studies play a role in determining health policy and medical practice. Educational scholars, however, contend that the two fields and their research constraints are not analogous. Social science is often contrasted with physical science, but as noted educational researcher David Berliner recently wrote (2002, p. 18), "We do our science under conditions that physical scientists find intolerable." In addition to a number of institutional and methodological constraints, cost is a "major concern in a field [i.e., education] that is widely considered to be underfunded" (Viadero, 1999, p. 34).

The development of a scientific basis for educational knowledge is limited by a set of features specific to education. Most practitioners are well aware of these features, but these aspects also affect research activities. Education is multilayered, constantly shifting, and involves interaction among institutions (e.g., schools, universities, families, communities, and government). It is value laden and embraces a diverse array of people and political forces. Because the U.S. educational system is so heterogeneous and the nature of teaching and learning so complex, research generalizations are limited in scope and thus application.

Furthermore, educational research relies on having relationships with professional practitioners. No study can be conducted without the participation of or cooperation of professionals. Educational research depends on its links with practice, which exist along a continuum: Some types of research involve only a short, distant, one-time interaction, whereas others require long-term, full partnerships or collaborations with schools or other agencies.

Educational research is limited by the following six constraints, which ultimately influence the knowledge gained about education through research (see Figure 1.3):

1. ***Legal and ethical considerations*** Educational research focuses primarily on human beings. The researcher is ethically responsible for protecting the rights and welfare of the subjects who participate in a study, which involves issues of physical and mental discomfort, harm, and danger. Most studies require that informed consent be obtained from the subjects, their parents, or a relevant institution, and laws are in place to protect the confidentiality of the data and the privacy of the subjects.[4] These principles often impose limitations on the kinds of studies that can be conducted in valid ways in education. For example, the physical and mental discomfort of subjects may affect the length of testing periods, the replication of studies, the types of treatments, and ultimately the research questions investigated.

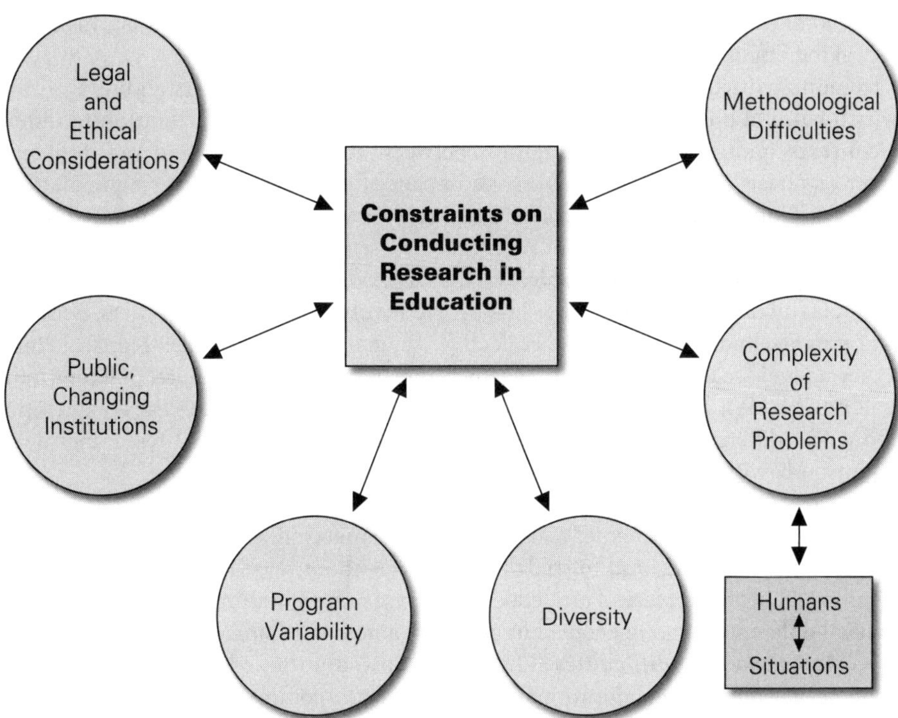

FIGURE 1.3 **Constraints on Educational Research**

2. ***Public institutions*** Education is a public enterprise that is influenced by the external environment. Since the report of a presidential commission, *A Nation at Risk*, was issued in 1983, the United States seems to be in a constant process of reforming its schools. Legislative mandates and judicial orders have changed the structure of schools and added, deleted, and modified programs. As waves of reform have swept the schools, instability has occurred in curriculum, standards, and accountability. Longitudinal and replication studies that evaluate changing clientele, programs, and institutions are difficult to conduct. In addition, the ultimate effects of these changes on schooling may not be known because such effects often occur years later, outside the educational setting.

The public nature of education also influences the kinds of research questions investigated. In most studies, the subjects and other groups are made aware of the research topic. Some topics may be too controversial for a conservative community or too divisive for a given institution's staff. Some studies are not conducted because the subsequent reactions may be detrimental to maintaining an educational organization.

3. ***Program variability*** A third constraint on research in education is the wide variety of programs that exist, often with the same core name. Even within reform movements, state and local control of education markedly shapes how instructional programs and other changes are implemented. Evaluations of curriculum changes may be influenced by high-stakes accountability systems and national college entrance exams. Researchers must specify the local and state conditions under which their findings were produced.

4. ***Diversity*** The U.S. population is becoming increasingly diverse, and this is mirrored in American neighborhoods and schools. The linguistic diversity that characterizes many schools is the most obvious manifestation of this trend. But beyond the common characteristic of lacking English fluency, there are notable differences between students from newly arrived immigrant families and those whose families have lived in this country for generations. Along with linguistic diversity come differences in culture, religion, academic preparation, and ties to the homeland. The parents' education and current

socioeconomic circumstances may affect a child's academic success more than his or her not speaking English.

Examining linguistic and sociocultural contexts is critical to understanding the ways in which cultural differences affect learning in diverse classrooms. Attention to different contexts implies close coordination between the researcher and practitioners. Greater emphasis should be placed on the impact of schooling on diverse populations of students. Contextual factors neccessitate a careful delineation of the limits of scientific generalization.

5. ***Complexity of research problems*** Another constraint on educational research is the complexity of research problems. The people involved—students, teachers, administrators, parents, and members of the collective community—are complex human beings, and they actively select the elements to which they respond. Furthermore, different individuals process ideas differently. Much of educational research illustrates the complexities of individual differences. Thus, within a single study, the educational researcher deals simultaneously with many, often ambiguous, variables.

In addition, most social scientists believe that individuals cannot be studied meaningfully by ignoring the context of real life. Behavior is determined by both individual and situational characteristics, and to study individuals without regard to situational characteristics would be incomplete. Thus, educational researchers must contend not only with individual differences among people but also with a myriad of situational elements.

6. ***Methodological difficulties*** The final constraint on educational research is methodological difficulties. Educational research measures complex human characteristics, as well as thinking and problem-solving skills. Moreover, to measure achievement, intelligence, leadership style, group interaction, or readiness skills involves formulating conceptual definitions and deciding issues of validity. Some educational research has become possible only as valid and reliable instruments have been developed. Other difficulties are the inappropriate use of methodology and reporting practices (Daniel, 1999).

Qualitative research also has methodological difficulties, especially those inherent in employing multimethod strategies, addressing the reflexive research role, and making explicit the data analysis techniques used. Qualitative research is sometimes criticized by the conventional viewpoint for its lack of reliable and generalizable findings, but case study designs provide context-bound summaries for understanding education and for future research (Peshkin, 1993).

Despite these difficulties, educational research has made considerable gains in evidence-based knowledge. The features of education and of educational research, in combination with the guiding principles of scientific inquiry, set the boundaries for the design of a study. As noted earlier, however, the actual design of the study does not make it scientific. A wide variety of legitimate scientific designs are available for education research, ranging from experiments to in-depth qualitative case study designs (National Research Council, 2002). To be scientific, the design must allow empirical investigation of an important question, account for the context in which the study occurred, use a conceptual framework, demonstrate a chain of logical reasoning, and disclose results to encourage public examination.

SUMMARY

This chapter has discussed the six guiding principles of scientific, evidence-based inquiry; the development of educational knowledge; the characteristics of educational research; distinctions between quantitative and qualitative research; the functions of research; and the limitations of educational research. The major ideas in this chapter can be summarized as follows:

1. Evidence-based inquiry uses systematically gathered, empirical data that are reported in such a way that the

logical reasoning that underlies them can be painstakingly examined.
2. The process of developing educational knowledge involves identification of research problems, empirical studies, replications, research synthesis, and practitioner adoption and evaluation.
3. The guiding principles of scientific inquiry are to pose significant empirical questions, to link research to theory, to use appropriate methods for investigating the research question, to demonstrate a specific chain of reasoning, to generalize or extend across studies, and to disclose results for professional scrutiny.
4. *Research* is the systematic process of collecting and logically analyzing data for some purpose.
5. Characteristics of research in education are objectivity, precision, verification, parsimonious explanation, empiricism, logical reasoning, and conditional conclusions.
6. Quantitative and qualitative research, differ in terms of their assumptions about the world, research purposes, research methods and processes, prototypical studies, research roles, and the importance of considering context in the physical, behavioral, and social sciences.
7. Applied research tests the usefulness of scientific theories in an applied field and investigates relationships and analytical generalizations common to that given profession.
8. Evaluation research assesses the merit and worth of a specific practice at a given site or several sites against one or more scales of value.
9. Action research involves teachers using research methods to study classroom problems.
10. The scientific quality of a study depends on the design and methods used, not the type of research (e.g., basic, applied, evaluation, or action research).
11. Education is an interdisciplinary field of inquiry—that is, educational researchers borrow concepts and methodologies from other academic disciplines and apply them in educational research.
12. Educational knowledge is limited by ethical and legal concerns, the public nature of education, program variability, diversity, the complexity of research problems, and methodological difficulties.

CHECK YOURSELF

Multiple-choice review items, with answers, are available on the Companion Website for this book.

www.ablongman.com/mcmillanschumacher6e

APPLICATION PROBLEMS

Research results can be used in a number of ways:

A. to influence the way the reader thinks or perceives a problem
B. to generate decision making that leads to action
C. to generate a new research question or problem

The following are examples of research results. In which of the ways just listed might each be used? Provide examples. There is not a single correct answer. For feedback, compare your answers with the sample answers in the back of the book.

1. A teacher reads a research study reporting that children from broken homes are more likely to exhibit deviant behavior in schools than are children from intact homes.
2. A study reports that a test measuring reading comprehension in grades 1 through 4 has been validated on students in grades 1 and 2 but not those in grades 3 and 4.
3. An educational historian notes that a well-known study of the organization of public schools from 1900 to 1950 stops short of the 1954 Supreme Court ruling on "separate but equal."
4. Upon reading the results of a survey of the parents of his school pupils, a principal realizes that the parents do not understand the new report card and grading system.
5. A curriculum developer field tests a pilot module of a strategy to help adult basic education teachers teach a reading strategy. The results of a representative sample of the teachers in the state suggest that the module should be revised to include a rationale for the strategy, a clear

specification of the type of student who would benefit from the strategy, and alternative techniques to respond to student difficulties.

6. Previous research indicates that school systems have been tightly structured organizations with hierarchical authority. A professor of school administration recalls that several superintendents and principals have seen many elements of autonomous behavior by principals and teachers at the school level, even though no empirical studies have reported this.

NOTES

1. Boldfaced key terms are defined in the Glossary at the end of the book.
2. Qualitative researchers debate whether the explanations are propositions, assertions, summaries, naturalistic/summary generalizations, or conclusions. See Stake (1995), Lincoln and Guba (1985), and LeCompte and Preissle (1993).
3. The authors recognize that the distinctions among basic, applied, evaluation, and action research are oversimplified and overemphasized in this discussion for illustrative purposes.
4. The laws, passed in 1974, are the Family Education Rights and Privacy Act, the National Research Act, and the Privacy Act. Although there is consensus about the intent of these laws, the interpretation of the regulations varies. A researcher abides by the procedures of the agency for which data are collected.

CHAPTER

2

Research Designs and Reading Research Reports

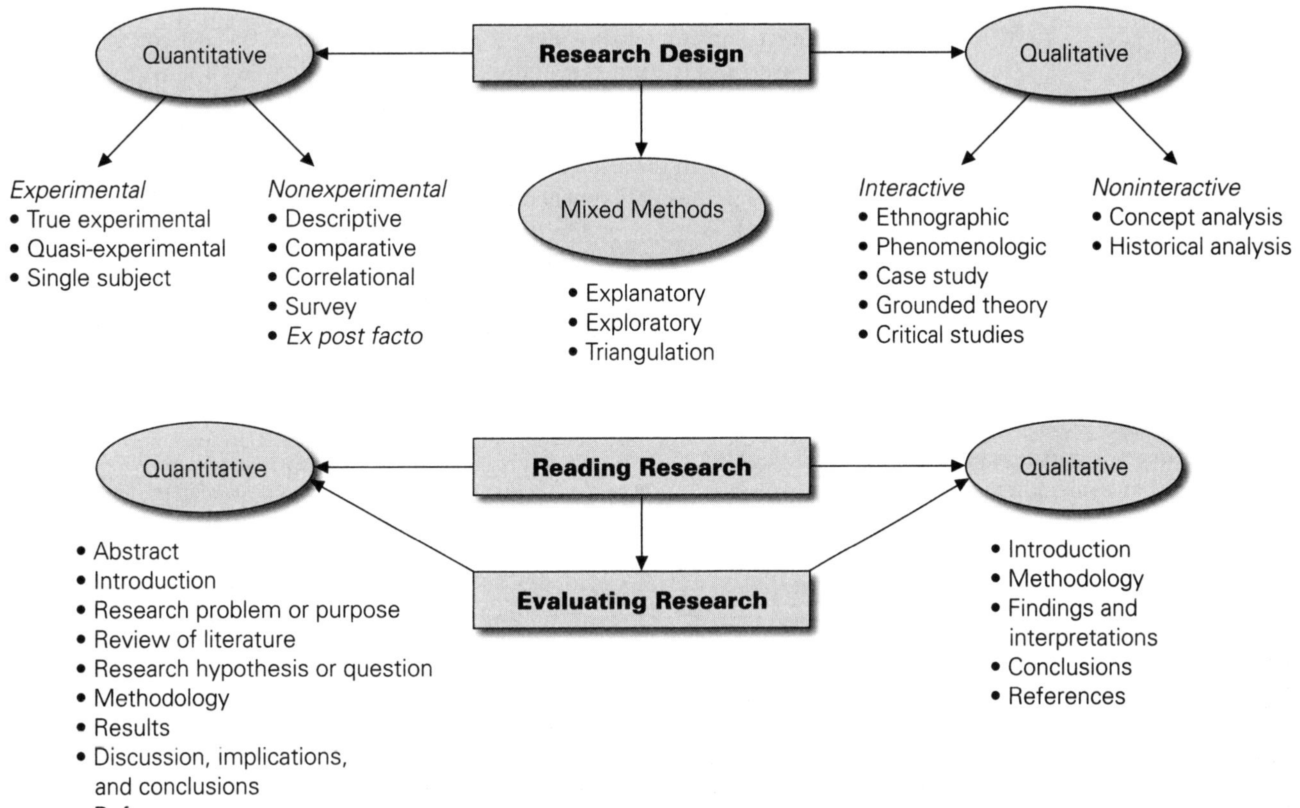

KEY TERMS

research design
experimental
true experimental
random assignment
quasi-experimental
single-subject
nonexperimental
descriptive
comparative
correlational
correlation
survey
ex post facto
secondary data analysis
qualitative
interactive
ethnography
phenomenological study
case study
grounded theory
critical studies
noninteractive
analytical research
concept analysis
historical analysis
mixed-method
explanatory
exploratory
triangulation

This chapter completes our overview of educational research. Its goals are to introduce terminology related to the way research is designed and to acquaint you with the organization of published research reports. Each of the research designs will be examined in greater detail in a later chapter. Our experience in teaching research is that it is best to become acquainted with these research design terms and concepts as early as possible. As they are reviewed in the context of actual studies and explained in greater detail, you will gain a more complete understanding and have increased retention.

RESEARCH DESIGNS

Chapter 1 examined how research can be viewed as scientific inquiry and disciplined inquiry, that approaches to research can be primarily quantitative or qualitative, and that research can be categorized as basic, applied, evaluation, or action. Another way to think about research is based on the research design of the study. A **research design** describes how the study was conducted. It summarizes the procedures for conducting the study, including when, from whom, and under what conditions the data will be obtained. In other words, the research design indicates the general plan: how the research is set up, what happens to the subjects, and what methods of data collection are used.

The purpose of a research design is to specify a plan for generating empirical evidence that will be used to answer the research questions. The intent is to use a design that will result in drawing the most valid, credible conclusions from the answers to the research questions. Since there are many types of research questions and many types of research designs, it is important to match the question to an appropriate design. Research design is a very important part of an investigation, since certain limitations and cautions in interpreting the results are related to each design and because the research design determines how the data should be analyzed.

To help you identify and classify different research designs, we have classified them as three major categories: quantitative, qualitative, and mixed method. The first two are the most common. Within each major category, there are different types. These types of designs, listed in Table 2.1, are often used to describe the research (e.g., "This is an experimental study," "This is a case study," "Correlational research was used"). The designs will

TABLE 2.1 Research Designs

Quantitative		Qualitative		
Experimental	**Nonexperimental**	**Interactive**	**Noninteractive**	**Mixed-Method**
True experimental	Descriptive	Ethnographic	Concept analysis	Explanatory
Quasi-experimental	Comparative	Phenomenologic	Historical analysis	Exploratory
Single-subject	Correlational	Case study		Triangulation
	Survey*	Grounded theory		
	Ex post facto	Critical studies		
	Secondary data analysis			

*Surveys are classified here as a type of research design. Surveys can also be classified as a type of data collection technique.

be reviewed briefly in this chapter and revisited in detail in later chapters. Once you become familiar with the primary orientation of each design it will help you identify that design when reading studies or when thinking about a study of your own.

ALERT! The debate as to whether using a quantitative, qualitative, or mixed-method approach is best has been resolved by matching appropriate designs to research questions.

It should be noted that these categories are independent of the classification of research as basic, applied, or evaluation. That is, for example, basic research can be experimental or nonexperimental, applied research can be single-subject or correlational.

QUANTITATIVE RESEARCH DESIGNS

Quantitative research designs were initially developed from research in agriculture and the hard sciences. These fields of study adopted a positivist philosophy of knowing that emphasized objectivity and quantification of phenomena. As a result, the research designs maximize objectivity by using numbers, statistics, structure, and control.

A very important subclassification of quantitative design is experimental/nonexperimental. Once you have determined that the study being reviewed is quantitative, then you should think about whether it is experimental or nonexperimental. This difference has major implications for both the nature of the design and the types of conclusions that can be drawn.

Experimental Designs

In an **experimental** design, the researcher manipulates what the subjects will experience. In other words, the investigator has some control over what will happen to the subjects by systematically imposing or withholding specified interventions. The researcher then makes comparisons either (1) between subjects who have had and others who have not had the interventions or (2) between subjects who have experienced different interventions. An experimental design also has a particular purpose in mind: to investigate cause-and-effect relationships between interventions and measured outcomes.

Here we will describe the three most common experimental designs.

True Experimental The unique characteristic of a **true experimental** design is that there is random assignment of subjects to different groups. With **random assignment,** every subject used in the study has an equal chance of being in each group. This procedure, when carried out with a large enough sample, helps ensure that there are no major differences between subjects in each group before intervention begins. This enables the researcher to conclude that the results are not due to differences in characteristics of the subjects or to most extraneous events.

The physical and biological sciences frequently use true experimental designs because they provide the most powerful approach for determining the effect of one factor on another. In these disciplines, it is also relatively easy to meet the conditions of random assignment and manipulation. For example, if a group of farmers wants to determine which of two fertilizers causes the best growth, they can divide large plots of land into smaller sections and randomly give some sections fertilizer A and the others fertilizer B. As long as the same amount of rain and sun and the same insect problems and other factors affect each section—which would probably be the case—the farmers can determine which fertilizer is best. In the social sciences, however, and especially in education, it is often difficult to meet these conditions. True experiments are especially difficult to employ in applied research, in which researchers minimize changes to naturally occurring conditions.

Quasi-Experimental A **quasi-experimental** design approximates the true experimental type. The purpose of the method is the same—to determine cause and effect—and there is direct manipulation of conditions. However, there is no random assignment of subjects. A common situation for implementing quasi-experimental research involves several classes or schools that can be used to determine the effect of curricular materials or teaching methods. The classes are intact, or already organized for an instructional purpose. The classes are not assigned randomly and have different teachers. It is possible, however, to give an experimental treatment to some of the classes and treat other classes as controls.

Single-Subject Research in education has been influenced heavily by a tradition in which groups of subjects, rather than individuals, are studied. In many situations, however, it is impossible or inconvenient to study entire groups of subjects. Furthermore, the researcher may be interested in one or two subjects, not large groups of subjects. **Single-subject** designs offer an alternative by specifying methods that can be used with a single individual or just a few subjects and still allow reasonable cause-and-effect conclusions. Similar to quasi-experimental research, there is direct manipulation but no random assignment in single-subject research.

Nonexperimental Designs

Nonexperimental research designs describe things that have occurred and examine relationships between things without any direct manipulation of conditions that are experienced. There are six types of nonexperimental designs: descriptive, comparative, correlational, survey, *ex post facto,* and secondary data analysis.

Descriptive Research using a **descriptive** design simply provides a summary of an existing phenomenon by using numbers to characterize individuals or a group. It assesses the nature of existing conditions. The purpose of most descriptive research is limited to characterizing something as it is.[1]

Comparative In a **comparative** design, the researcher investigates whether there are differences between two or more groups on the phenomena being studied. As with descriptive designs, there is no manipulation or direct control of conditions experienced; even so, the comparative approach takes descriptive studies a step further. For example, rather than simply describe pupil attitudes toward discipline, a comparative study could investigate whether attitudes differed by grade level or gender. Another example would be to compare the grades of athletes and nonathletes. Often, comparative modes of inquiry are used to study relationships between different phenomena, for example, the relationship between participation in athletics and grade-point average.

Correlational **Correlational** research is concerned with assessing relationships between two or more phenomena. This type of study usually involves a statistical measure of the degree of relationship, called **correlation.** The relationship measured is a statement about the degree of association between the variables of interest. A *positive correlation* means that high values of one variable are associated with high values of a second variable. The relationship between height and weight, between IQ scores and achievement test scores, and between self-concept and grades are examples of positive correlation. A *negative correlation* or relationship means that high values of one variable are associated with low values of a second variable. Examples of negative correlations include those between exercise and heart failure, between successful test performance and feelings of incompetence, and between absence from school and school achievement.

Survey In a **survey** research design, the investigator selects a sample of subjects and administers a questionnaire or conducts interviews to collect data. Surveys are used frequently in educational research to describe attitudes, beliefs, opinions, and other types of information. Usually, the research is designed so that information about a large number of people (the population) can be inferred from the responses obtained from a smaller group of subjects (the sample).

Ex Post Facto An ***ex post facto*** design is used to explore possible causal relationships among variables that cannot be manipulated by the researcher. The investigator designs the study to compare two or more samples that are comparable except for a specified factor. The possible causes are studied after they have occurred. Rather than manipulate what *will* happen to subjects, as in experimental designs, the research focuses on what has happened differently for comparable groups of subjects, then explores whether the subjects in each group are different in some way. For example, an important question concerning day care for children is the relative effect the type of day-care program may have on school readiness. Some day care programs are more academic than others. Since it would be very difficult to manipulate experimentally the type of day care a child attends, an ex post facto mode of inquiry would be appropriate. The investigator would identify two groups of children who have similar backgrounds but who have attended different types of day care. The subjects would be given a school readiness test to see whether those who attended a highly academically oriented day-care facility differ from children who attended a less academically oriented day-care facility.

Secondary Data Analysis Often, researchers have access to data that others have gathered and conduct analyses using these data. This type of research design is called **secondary data analysis.** Secondary analysis is becoming more popular as large federal and state data sets are released to the public. Good examples include test score data and data relevant to the No Child Left Behind (NCLB) Act, passed in 2001. According to the NCLB, for example, student test score data must be reported for different types of students (e.g., students with disabilities, English-language learners, African American students). Researchers can take these data and conduct studies that compare achievement among the groups or that examine trends.

QUALITATIVE RESEARCH DESIGNS

Qualitative research designs use methods that are distinct from those used in quantitative designs. To be sure, qualitative designs are just as systematic as quantitative designs, but they emphasize gathering data on naturally occurring phenomena. Most of these data are in the form of words rather than numbers, and in general, the researcher must search and explore with a variety of methods until a deep understanding is achieved. Qualitative designs can initially be classified as *interactive* or *noninteractive* and then further delineated within each of these major types.

ALERT! Researchers use a number of different terms to describe methods that are *qualitative.* Be sure to check the meanings of terms used by individual researchers.

Interactive Methods

Interactive qualitative methods use face-to-face techniques to collect data from people in their natural settings. Five interactive designs (as listed in Table 2.1) are ethnographic, phenomenological, case study, grounded theory, and critical studies. These designs can be organized by (1) a focus on *individual lived experience,* as seen in phenomenology, case study, grounded theory, and some critical studies, and (2) a focus on *society and culture,* as defined by ethnography and some critical studies.

Ethnography An **ethnography** is a description and interpretation of a cultural or social group or system. Although there is considerable disagreement about the meaning of the term *culture,* the focus is on learned patterns of actions, language, beliefs, rituals, and ways of life. As a process, ethnography involves prolonged field work, typically employing observation and casual interviews with participants of a shared group activity and collecting group artifacts. A documentary style is employed, focusing on the mundane details of everyday life and revealing the observation skills of the inquirer. The collective informants' point of view is painstakingly produced through extensive, closely edited quotations to convey that what is presented is not the fieldworker's view but authentic and representative remarks of the participants. The final product is a comprehensive, holistic narrative description and interpretation that integrates all aspects of group life and illustrates its complexity.

There are several variants of ethnography. Whereas many anthropologists employ participant observation in ethnographic studies of a culture, educational researchers utilize the technique to produce micro-ethnographies (Erickson, 1973; LeCompte & Preissle, 1993; Wolcott, 1995). A *micro-ethnography* is a participant observation study of one aspect of a cultural component (e.g., education) such as participants in an educational activity (an urban classroom or principals in an innovative program).

Phenomenology A **phenomenological study** describes the meanings of a lived experience. The researcher "brackets," or puts aside, all prejudgments and collects data on how individuals make sense out of a particular experience or situation. The aim of phenomenology is to transform lived experience into a description of "its essence—in such a way that the effect of the text is at once a reflexive reliving and reflective appropriation of something meaningful" (Van Manen, 1990, p. 36). The typical technique is for the researcher to conduct long interviews with the informants directed toward understanding their perspectives on their everyday lived experience with the phenomenon.

Case Study A **case study** examines a *bounded system,* or a case, over time in detail, employing multiple sources of data found in the setting. The case may be a program, an event, an activity, or a set of individuals bounded in time and place. The researcher defines the case and its boundary. A case can be selected because of its uniqueness or used to illustrate an issue (Stake, 1995). The focus may be one entity (within-site study) or several entities (multisite study).

Grounded Theory Although the hallmark of qualitative research is detailed description and analysis of phenomena, **grounded theory** goes beyond the description to develop *dense* (detailed) concepts or conditional propositional statements that relate to a particular phenomenon. The term *grounded theory* is often used in a nonspecific way to refer to any approach to forming theoretical ideas that somehow begins with data. But grounded theory methodology is a rigorous set of procedures for producing substantive theory. Using a constant comparative method, the data analysis simultaneously employs techniques of induction, deduction, and verification. The researcher collects primarily interview data, making multiple visits to the field. The initial data collection is done to gain a variety of perspectives on the phenomena; then, the inquirer uses constant comparison to analyze across categories of information. Data are collected until the categories of information are *saturated*. At this point, the researcher selects the central phenomenon, develops a *story line*, and suggests a conditional matrix that specifies the social and historical conditions and consequences influencing the phenomenon.

Critical Studies Researchers who conduct **critical studies** draw from critical theory, feminist theory, race theory, and postmodern perspectives, which assume that knowledge is subjective. These researchers also view society as essentially structured by class and status, as well as by race, ethnicity, gender, and sexual orientation. Thus, a patriarchal society maintains the oppression of marginalized groups (Lather, 1991). Critical researchers are suspicious of most research designs for ignoring the power relations implicit in the data collection techniques and for excluding other ways of knowing. Whereas feminist and ethnic research focus on gender and race as the problem of a study, postmodernism and critical theory tend to focus more on society and social institutions.

Noninteractive Methods

Noninteractive designs, sometimes termed **analytical research,** investigate concepts and events through an analysis of documents. The researcher identifies, studies, and then synthesizes the data to provide an understanding of the concept or a past event that may or may not have been directly observable. Authenticated documents are the major source of data. The researcher interprets facts to provide explanations of the past and clarifies the collective educational meanings that may be underlying current practices and issues.

Examples of analytical research include concept analysis and historical analysis. **Concept analysis** is the study of educational concepts such as *cooperative learning, ability grouping,* and *leadership* to describe the different meanings and appropriate use of the concept. **Historical analysis** involves a systematic collection and criticism of documents that describe past events. Educational historians study past educational programs, practices, institutions, persons, policies, and movements. These are usually interpreted in the context of historical economic, social, military, technological, and political trends. The analysis examines causes and the subsequent events, often relating the past to current events.

MIXED-METHOD RESEARCH DESIGNS

The use of **mixed-method** research designs, which combine quantitative and qualitative methods, is becoming increasingly popular because many situations are best investigated using a variety of methods. With mixed-method designs, researchers are not limited to using techniques associated with traditional designs, either quantitative or qualitative. For example, a study of how teachers apply the results of high-stakes tests to their instruction might use a written questionnaire to survey a large number of teachers, as well as qualitative interviews to probe the reasons for the use documented in the survey. An important advantage of mixed-method studies is that they can show the result (quantitative) and explain why it was obtained (qualitative).

ALERT! The overall credibility of a mixed-method study depends on the independent quality of the quantitative and qualitative designs used as well as the interplay between them.

Explanatory Designs

How mixed-method designs are used can vary considerably, depending on the weight given to each approach and when each is used. It is common, for instance, to use methods sequentially. In an **explanatory** design, which may be the most common type, quantitative data are collected first and, depending on the results, qualitative data are gathered second to elucidate, elaborate on, or explain the quantitative findings. Typically, the main thrust of the study is quantitative, and the qualitative results are secondary. For example, this kind of design could be used to study classroom assessment and grading. A large sample of teachers could be surveyed to determine the extent to which they use different factors in classroom assessment and grading; this would provide a general overview of the teachers' practices. In a second phase, teachers could be selected who represent extremely high or low scores on the factors in the survey. These teachers could then be interviewed using a qualitative method to determine why they used certain practices. Thus, the qualitative phase would be used to augment the statistical data and thus explain the practices.

Exploratory Designs

In a second type of mixed-method design, the qualitative data are gathered first and a quantitative phase follows. The purpose of this kind of study, which is called an **exploratory design,** is typically to use the initial, qualitative phase with a few individuals to identify themes, ideas, perspectives, and beliefs that can then be used to design the larger-scale, quantitative part of the study. Often, this kind of design is used to develop a survey. By using a qualitative component in the beginning, researchers are able to use the language and emphasis on different topics of the subjects in the wording of items for the survey. Doing so increases the validity of the scores that result because they will be well matched with how the subjects, rather than the researchers, think about, conceptualize, and respond to the phenomenon being studied.

Triangulation Designs

The third kind of mixed-method study is called a **triangulation** design. In this design, both qualitative and quantitative data are collected at about the same time. Triangulation is used when the strengths of one method offset the weaknesses of the other, so that together, they provide a more comprehensive set of data. To the extent that the results from each method converge and indicate the same result, there is triangulation and thus greater credibility in the findings. Theoretically, the triangulation design is used because the strengths of each approach can be applied to provide not only a more complete result but also one that is more valid. An example of a triangulation design would be a study on school culture. A quantitative survey of school culture could be used in conjunction with focus groups of students, teachers, and administrators. The more the survey results match the focus group results, the greater the validity of the conclusion that a certain type of culture exists in the school. The advantage of using the survey is that a large number of students, teachers, and administrators can be represented, and the advantage of using the focus groups is that descriptions are provided in voices specific to each group.

READING AND UNDERSTANDING RESEARCH REPORTS

Research is reported in a variety of ways, most commonly as a published article or as a paper delivered at a conference. The purpose of the report is to indicate clearly what the researcher has done, why it was done, and what it means. To do this effectively, researchers use a more or less standard format. This format is similar to the process of conceptualizing and conducting the research. Since the process of doing research is different for quantitative compared with qualitative methods, there are differences in the reporting formats used for each approach. Mixed-method studies, as might be expected, combine elements of both quantitative and qualitative report formats. While there is typically one review of the literature, there are often separate Methodology sections for the quantitative and qualitative parts of the study. Explanatory studies present quantitative methods first, exploratory studies present qualitative methods first, and triangulation studies present both at the same time.

All research reports, however, share this common, simple sequence:

Question → Method → Conclusion

The article or paper will begin with a question, summarize the methods used, and end with one or more conclusions.

At this point, it will be helpful simply to jump in, so to speak, and to begin reading research reports. Two articles have been provided in this chapter to get you started: one quantitative study and one qualitative study. Each contains notes to help you understand what you read, but you are not expected to comprehend everything. That will come with further experience and study. Each type of research is introduced with a description of the major parts, and each article is followed by questions that will help you understand what is being reported.

In reading research it is important to judge the overall credibility of the study. This judgment is based on an evaluation of each of the major sections of the report. *Each part of the report contributes to the overall credibility of the study.*

How to Read Quantitative Research: Anatomy of an Experimental Example

Although there is no universally accepted format for reporting quantitative research, most studies adhere to the sequence of scientific inquiry. There may be variation in the terms used, but the components indicated below are included in most studies:

1. Abstract
2. Introduction
3. Statement of research problem or purpose
4. Review of literature
5. Statement of research hypotheses or questions
6. Methodology
   a. Subjects
   b. Instruments
   c. Procedure
7. Results
8. Discussion, implications, conclusions
9. References

Abstract The *Abstract* is a short paragraph that summarizes the entire journal article. It follows the authors' names and is usually italicized or printed in type that is smaller than the type in the article itself. Most abstracts contain a statement of the purpose of the study, a brief description of the subjects and what they did during the study, and a summary of important results. The abstract is useful because it provides a quick overview of the research, and after studying it, the reader usually will know whether to read the entire article.

Introduction The *Introduction* is typically limited to the first paragraph or two of the article. The purpose of the introduction is to put the study in context. This is often accomplished by quoting previous research in the general topic, citing leading researchers in the area, or developing the historical context and/or theoretical rationale of the study. The introduction acts as a lead-in to a statement of the more specific purpose of the study. In Excerpt 2.1, the introduction includes the first nine paragraphs.

Research Problem or Purpose The first step in planning a quantitative study is to formulate a research problem or purpose: that is, a clear and succinct statement that indicates the purpose of the study. Researchers begin with a general idea of what they intend to study, such as the relationship of self-concept to achievement, and then they refine this general goal to a concise sentence that indicates more specifically what is being investigated—for example, What is the relationship between fourth graders' self-concept of ability in mathematics and their achievement in math as indicated by standardized test scores?

The *Research Problem* or *Statement of Purpose* can be found in one of several locations in articles. It can be the last sentence of the introduction, as in Excerpt 2.1, or it may follow the review of literature and come just before the methods section.

Review of Literature After researchers formulate a research problem, they conduct a search for studies that are related to the problem. The *Review of Literature* summarizes and analyzes previous research and shows how the present study is related to this literature. Often, the theoretical rationale for the study is included. The length of the review can vary, but it should be selective and concentrate on the way the present study will contribute to existing knowledge. As in the example, it should be long enough to demonstrate to the reader that the researcher has a sound understanding of the relationship between what has been done and what will be done. There is usually no separate heading to identify the review of literature (Excerpt 2.1 does have one, however), but it is always located before the methods section.

Research Hypothesis or Question Following the literature review, researchers state the hypothesis or question. Based on information from the review, researchers write a *Hypothesis* that indicates what they predict will happen in the study. A hypothesis can be tested empirically, and it provides focus for the research. For some research, it is inappropriate to make a prediction of results, and in some studies, a research question rather than a hypothesis is used. Whether it is a question or a hypothesis, the sentence should contain objectively defined terms and state relationships in a clear, concise manner, as do the hypotheses in our example (i.e., the last two sentences before the *Method* section).

Methodology In the methods or *Methodology* section, the researcher indicates the research design, subjects, instruments, and procedures used in the study. Ideally, this section contains enough information to enable other researchers to replicate the study. There is usually a subheading for each part of the methods section.

In the *Subjects* subsection (sometimes referred to as the *Participants* or *Data Source*), the researcher describes the characteristics of the individuals from whom information was gathered. There is an indication of the number of subjects and the way they were selected for the study.

The *Instruments* subsection describes the techniques used to gather information. There should be an indication of the validity and reliability of the results for each measuring device to show that the techniques are appropriate for the study. Sometimes examples of items are included to help the reader understand the nature of the instrument.

The *Procedure* or data collection subsection is used to explain how the study was conducted. The authors describe when the information was collected, where, and by whom. They describe what was done to the subjects (i.e., the intervention) and the manner in which the data were collected. It is important to provide a full description of the procedures. There needs to be sufficient information so that the reader would know how to proceed in replicating the study. The procedures may also affect the ways subjects respond. Readers thus need to examine the procedures carefully in interpreting the results.

Results A summary of the analyses of the data collected is reported in the *Results* or *Findings* section. This section may appear confusing to the beginning researcher because statistical language, symbols, and conventions are used in presenting the results. The results are usually indicated in tables and graphs within the text of the article. The results should be presented objectively without interpretation or discussion, summarizing what was found. (Sometimes, interpretation will follow the results in this section.) Since the Results section contains crucial information in the article, the reader must be able to understand and evaluate the material. This is important in order to avoid uncritical acceptance of the conclusions. At this point readers should not be concerned with understanding all statistics presented in Excerpt 2.1.

Discussion, Implications, and Conclusions In this section, the researchers indicate how the results are related to the research problem or hypothesis. It is a nontechnical interpretation of whether the results support a hypothesis or answer a research question. If the study is exploratory or contains unexpected findings, the researchers explain why they believe they obtained these results. The explanation should include an analysis of any deficiencies in the methodology utilized and an indication of other research that may explain why certain results were obtained. This section is also used to indicate implications of the study for future research and practical applications and to give overall conclusions. This section is identified by several different labels. The most common are *Discussion*, *Conclusion*, and *Summary*.

References A list of references and reference notes that are cited in the article follows the discussion. The style of the notation will vary. The journal in which Excerpt 2.1 was published uses the most recent APA (American Psychological Association, 2001) format.

Guidelines for Evaluating Quantitative Research

There is no agreed-upon method for or approach to reading research articles. Some readers begin with the conclusion, and others follow the written sequence of the article. Our experience suggests that a reader should begin with the abstract and then scan the introduction, research problem, and conclusion sections. If after reading these sections, the reader is still interested in the article, then he or she should start at the beginning and read the entire article more carefully. Whenever reading research, one should keep in mind the practical or meaningful significance of the study. Research is significant if there are no serious weaknesses in the design and the differences obtained between groups or individuals or relationships reported are large enough to suggest changes in theory or practice.

Other questions also should be kept in mind in reading research. While readers need to become acquainted with these considerations now, a full understanding and application of the questions is expected only after further study of each topic. The following questions, organized according to each major section of a quantitative research article, constitute a guideline for evaluating quantitative investigations.

Research Problem or Purpose

1. How clearly and succinctly is the problem or purpose stated?
2. Is it sufficiently delimited to be amenable to investigation? At the same time, does it have sufficient practical or theoretical value to warrant study?
3. Does it have a rationale? Has the problem been studied before? If so, should this problem be studied again? Is the study likely to provide additional knowledge?
4. Will the findings give rise to further hypotheses, thereby increasing the probability of adding to existing knowledge?

Review of Literature

1. How adequately has the literature been surveyed?
2. Does the review critically evaluate previous findings and studies, or is it only a summary of what is known?
3. Does the review support the need for studying the problem?
4. Does the review establish a theoretical framework for the problem?
5. Does the review relate previous studies to the research problem?

Hypotheses or Questions

1. Are any assumptions advanced with respect to the hypotheses or questions?
2. Are hypotheses consistent with theory and known facts?
3. Are they testable?
4. Do they provide an expected result?

Methodology

1. Are the procedures, design, and instruments employed to gather the data described with sufficient clarity to permit another researcher to replicate the study?
2. Is the population described fully? Did the researcher use the total population, or was there a sample used? If a sample is used, is it representative of the population from which it was selected?
3. Is evidence presented about the validity and reliability of the scores?
4. Was a pretest used? Was there a pilot study? If so, why? What were the results? Was the problem or question or procedure changed as a result of the pretest or pilot study, and if so, was this modification justifiable or desirable?
5. Are there any obvious weaknesses in the overall design of the study?

Results

1. Were statistical techniques needed to analyze the data? If so, were the most appropriate and meaningful statistical techniques employed?
2. Have the results been adequately and clearly presented?
3. Is there reference to *practical* as well as *statistical* significance?

Discussion, Implications, Conclusions

1. Are the conclusions and generalizations consistent with the findings? What are the implications of the findings? Has the researcher overgeneralized the findings?
2. Does the researcher discuss the limitations of the study?
3. Are there any extraneous factors that might have affected the findings? Have they been considered by the researchers?
4. Are the conclusions presented consistent with theory or known facts?
5. Have the conclusions (both those relevant to the original hypothesis and any serendipitous findings) been presented adequately and discussed?

EXCERPT 2.1 Anatomy of a Quantitative Research Article

The Effects of Computer-Assisted Instruction on First Grade Students' Vocabulary Development

Charlotte Boling, *The University of West Florida*
Sarah H. Martin, *Eastern Kentucky University*
Michael A. Martin, *Eastern Kentucky University*

The purpose of the present study was to determine the effect of computer-assisted instruction on first grade students' vocabulary development. Students participating in this study were randomly divided into experimental and control groups. The students in both groups were involved in DEAR (Drop Everything And Read) as part of their instruction in a balanced literacy program. During their normal DEAR time, the control group used a book and tape to explore stories. The experimental group explored stories using computerized storyboards. The results of the study show a significant difference for both groups on pre and posttests. However, the mean difference demonstrates a much larger gain for students in the experimental group.

Abstract

What can teachers do to insure that the children they teach will develop into successful readers? This is a question that has puzzled the educational community for years. Most educators have their individual opinion as to how the reading process occurs. Morrow and Tracey (1997) state that some educators believe in a behavioristic approach where reading is taught in a skills-based environment through a prescribed curriculum. Others believe in a more constructivist approach where a relationship between the context and child must be developed where students build knowledge and gain skills through immersion in a literature-rich environment (Czubaj, 1997; Daniels & Zemelman, 1999). Whatever one believes, these approaches to reading instruction—behaviorist or constructivist—continue to be the subject of debates in our classrooms and communities.

Introduction—Significance of topic

The core beliefs that teachers possess have a great impact on students learning to read. Teacher's personal beliefs concerning the processes involved in learning to read greatly influence their instructional choices. A teacher's beliefs are based on his or her personal knowledge, experiences with instructional techniques, and the way students respond to the instructional strategies in classroom situations (Dillon, 2000; Howard, McGee, Purcell, and Schwartz, 2000; Kinzer and Leu, 1999). Therefore, while teachers maintain their core beliefs about how children best learn to read, they are continuously striving to find the technique(s) that will have the greatest impact on their students.

Since the early 1920s, educators have used a multi-sensory approach to teaching reading by combining reading, writing, and speaking in a natural context and not through deliberate teaching (Chall, 1992). This has been particularly useful in the teaching of vocabulary. It stands to reason then that the most active vocabulary growth occurs in the early years of life. A child learns to connect an object with the sight, sound, smell, taste, and feel associated with the object. This experience is followed by certain sounds made to represent the object. Thus, communication begins and the concept associated with the object develops into vocabulary. For example, a child understands the physical properties of an apple. He knows how the object looks, tastes, feels, smells, and sounds. A loving parent then builds vocabulary in a natural context by adding the word associated to this object—apple. Then, this label is connected to the experience. "You are eating an apple."

As the vocabulary increases, children realize words are used in many contexts. Children must then reach beyond the actual word and activate their schema of the context in which the word is used to understand the meaning. For example, the word "mouse" can have different meanings, such as, a small rodent or a computer device. A child needs to

Introduction—Background on importance of vocabulary

(continued)

excerpt 2.1 *(continued)*

experience words being used in different contexts to understand the complexity of our language. The more children experience vocabulary in context, the sooner they will begin to realize that it is the concept of the word in question in the given context that provides meaning.

As a child progresses through the various aspects of literacy development (listening, speaking, reading, and writing), their communication skills become more interdependent upon vocabulary development. Vocabulary development involves understanding the 'labeling' that goes with the 'concept' that makes the word meaningful. It is acquired through direct experience, multiple exposure, context, association, and comprehension. As students become comfortable with new vocabulary words, they are more likely to use the words when communicating.

Introduction—Background on importance of vocabulary (continued)

Elements of our 'Technological Age' often influence the instructional decisions that teachers make in the classroom. One such decision is the role that computers will play in the reading development of the children one teaches. Computer-based teaching and learning has produced positive effects in the classroom. Students seem to be motivated by learning through this medium (Forcier, 1999). Therefore, it is essential that today's teachers change as our society changes (Hoffman & Pearson, 2000). Children who enter today's primary classrooms have been processing multi-sensory concepts for most of their young lives. Home computers, interactive games, television, the Internet, and software companies capitalize on this multi-sensory concept.

Software companies have developed many programs for beginning reading that appeal to the senses and interests of the young child who is learning to read. This multimedia concept stimulates the learner with sight, sound, and action while integrating skills necessary for language development. Instructional technology offers virtual multi-sensory perception that should provide meaningful instruction.

Introduction—Background on importance of technology

Teacher-centered instruction is one approach to the use of instructional technology in the classroom (Forcier, 1999). The teacher-centered approach is similar to the direct-instruction approach in that the teacher is directing the children through the learning in order to achieve the goals of the lesson. One category of the teacher-centered approach is computer-assisted instruction. When using computer-assisted instruction the teacher organizes the learning situation. He/she selects the targeted learning goal, situates the learning environment, and then allows exploratory time as students engage in learning. The teacher then monitors the learning activities and modifies the instructional level as needed to meet the various needs of the children involved.

Introduction—Importance of teacher-centered instruction

Classroom teachers have the unique opportunity to infuse a variety of technological components with multi-sensory learning while situating the learning situation. One area where this is especially true is in the teaching of reading to young children. The research study being reported employed a teacher-centered, computer-assisted instructional technique that situated progressive reading material in an attempt to answer the following question:

Will a computerized multi-sensory approach to the teaching of reading increase first-graders' vocabulary development?

Research question

Review of Literature

Major heading

Many software programs offer 'read alongs' and 'edutainment' that assist students as they learn letter sounds, vocabulary concepts, comprehension, and to enjoy literature. Interactive multimedia allows the printed word to take on sight, sound, and action which visually and mentally stimulates the individual.

One such program is DaisyQuest I and II (Mitchell, Chad & Stacy, 1984–2000). An in-depth study investigated the phonological awareness in pre-school children utilizing this software (Brinkman and Torgesen, 1994). Each child in the treatment group interacted with a computerized story concerning "Daisy the friendly dragon". A computer, monitor,

Summary of findings from previous study

excerpt 2.1 *(continued)*

mouse, and standard headphone were provided to allow the child, as he/she listened to the story, to discover clues revealing where the dragon was hiding. The clues were revealed by correctly answering at least four correct answers in a row. The skills assessed were rhyming words, beginning sounds, ending sounds, middle sounds, and whether a word contained a given number of sounds. This study revealed that children in the treatment group responded at a higher and faster rate of reading readiness than children in the control group. Not only did the children in the treatment group gain knowledge to aid in their ability to read; these pre-schoolers had fun!

Summary of findings from previous study (continued)

In another study, two literacy teachers (one a Reading Recovery teacher, the other a Title 1 Reading Teacher) wrote simple, predictable texts using a multimedia software, HyperStudio (Wagner, 1978–2000). These teachers created 'talking books' for their students with a focus on high-frequency words with graphics and animation to offer sight, sound, and movement. Students enjoyed experiencing the stories as the computer 'read' the story to them as the cursor (pointing finger) touched each word. This process came full circle by the end of the school year, as these students were writing and reading their own stories. Students were then encouraged to use invented spelling, graphics, and sounds, while they created their own stories using the Kid Pix Software program (Hickman, 1984–2000). "The computer serves as a motivational tool in their journey to literacy" (Eisenwine & Hunt, 2000, p. 456).

Summary of findings from previous study

There are many reasons why computer-assisted reading instruction has been effective. The computer provides immediate responses and practice for the child learning a skill. Struggling readers interface with the computer and practice a skill without embarrassing situations in the classroom. Interaction with a multi-sensory format provides motivation and a positive attitude toward reading and learning (Case & Truscott, 1999; Forcier, 1999).

Shows significance of technology

A word of caution accompanies much of the literature warning educators to focus on the targeted instructional goals and not be 'enchanted' by the entertainment that makes software packages so appealing (Case and Truscott, 1999; Sherry, 1996). While this multisensory approach is highly motivating for young readers, the instructional purpose is to enable them to become better readers. Educators should choose the types of software and technological resources carefully in order to maximize learning without being entangled in the 'bells and whistles'.

Indicates criteria for selecting software

The benefits of using instructional technology include "an intrinsic need to learn technology . . . motivation increases engagement time . . . students move beyond knowledge and comprehension and into application and analysis . . . and students develop computer literacy by applying various computer skills as part of the learning process" (Dockstader, 1999, p. 73). As Ray and Wepner (2000) suggest, the question as to whether or not technology is the valuable educational resource we think it is may be a moot point since it is such an integral part of our lives. However, the question concerning the most productive methods of using technology in the classroom still needs to be addressed. Therefore, the purpose of this study was to investigate the effects of computer-assisted instruction on first grade students' vocabulary development. Specifically, this study investigated the impact of the WiggleWorks program (CAST & Scholastic, 1994–1996) on first grade students' vocabulary development.

Shows need for study

Purpose

Research problem

Method

Sample

Identifies subjects

A first grade classroom at a mid-Atlantic elementary school was selected for this research project. The subjects were 21 first-grade students. There were 10 boys and 11 girls involved in this study. The ethnic background of this class was as follows: 13 Caucasian students, six African American students, one Hispanic student, and one Pakistani student. Students were from a lower socioeconomic status and had limited exposure to educational experiences

Convenience sample

Description of subjects

(continued)

excerpt 2.1 *(continued)*

outside the school. The subjects were assigned to either the control or experimental group by using a table of random numbers and applying those numbers to the students. Ten students were assigned to the control group and 11 to the experimental group.

Random assignment (low number of students in each group)

Computer Assisted Program

The WiggleWorks (1994–1996) software program was used in this study. Co-developed by CAST and Scholastic, Inc., this program offers a literacy curriculum based on a combination of speech, sounds, graphics, text, and customizable access features. The software program features 72 trade books, audiocassettes, and a variety of computer-based activities. Students use the trade books and audiocassettes to read independently with or without the support of the audiocassette. Using the software program, students may listen to a story, read along with a story, or read a story silently. As they read, students are encouraged to review the suggested vocabulary words by selecting My Words. Students may listen to a pronunciation of the word by clicking on it or hear the word contextually in the story. Students may add new words to their vocabulary list by clicking on the selected word and the plus sign or remove words by clicking on the subtraction sign. Students may read and reread the story as they wish. Students may also create word families or practice spelling using a magnetic alphabet.

After listening to or reading a story, students have the option of composing their own stories. WiggleWorks provides a story starter, cloze-structured text, or free writing to help young students write their story. After composing a story, students may illustrate personal stories using basic drawing tools, stamps of the story characters, and/or story event backgrounds. Students may share their stories with others by recording their stories or printing the story and creating a book. These functions are available in a Read Aloud, Read, Write, My Book, and Magnet Board menu available to the individual user.

WiggleWorks is a managed instructional system. The management functions allow the teacher the opportunity to customize the computer-assisted instruction for each child. For instance, in Read Aloud, the settings can be adjusted so that the story is read to the student using a word-by-word, line-by-line, or whole-page approach. The management system also keeps a running log of individual and class activities. The Portfolio Management feature provides a reading record for each child (tracks the stories read, date and time individual stories were read, etc.), including reading and writing samples. The WiggleWorks software program provides a multimedia approach to literacy while supporting traditional methods with the accompanying trade books and audiocassettes.

Detailed description of intervention

Variables

The research project tested the independent variable of computer-assisted instruction on reading vocabulary development. Eleven students received the treatment monitored by one of the researchers. The dependent variable was a pre and post vocabulary test. The test was an independent word list administered by the researcher to the experimental and control group at the beginning and end of each session.

Intervention (independent) and outcomes (dependent)

Measurement

How data are collected

The instrument used to determine the effect of computer-assisted instruction on vocabulary was a pre and posttest designed by one of the researchers. Six high-frequency vocabulary words from each of the seven stories were selected by the researcher and placed on an independent list. The independent list of words served as the pre and post vocabulary test for each. All results were compared to determine the effect the treatment had on these subjects.

Locally developed instrument

Procedure

How intervention was implemented

As a part of the regular curriculum, all students received reading vocabulary instruction. The teacher utilized the reading instructional curriculum adopted by the county which consist of reading text books, related materials, and charts provided by the publishing company. Students participated in daily reading instruction. Each student in the class was

excerpt 2.1 *(continued)*

randomly assigned into two groups: a control group and an experimental group. In an attempt to limit extraneous learning, both groups continued to receive regular reading instruction by the researcher/teacher. The regular reading curriculum had a twenty minute time block where students participated in a DEAR (Drop Everything And Read) program. The researchers used this block of time to implement this research project.

Seven pre-determined stories were used for this research project. The stories were available on book and tape as well as interactive, computerized storyboards. The control group experienced the story in a variety of ways. First, they listened to the assigned story as the teacher/researcher read the story to them. Next, students listened to the story on tape and read along with an accompanying book. Lastly, students were provided with an assortment of literature: library books, classroom literature, or the student's personal books to read at their leisure after the pre-determined book and tape assignment had been completed. During that twenty-minute time span, the 10 students in the experimental group visited the Media computer lab and explored the same story using the computerized storyboard. A computer, monitor, mouse, and headphone were provided for each subject. During the first session, the teacher/researcher explained the working mechanics of the computer laboratory and answered any questions from the students. Then, the lessons began as students listen to enjoy the story. Next, the students revisited and identified words unknown to them by clicking on the word. The computerized storyboards serve as a remediator. These subjects saw the printed word highlighted and heard as the word was produced in sound. Students were required to listen to the story once while reading along. After completing those requirements, students could listen and/or read any story previously read or any story at a lower level. Students were introduced to a new WiggleWorks story every other day. During this project, students experimented with seven different stories that became progressively more challenging. The ability levels of the stories ranged from Kindergarten to second grade. The project continued for six weeks.

More detail about intervention and procedure

Results

The results were analyzed using a Paired-Samples T-test. An alpha level of .05 was set incorporating a two-tailed significance level. The analyses showed significant positive changes for both groups. The mean scores confirm that students using computerized storyboards demonstrate significant gains in their ability to recall a greater amount of new vocabulary words (See Table 1). The pre and posttest were analyzed using a Paired-Samples T test. The results demonstrate a statistically significant difference (p > .002) in the experimental (computer) group. A significant difference (p > .01) was also found (See Table 2) in the control group (Book/Tape).

Pretest-posttest analysis

Description of results

The mean scores of the pre and post vocabulary tests indicate a significant gain in the experimental (computer story board) group (MeanPre = 3.7; MeanPost = 16.9). A further analysis involving the reading ability of the individual students demonstrated that students with higher reading ability scored higher in the experimental and control groups than

Introduction of second independent variable

TABLE 1 Means and Standard Deviations

	Pretest		Posttest	
Group	M	SD	M	SD
Computer	3.7	4.37	16.9	13.17
Book/Tape	1.8	2.68	5.45	6.07

Mean scores
Standard deviation

(continued)

excerpt 2.1 *(continued)*

TABLE 2 Paired-Samples T-test

Group	df	t	P
Computer	9	4.18	0.002
Book/Tape	10	3.17	0.010

Inferential statistical test

average ability or low ability student. Those students who were performing successfully in their reading scored significantly higher than those students who were performing at a lower level.

Introduction of second independent variable (continued)

Discussion

The stories selected for this project were progressively more challenging so as to meet the needs of as many young readers as possible. Students with greater reading ability scored higher on the pretests and showed greater improvement on the posttests. These students seemed to possess a greater command of reading and technological skills required in maneuvering the storyboards.

Summary of results

Students with less reading ability did not gain as much from the experience. While they seemed to enjoy the stories, they were greatly challenged by the pre and posttest. These students would have been more successful with stories developmentally appropriate for their reading ability. Overall, the ability level of the students in the classroom seemed to mirror their performance in the computer-based reading instruction. Strong readers worked somewhat independently, average-ability students were at an instructional level with reading and technology skills, while students with less reading ability needed assistance with reading and technology. Students in the experimental group (computer storyboards) were greatly motivated by the use of computers. They enjoyed the interactive, multi-sensory aspect of learning. This was evidenced by the students' request to spend more time listening to stories on the computers. Multi-sensory teaching seemed to make their learning fun.

Additional results and explanation of results

Implications and Significance

This research project was designed to investigate the effects of computer-assisted instruction on first grade students' vocabulary development. With the integration of sights, colors, sounds, actions, plus the printed word, vocabulary lessons took on a new meaning. Students recognized the word on sight, remembered the word through association and phonemes, and quite a few could use the word as a part of their spoken and written vocabulary. Students were able to recognize the words in isolation and in text.

Conclusions

Overall, implications of this research project are that a 20-minute DEAR time using computerized storyboards directly results in improved vocabulary development among first grade students. Learning new vocabulary words took place at a faster pace with greater accuracy than with the direct teaching format. "Technology brings to your classroom the capability of connecting dynamic, interactive vocabulary learning with reading, writing. spelling, and content learning." (Fox and Mitchell, 2000, p. 66)

Findings related to previous research

Computerized classroom instruction does not infer inflated test scores or a magic potion for teaching. It is a motivating medium that enhances good teaching. The infusion of technology and literacy is a lifelong learning gift we create for our students.

Significance

excerpt 2.1 *(continued)*

Recommendations

Computer-assisted instruction has a positive influence on student's motivation, interest, and learning. This research project validates the effect that computer-assisted instruction has on first graders vocabulary development during a crucial time when they are learning to read. To improve upon this study, a concentrated effort should be made to determine the developmental reading level of each student. Students could then receive more individualized instruction at their appropriate reading level. Additionally, teachers/researchers need to move students from dependent direct instruction to more independent learning. A natural follow-up to this study could be to see if this move to more independent learning is facilitated by differing uses of technology in the classroom.

Restatement of conclusion

Suggestions for future research

References

Brinkman, D. & Torgeson, J. (1994). Computer administered instruction in phonological awareness: evaluation of the DaisyQuest program. *The Journal of Research and Development in Education, 27* (2), 126–137.

Case, C. & Truscott, D. M. (1999). The lure of bells and whistles: choosing the best software to support reading instruction. *Reading and Writing Quarterly, 15,* (4), p. 361.

Chall, J. (1992). The new reading debates: evidence from science, art, and ideology. *Teachers College Record, 94,* (2), 315.

Czubaj, C. (1997). Whole language literature reading instruction. *Education, 117* (4), 538.

Daniels, H. and Zemelman, S. (1999). Whole language works: sixty years of research. *Educational Research, 57,* (2), 32.

Dillon, D. R. (2000). Identifying beliefs and knowledge, uncovering tensions, and solving problems. *Kids insight: reconsidering how to meet the literacy needs of all students* (pp. 72–79). Newark, DE: International Reading Association.

Dockstader, J. (1999). Teachers of the 21st century know the what, why, and how of technology integration. *T.H.E. Journal, 26* (6), 73–74.

Eisznwine, M. J. & Hunt, D.A. (2000). Using a computer in literacy groups with emergent readers. *The Reading Teacher, 53* (6), 456.

Forcier, R. C. (1999). Computer applications in education. *The computer as an educational tool* (pp.60–93). Upper Saddle, NJ: Prentice-Hall. Inc.

Fox, B. J. & Mitchell, M. J. (2000). Using technology to support word recognition. spelling. and vocabulary acquisition. In R. Thurlow, W. J. Valmont, & S. B. Wepner (Eds.). *Linking Literacy and Technology.* Newark, DL: International Reading Association. Inc.

Hickman, C. (1984–2000). Kid Pix. Deluxe Version. [Unpublished computer software], Available: http://www.pixelpoppin.comlkid-pix/index.html

Hoffman, J. & Pearson, P. D. (2000). Reading teacher education in the next millennium: what your grandmother's teacher didn't know that your granddaughter's teacher should. *Reading Research Quarterly, 35,* (1), 28–44.

Howard, B. C., McGee, S., Purcell, S., & Schwartz, N. (2000). The experience of constructivism: transforming teacher epistemology. *Journal of Research on Computing in Education, 32,* (4), 455–465.

Kinzer, C. K. & Leu, D. J. (1999). *Effective Literacy Instruction.* Upper Saddle River, NJ: Prentice-Hall, Inc.

Mitchell, C. & S. (1984–2000). DaisyQuest. [Unpublished computer software]. Available: http://www.greatwave.com/html/daisys.html

Morrow, L. M. & Tracey, D. H. (1997). Strategies used for phonics instruction in early childhood classrooms. *The Reading Teacher, 50,* (8), 644.

Ray, L. C. & Wepner, S. B. (2000). Using technology for reading development. In R. Thurlow, W. J. Valmont, & S. B. Wepner (Eds.). *Linking Literacy and Technology.* Newark, DL: International Reading Association, Inc.

Sherry, L. (1996). Issues in distance learning. International *Journal of Educational Telecommunications, 1* (4), 337–365.

Wagner, R. (1978). HyperStudio. [Unpublished computer software]. Available: http://www.hyperstudio.com/

WiggleWorks [Computer Software]. (1994–1996). New York: CAST and Scholastic, Inc.

References in APA format

Title of journal article: initial cap only

Title of journal: cap each word

Year published

Pages

Volume

Title of book: initial cap only

Chapter in a book

Publisher

Journal title and volume number italic

Web reference

Source: From Boling, C., Martin, S. H., & Martin, M. A. (2002). The effects of computer-assisted instruction on first grade students' vocabulary development. *Reading Improvement, 39*(2), 79–88. Provided by Reading Improvement, Phillip Feldman, Ed. Reprinted by permission.

How to Read Qualitative Research: Anatomy of a Qualitative Example

There is greater diversity in the formats used to report qualitative research than in the formats typical of quantitative studies. While there is not a single mode for representing qualitative research, many published reports have four major sections: Introduction, Methodology, Findings, and Conclusions. In contrast to those found in quantitative studies, however, these sections may not be identified clearly or may be identified by descriptive terms related to the topic. Excerpt 2.2 provides an example of a qualitative research article.

Introduction The *Introduction* provides a general background of the study, indicating the potential importance of the research. It summarizes the general intentions of the investigator, along with a general statement of the research problem or purpose. For a journal article, usually only one of many research foci are reported. The introduction includes a preliminary literature review to present possible conceptual frameworks that will be useful in understanding the data and results. The review justifies the need for a descriptive case study. The introduction may also indicate the structure of the rest of the report.

Methodology The *Methodology* section describes the design of the study, including the selection and description of the site, the role of the researcher, initial entry for observation, the time and length of the study, the number of participants and how they were selected, and data collection and analysis strategies. This information is needed to evaluate the soundness of the procedures. The amount of detail contained in this section will vary, depending on the type of research report. In relatively short published articles the methodology may be part of the introduction.

Findings and Interpretations In this section, the researcher presents the data that were gathered, usually in the form of a lengthy narrative, and analyzes the data. This should be done in sufficient detail to allow the reader to judge the accuracy of the analysis. The data are used to illustrate and substantiate the researcher's interpretations. Analysis is often intermixed with the presentation of data. The data are often in the form of quotes by participants. It is important to indicate the purpose of data analysis and to describe what has been learned by synthesizing the information. Because the presentation is in narrative form, there are frequently a number of descriptive subtitles connoting different findings.

Conclusions The *Conclusion* usually includes a restatement of the initial focus of the study and how the data results and analyses impinge on that focus. Implications of the results can be elaborated, as well as implications for further research.

References The References section provides full bibliographic information for all previously completed work that is cited in the article. While APA format is common, some journals have a unique style.

Guidelines for Evaluating Qualitative Research

To understand qualitative research, it is necessary to carefully read the entire report. This is how readers are able to identify with the investigators and understand how they have come to their conclusions. The process by which this occurs is important, and to understand this process, it is necessary to read from beginning to end. As with quantitative studies, certain questions should be asked about the report to judge its quality.

Introduction

1. Is the focus, purpose, or topic of the study stated clearly?
2. Are there situations or problems that lead to the focus of the study? Is there a rationale for the study? Is it clear that the study is important?
3. Is there background research and theory to help refine the research questions?

4. Does the introduction contain an overview of the design?
5. Is the literature review pertinent to the focus of the research? Is the literature analyzed as well as described?

Methodology

1. Are the particular sites described to identify their uniqueness or typicality?
2. How was initial entry into the field established?
3. How was the researcher's presence in the field explained to others? What was the role of the researcher?
4. Who was observed? How long were they observed? How much time was spent collecting data?
5. Does the researcher report any limitations to access of pertinent data?
6. Are the data representative of naturally occurring behavior?
7. Are limitations of the design acknowledged?

Findings and Interpretations

1. Are the perspectives of the different participants clearly presented? Are participants' words or comments quoted?
2. Is contextual information for participants' statements provided?
3. Are multiple perspectives presented?
4. Are the results well documented? Are assertions and interpretations illustrated by results?
5. Is it clear what the researchers believe the data indicated? Are personal beliefs kept separate from the data?
6. Are the interpretations reasonable? Were researcher preconceptions and biases acknowledged?

Conclusions

1. Are the conclusions logically consistent with the findings?
2. Are limitations of the research design and focus indicated?
3. Are implications of the findings indicated?

EXCERPT 2.2 Anatomy of a Qualitative Research Article

The Developmental Progression of Children's Oral Story Inventions

Eugene Geist Jerry Aldridge

This study investigated stories that children created after being told the Grimm version of selected tales. These stories were told as an instruction to the children on story structure and to familiarize children with ideas of plot, character, and conflict in stories. This cross-sectional study considered what differences are evident in the oral fairy tales that children tell at different ages. Stories from children in kindergarten, first grade, second grade, and third grade were collected and analyzed. For the purpose of this study, the following research questions were asked. These questions guided the research and eventually became the major coding categories.

1) Is there a developmental difference in the type of story (i.e., personal narrative, fantasy, realistic fiction) children tell when they are asked to invent a fairy tale?
2) Are there developmental differences in the content of children's stories among age groups?
3) Are there developmental differences in how children organize the content of their invented fairy tales?

Abstract (rather long)

(continued)

excerpt 2.2 *(continued)*

A qualitative research methodology was used for this study. Children's orally invented stories were tape recorded and transcribed. The data were analyzed using content analysis of the transcripts.

This study indicates that children's orally told invented fairy tales can be used (a) to promote cognitive development, (b) to assess cognitive development, and (c) to identify emotional conflicts that children are experiencing. This study also indicates that second grade is a good time to promote creativity and imaginations as this was the age in which children were most confident in their imaginative abilities.

Abstract (continued)

Few studies have been conducted on children's oral story inventions (Aldridge, Eddowes, Ewing, & Kuby, 1994). Studies on children's interest in folk and fairytales have not touched on children's invented "fairy tales" and how they can reflect developmental issues. There have been many examinations of written retellings of fairy tales (Boydston, 1994; Gambrell, Pfeiffer, & Wilson, 1985; Morrow, 1986). However, few works have examined oral stories invented by children. Invented oral stories can give a valuable insight into a child's cognitive, affective, and creative development (Allan & Bertoia, 1992; Markham, 1983; Sutton-Smith, 1985).

Suggests need for study

This study investigated stories that children created after being told the Grimm version of selected tales. These stories were told as an instruction to the children on story structure and to familiarize children with ideas of plot, character, and conflict in stories. The Grimm (1993) versions were chosen because the literature suggests that they are the closest to the oral tradition (Zipes, 1988). This cross-sectional study considered what differences are evident in the oral fairy tales that children tell at different ages. Stories from children in kindergarten, first grade, second grade, and third grade were collected and analyzed (Geist & Aldridge, 1999).

General research problem

For the purpose of this study, the following research questions were asked. These questions guided the research and eventually became the major coding categories.

1) Is there a developmental difference in the type of story (i.e., personal narrative, fantasy, realistic fiction) children tell when they are asked to invent a fairy tale?
2) Are there developmental differences in the content of children's stories among age groups?
3) Are there developmental differences in how children organize the content of their invented fairy tales?

Research questions

Method

A qualitative research methodology was used for this study. Children's orally invented stories were tape recorded and transcribed. The data were analyzed using content analysis of the transcripts. According to Carney (1972), "content analysis is any technique for making inferences by objectively and systematically identifying specified characteristics of messages" (p. 25).

Overall research design

A semistructured interview format was used to collect data. The children were asked to make up a fairy tale and tell it to the researcher. The researcher prompted the subject if there was a long pause. The researcher also had the child start over if the child was engaging in a retelling of a story that the researcher recognized. The data were then analyzed using a content analysis.

Researcher conducted all interviews

Participants

Not "subjects"

Convenience sampling was the method used to select study participants. The classrooms chosen were believed to facilitate the expansion of a developing theory because the sample was homogeneous. All subjects were African American and from low socioeconomic families. The subjects for this study were students in four classrooms at an elementary

Indicates characteristics of participants

excerpt 2.2 *(continued)*

school in a low socioeconomic area of an urban city in the Southeastern United States. The racial make up of the sample was 100% African American.

Indicates characteristics of participants (continued)

Data Collection

Each classroom participated in a 45-minute lesson on fairy tales and story structure each day for 4 days. The lesson consisted of reading and discussing the plots and characters of fairy tales. After the 4 days, the children were asked, individually, to make up a fairy tale and tell it orally. The stories were tape recorded and transcribed. A content analysis of the transcripts was performed as described by Carney (1992).

Data gathered as tape-recorded interviews

Data analysis

One kindergarten, one first-grade, one second-grade, and one third-grade classroom, each with approximately 15 students, participated in this study. Each classroom was given an identical session on fairy tales and story structure. This session consisted of reading fairy tales to the students and discussing the aspects of the story. The specific description of the 5 days of storytelling and discussion are found in Geist and Aldridge (1999). These procedures were modified from Allan and Bertoia (1992) by Boydston (1994). Allan and Bertoia developed a procedure to initiate the discussion of fairy tales. This outline was used for seventh graders, however, because this study was interested in students in kindergarten, first, second, and third grades, a procedure modified by Boydston (1994), was used for this study. Boydston's outline was developed for second graders but is appropriate for the ages targeted in this study.

Shows modification of previously used methods

Data Analysis

Analysis of the data was generated from the transcripts of the audiotapes. The research questions served as a guide for conducting the analysis. Each question became a major coding category broken down by age. The results of each age were then compared to each other to build a model of children's invented fairy tales. Bogdan and Biklen (1992) stated that preassigned coding systems are developed when researchers explore particular topics or aspects of the study.

Coding emerges from the data for many qualitative studies

Inter-rater reliability was conducted on this study by having an educational professional with extensive knowledge of fairy tales and their form, function, and uses independently categorize the data. Another rater was trained in content analysis and was experienced in the content analysis method. This researcher had performed qualitative studies on fairy tales and children's storytelling in the past. The two raters participated in two practice sessions of reading and analyzing children's oral invented stories.

The recordings were transcribed and copied. The independent rater and the researcher received identical copies of the transcripts. Because the three foreshadowed questions were used as a framework for the categories, the independent rater was given a copy of the foreshadowed questions. Each rater read the transcripts as many times as needed and noted themes related to genre, content, and organization. Each rater then independently compared the common themes from each grade and constructed a model for genre, content, and organization.

Use of trained, independent rater improves credibility

Both raters discussed the method for analysis before beginning. When a theme or thread was identified, it was highlighted by a colored marker that identified it with other items that belonged with that thread. The rater wrote notes in the margin next to this highlighted text. Then all of the text passages with the same color highlight were collected by grade. The rater then reread the passages and came up with a phrase or word that best described the common characteristics of those passages. The descriptive phrases were then compared to the phrases for the other grades to determine if a model could be constructed. Often, there was more than one model that was evident in each of the categories.

These themes and models were then compared. The themes and models that were consistent between the two raters were retained and clarified. The themes and models that were not consistent between the two raters were not included. Each story

(continued)

excerpt 2.2 *(continued)*

was then categorized independently by each rater into the rough model that had been developed.

Results

Findings from this study suggest a developmental shift in the genre, content, and organization of children's oral invented stories. The genre of the children's stories moved from the fantastical to stories based on personal experiences. Kindergarten children told mostly fantasy stories, first and second graders told mostly realistic fiction, and third graders told mostly personal narratives.

Results directly related to research question

The content of the children's stories showed development in two areas. First, there was development in the basis of their stories. Kindergarten children based their stories on previously heard material, first graders based theirs on familiar surroundings, second graders based their inventions on their imagination, and third graders tended to base their stories on personal experiences.

Second, there was development in how parents were depicted in the stories. Kindergartners, first, and second graders depicted parents as heroes and comforters. Third graders depicted parents as authority figures.

The content of the stories of all the grades contained reflections of the children's fears and concerns from everyday life. Fears about being kidnapped or other stresses, such as performance anxiety and social pressures, were reflected in their stories.

Examples from participants

The organization of the stories moved from disjointed sentences to a coherent whole story. States that could be delineated were (a) disjointed, (b) phrase disjointed, (c) short-utilitarian, (d) sidetracked, and (e) coherent whole.

Genre

Inquiry paradigm

The development of genre moved from the fantastical notions of kindergartners to the realistic personal narratives of third graders. Kindergartners told fantastical stories of talking umbrellas, flying to Mars, magic, and evil witches that turned children into food. First and second graders told realistic fiction stories about hunters, kings, queens, and an occasional witch; however, almost all of the actions of the characters were in the realm of possibility. Third graders tended to tell personal narratives that related directly to their life experiences; they were simply retelling events that happened to them or to someone they knew.

Detail provided to show depth of understanding

The study suggests the genre was influenced by 3 things. First it was influenced by the classroom context. In the kindergarten classroom, the researcher observed a lot of fantasy literature. Children heard stories daily about talking animals and fantastical actions in the books the teachers read to them. However, as the grades progressed, the researcher observed that the teachers provided more realistic literature and less fantasy. This, in turn, affected the genre of the stories that the children told. Second was the children's developing understanding of the difference between fantasy and reality. As children begin to understand the concept of causality and move into concrete operations, the concept of what is possible and logical versus what is illogical, magical and impossible becomes more delineated. The second and third grade stories reflect this move toward reality based stories. Third, was the base material that children chose. As we have already mentioned, children tended to choose more personal material as they got older until at third grade, they tell personal, true to life personal narratives. Obviously, this shift is going to affect the genre of the story that they tell. This will be discussed further in the examination of the content of the children's stories.

Explanation of overall findings concerning genre

Content

There were two developmental themes that could be delineated in the content of the children's stories. The first was the basis that the children used to construct their stories. The

excerpt 2.2 *(continued)*

second was the role of parents in the children's stories. Third, the content of all the grades contained reflections of children's fears and concerns.

Children in kindergarten based their stories on previously heard material. They did not appear confident in their ability to be successful in making up a story on their own, so they used stories that they had heard or read recently to build their story around. First graders were a little more sure of themselves so they did not need specific stories on which to base their inventions. However, they still needed to base the settings and characteristics on things that were familiar to them. This gave them the framework for their stories. By second grade, the children did not need outside structure on which to build their stories. They could rely on their imagination completely as the basis for their stories. In third grade, the surge of imagination noted in second grade appeared to be gone. Either by discouragement or development, children had given up on imagination as the basis of their stories. These children told personal narratives that used personal experiences as the basis for their inventions. These types of stories required little or no imagination.

Researcher opinion

A second developmental theme evident in the content of the children's orally invented stories was that at around third grade children began to consider peers, rather than parents, as their primary social contacts. This transition was reflected in their stories. In kindergarten and first grade, children were still primarily dependent on their parents for social and emotional interaction. However, around second grade they began to bond with peers, and the peer group became their primary social group with many third graders.

Researcher synthesis of findings from each grade level

Before third grade, parents in children's stories were heroes and comforters. It was they who rescued the child from the grasp of the monster. A major shift had occurred In the third graders' stories, when parents were depicted as strict authority figures who were present to judge and punish. Third grade children's stories showed a common theme of fear of parental reprisals in this sample.

The stories also show a reflection of children's fears and anxieties. Children are surrounded with stress that is often not released. Stories offer children this release. The stories of all the grades contained personal reflections of fears and stresses. Especially prevalent were fears of kidnap and murder. The children in this particular school had experience with a classmate being kidnapped and murdered so it is not surprising that this fear appeared in their stories.

Researcher reflection on characteristics of participants

Organization

Three developmental aspects of children's organization of invented stories were determined in this study. These included:

1) There was a clear developmental sequence to the way children organized their stories.
2) Egocentrism decreased through interactions in the social environment.
3) The distinction of the difference between fantasy and reality developed with age.

Even after the children were involved in the 4-day workshop on fairy tales, a developmental pattern still emerged. This suggests that there are aspects to children's understanding of story structure that is developmental and cannot be totally directly taught. The workshop focused on the characters, settings, plot, and organization of fairy tales. The children were instructed that fairy tales have a clear beginning, middle, and end; the beginning contains an introduction of the characters, setting, and problems; the middle of the story discusses how the characters go about solving the problems; and the end of the story contains the resolution. Thus, the children were familiar with the parts of the stories, and still a majority of the children were unable to use the information gen in the workshops to construct a coherent whole story. This suggests that the progression through stages of organization is developmental and not based on training.

Review of salient characteristics of context

Conclusion

Implication of conclusion

(continued)

excerpt 2.2 *(continued)*

There was a cognitive developmental sequence in the organization of children's oral invented stories. So distinct were the differences, a developmental model can be proposed based on the data. The first stage can be characterized by the children's being unable to form a coherent ordered whole story. They told disjointed stories in which individual thoughts were juxtaposed. This is consistent with the findings of Piaget (1958) that children could not order a story into a coherent whole until about the age of 8.

Synthesis of data to suggest model

In the second stage, the children could string a series of thoughts together into coherent phrases, however, the phrases of about two or three sentences were juxtaposed against other phrases to which they had little relationship. In the third stage, children told short, utilitarian stories that just included the basics of a story with no elaboration. The children were attempting to keep their stories ordered and coherent and, if there was too much information, they got confused.

The fourth stage showed the result of this confusion. Children got sidetracked because they included more elaboration and lost track of the original story line. Eventually, they got back on track, and ended the story on the same theme with which they started. The final stage was characterized by children telling a coherent, elaborate story from beginning to end without getting sidetracked.

Conclusions and Implications

This study showed that literacy is not totally in the domain of social knowledge. The learning of words, letters, and rules of language must be passed down through the culture; these aspects of literacy cannot be invented by children without help. However, there are aspects of literacy that involve what Piaget deemed logico-mathematical knowledge. This study suggests that story structure is, at least partially, logico-mathematical knowledge. The part-whole relationship (Piaget, 1970) plays a part in the structure of children's stories. The children in this study all received direct instruction on story structure, but still a developmental sequence was evident. Children's understanding of story structure Is dependent on more than direct instruction.

Findings related to previous research

Story structure is learned through interaction with text and words rather than through direct instruction. Children will invent story structure by telling and writing stories. The reactions from the audience and from their rereading or listening to other students' stories cause disequilibrium, which according to Piaget (1970), leads to development.

This study indicates that children's orally told invented fairy tales can be used (a) to promote cognitive development, (b) to assess cognitive development, and (c) to identify emotional conflicts that children are experiencing. This study also indicates that second grade is a good time to promote creativity and imaginations as this was the age in which children were most confident in their imaginative abilities.

Overall conclusions

Orally invented stories can be used to promote cognitive development. Each time children tell a story, they must attempt first to order it mentally. This mental activity promotes the construction of knowledge. A developmental sequence to the organization of orally told stories appears evident from the stories children told in this study. To promote the movement through these developmental stages, children must be provided with the opportunity to tell stories to an audience and receive social interaction. Each time the child tells a story, the reaction from the audience causes disequilibrium. If the audience does not understand the story, the child must examine why the audience did not understand it. This type of construction through social interaction was also described by Kamii (2000) in math development. This works just as well for storytelling. The feedback from peers helps the child to overcome the limitations of egocentrism and egocentric thought.

Implications

Points related to previous research

Orally told invented fairy tales can also be used for assessment of children's cognitive abilities. This can give a teacher an idea of the areas in which a child might need work. This study was consistent with Piaget (1952) with regard to developmental sequences through which children must progress. This sequence can be used to assist in screening students who might need assistance.

Implications

excerpt 2.2 *(continued)*

These stories can be used to identify emotional differences or possible traumas in children's lives. As this study and others have shown (Allan, 1988; Allan & Bertoia, 1992), children include stressful events and emotional problems they are dealing with in their stories. These orally told stories could help screen for physical and sexual abuse, fears and concerns, and emotional problems.

Implications (continued)

Points related to previous research

While this study showed promise for identifying developmental changes in children's oral storytelling inventions from kindergarten through third grade much more research needs to be done. Researchers should also seek to "identify individual and cultural variations in the discourse and oral inventions of young children" (Geist & Aldridge, 1999, p. 822).

Suggestion for subsequent studies

References

Not APA style

Aldridge, J., Eddowes, A., Ewing, J., & Kuby, P. (1994) Analytical psychology, constructivism, and education. Journal of Instructional Psychology, 21, 59–367.

Allan, J. (1988). Inscapes of the child's world. Dallas, TX: Spring Publications.

Allan, J., & Bertoia, J. (1992). Written paths to healing. Dallas, TX: Spring Publications.

Bogdan, R., & Biklen, S. (1992). Qualitative research for educators (2nd ed.). Boston: Knopp.

Boydston, R. (1994). Written retellings of fairy tales. Unpublished doctoral dissertation, University of Alabama at Birmingham, Birmingham, Alabama.

Camey, T. F. (1972). Content analysis: A technique for systematic inference from communication. Winnepeg, Manitoba: University of Manitoba Press.

Gambrell, L. B., Pfeiffer, W. R., & Wilson, R. M. (1985). The effects of telling upon reading comprehension and recall of text information. Journal of Educational Research, 78, 216–220.

Geist, E. A., & Aldridge, J. (1999). Genre, content, and organization of kindergarten children's oral story inventions. Psychological Reports, 85, 817–822.

Grimm Brothers (1993). The complete Brothers Grimm fairy tales. New York: Pantheon Books.

Kamii, C. (2000). Young children reinvent arithmetic (2nd ed.). New York: Teachers College Press.

Markham, R. H. (1983). The fairy tale: An introduction to literature and the creative process. College English, 45, 31–45.

Morrow, L. M. (1986). The effect of structural guidance in story retellings of children's dictation of original stories. Journal of Reading Behavior, 18, 135–151.

Piaget, J. (1952). The thought and language of the child. London: Humanities Press.

Piaget, J. (1958). The growth of logical thinking from childhood to adolescence. New York: Basic Books.

Piaget, J. (1970). Structuralism. New York: Basic Books.

Sutton-Smith, B. (1985). The development of fictional narrative performances. Topics In Language Disorders, 7, 1–10.

Zipes, J. (1988). The Brothers Grimm. New York: Routledge.

Year published

Pages

Volume

Journal title: cap each word

Location of publisher

Source: From Geist, E., & Aldridge, J. (2002). The developmental progression of children's oral story inventions. *Journal of Instructional Psychology, 29,* 33–39. Reprinted with permission of the Journal of Instructional Psychology.

SUMMARY

This chapter has provided an overview of common terminology of types of research designs and the standard formats of published articles. The major points in this chapter are as follows:

1. Research design is the general plan of the study, including when, from whom, and how data are collected.
2. In experimental research, the investigator studies cause-and-effect relationships by manipulating a factor and seeing how that factor relates to the outcome of the study.
3. True experimental research is characterized by random assignment of subjects to groups.
4. Quasi-experimental research investigates causation without random assignment.
5. Single-subject research investigates the causal relationship between a factor and the behavior of a single individual.
6. *Nonexperimental* is a generic term that refers to research in which there is no direct control over causation. Nonexperimental designs can be classified as descriptive, comparative, correlational, survey, ex post facto, and secondary data analysis.

7. Interactive qualitative modes of inquiry use face-to-face data collection to construct in-depth understandings of informants' perspectives.
8. An ethnography is a detailed description and interpretation of a culture or system.
9. A phenomenological study describes the meanings of a lived experience from the perspective of the informants.
10. A case study investigates a single bounded system over time using multiple sources of data.
11. Grounded theory is used to develop detailed concepts or propositions about a particular phenomenon.
12. Critical studies emphasize the subjectivity of knowledge and contemporary perspectives of critical, feminist, and postmodern theory.
13. Noninteractive qualitative modes of inquiry, or analytical research, investigates concepts and events through document analysis.
14. Mixed-method studies use elements of both quantitative and qualitative designs.
15. Quantitative studies follow a well-established format and contain similar sections. In qualitative studies, the format will vary but will usually include an introduction and literature review, methodology, findings and interpretation, and conclusions.

CHECK YOURSELF

Multiple-choice review items, with answers, are available on the Companion Website for this book.

www.ablongman.com/macmillanschumacher6e.

APPLICATION PROBLEMS

1. Classify each study described below as a type of research design: experimental, nonexperimental, quantitative, qualitative, or mixed-method.
   a. A pilot investigation of the validity of the Back Stroke Test to identify problem swimmers
   b. A comparison of the effect of two reading programs on fourth-grade classes in Kalamazoo
   c. An investigation of the structure of attitudes of college students
   d. The effect of extrinsic rewards on the motivation of randomly assigned children to play groups
   e. A survey of principals' general attitudes toward collective bargaining as well as interviews with a small number of principals
   f. A study of the relative effectiveness of different counseling techniques used by counselors over the past five years
   g. An investigation of the difference in attendance between students in two high schools with different leadership styles
   h. A posttest-only study of the effect of humorously written review sentences on comprehension for two groups of children
   i. A study of the meaning of merit pay to teachers
2. Locate one quantitative and one qualitative journal article. For each article, identify the major sections and answer the questions provided in the guidelines for evaluating each type of article. Rate the overall credibility of each article.

3. Write a brief statement that indicates which type of research design—quantitative or qualitative—is used most commonly in your field of study.
4. Ask a professor in your field of study how he or she reads a research article. Ask about what he or she reads first, second, and so forth. Also ask what your professor does about statistical procedures included that he or she does not understand and what features he or she focuses on to judge the overall credibility of the study.

NOTE

1. We restrict the use of descriptive design to situations in which comparisons or correlations are not used only to provide a way to distinguish these designs from others. It would not be uncommon to find researchers using descriptive and nonexperimental designs interchangeably.

CHAPTER

3 Research Problems: Statements, Questions, and Hypotheses

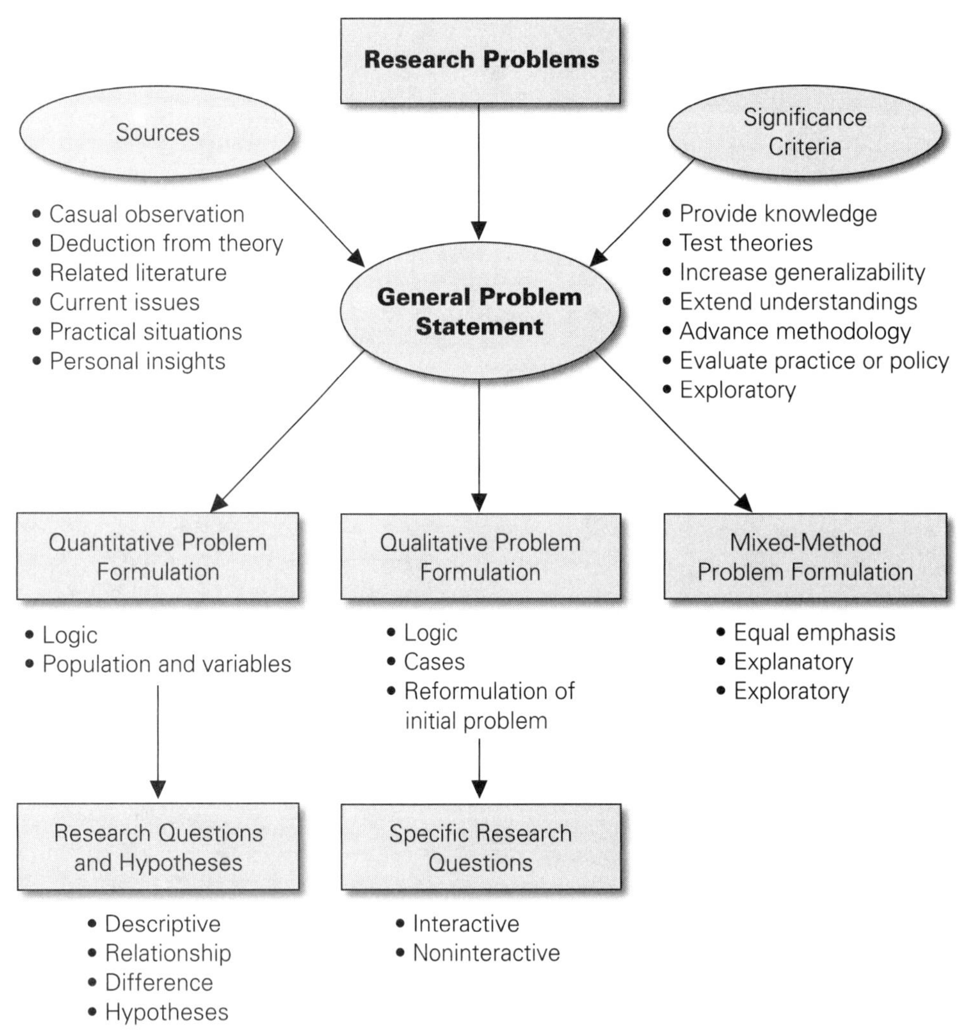

KEY TERMS

research problem
quantitative:
- construct
- variable
- categorical variable
- continuous or measured variable
- independent variable
- manipulated or experimental variable
- dependent variable
- predictor variable
- criterion variable
- operational definition
- research hypothesis

qualitative:
- case
- qualitative field records
- narrative descriptions
- synthesized abstractions
- foreshadowed problems
- significance of the problem

Perhaps the most difficult aspect of research is formulating a clear, concise, and manageable research problem. As explained in this chapter, the statement of the research problem is crucial because it communicates to others the focus and importance of the problem, the educational context and scope, and the framework for reporting the results.

This chapter also discusses common sources used to generate research problems and criteria for evaluating their significance. Quantitative problem formulation uses reasoning to link the constructs, variables, and instruments. Qualitative problems are reformulated as the researcher builds from field records of social situations of a selected case and later relates them to broader phenomena. Criteria for judging the adequacy of the problem statement are addressed in this chapter, as well.

THE NATURE OF RESEARCH PROBLEMS

Asking questions about educational practices constitutes the initial step in research. Some questions, although important, may not connote research problems as stated. A **research problem** implies the possibility of empirical investigation—that is, of data collection and analysis.

Vague propositions and value questions are not research problems per se. Questions such as How can we prevent student dropout? and propositions such as Democratic institutions are a natural manifestation of the American culture are too vague to be researchable. Value questions ask which of two things should or should not be done. As stated, value questions, cannot be investigated empirically. In the process of asking such questions, however, a researchable problem may emerge.

A research problem is formally stated to indicate evidence-based inquiry. Quantitative research problems may be phrased as statements, questions, or hypotheses. Some examples of quantitative research problems are:

- What are the attitudes of the parents toward a school's student retention policy?
- Is there a difference in motivation between age cohorts of male and female graduate students?
- There is a positive relationship between school climate and student achievement.
- The purpose of this research is to study adolescent loneliness.

Each of these statements implies data collection and analysis.

Qualitative research problems are phrased as research purposes or questions but *never* as hypotheses. Qualitative problems usually are phrased more broadly than quantitative problems by using terms such as *How? What?* and *Why?* Stating the situation or context limits the problem. A qualitative study might examine in detail, for instance, one specific situation, person, state, or historical period. Some examples are:

- An interpretative research design was used to examine urban middle school students' meanings attributed to teachers' caring relationships.
- What does being a "single parent" mean to teachers who have young children to rear—how does being a single parent affect their parenting, job, and social roles?
- The purpose of this study is to examine and analyze the development of female academies in Vermont.

Sources of Problems

A problem is identified initially as a *general topic*, and after much preliminary work, the general topic is focused as a *specific research problem*. But where does one begin to find even general topics? The most common sources are casual observations, deductions from theory, reviews of the literature, current social issues, practical situations, and personal experiences and insights:

- **Casual observations** are rich sources of questions and hunches. Decisions frequently are made based on assumptions about the effects of practices on pupils or staff, without empirical data. Evidence-based inquiries often start with observations of certain relationships, routine ways of doing things, and innovations. Each of these inquiries may solve a practical problem, propose a new theory, or identify variables not yet in the literature.
- **Deductions from theory** also can suggest research problems. The applicability of a theory to a specific educational problem is unknown until tested empirically. Such a study could verify the usefulness of a theory for explaining one or more educational occurrences.
- **Related literature** may suggest a need to replicate a study to increase the generalizability and validity of those previous findings. In many instances, it is impossible to randomize the subjects, which limits the generalizability of the findings. When studies have been replicated, researchers can have more confidence in the findings. Citing related literature enables qualitative studies to extend the empirical understandings to other situations.
- **Current social and political issues** in U.S. society often lead to educational research. For example, the women's movement raised questions about sexual equity in general and about gender stereotyping in educational materials and practices. Similarly, recent immigration policies have suggested research questions about multiculturalism in education.
- **Practical situations** may suggest evaluation and policy studies. Questions for such research may focus on educational needs; information for program planning, development, and implementation; and the effectiveness of a given practice.
- **Personal experience and insights** may suggest research problems that can be examined in depth through qualitative methodologies. For example, a teacher who has worked with exceptional children can recognize more readily the meanings in a situation involving such children than an ethnographer who has had no prior contact with exceptional children. Being able to empathize and being able to recognize the subtle meanings in a situation are important skills in most qualitative research.

Formal Problem Statements

Researchers use formal problem statements to guide their research. Such a statement introduces the reader to the importance of the problem, places the problem in an educational context, and provides the framework for reporting the results. The problem statement orients the reader to the significance of the study and the research questions or hypotheses to follow.

The Focus, Educational Context, and Significance of the Problem In any well-written problem statement, the reader is not kept in suspense but rather told directly and immediately the general focus, educational context, and significance of the problem. For example, in Excerpt 3.1 the reader is told about the expected shortage in the number of

EXCERPT 3.1 Problem Statement: Framework

Who will lead the schools during the 21st century? . . . The problem is exacerbated by . . . teacher reluctance to enter administration coupled with the number of administrator retirements present a significant challenge to boards, superintendents, and communities. . . .

To help find a solution to this problem, a study was conducted of 189 master's students enrolled in a Midwestern university's educational leadership program. Students completed a survey identifying factors that influenced their decision to apply for an administrative position. (p. 75)

Source: From Cooley, V., & Shen, J. (1999). Who will lead? The top 10 factors that influence teachers moving into administration. *NASSP Bulletin, 83*(606), 75–80.

school administrators and about teachers' reluctance to enter administration. The study was conducted to identify factors that influenced teachers' decisions to apply for an administration position.

A Framework for Results and Conclusions The problem statement also provides the framework for reporting the conclusions (e.g., what information will be presented). Excerpt 3.1 exemplifies the framework for the findings of a study. Ten factors that teachers consider in applying for administrative positions were reported and discussed in that study, with implications for recruiting and retaining a new generation of school leaders.

Qualitative problem statements also provide the framework for reporting the findings and interpretations. For example, in a recent study, the research problem was to report the "findings on the perception of poor single mothers regarding the helpfulness of their support systems in enabling them to work" (Wijnberg & Weinger, 1998). The findings were organized as early dreams, perceived network support and resources, coping styles, and social support when ill.

The introductory paragraphs of a study are difficult to write, as they must convey a lot of information succinctly. Researchers frequently rewrite these paragraphs as they formulate the significance of the study and research questions. They may even write the final version of the introduction after the study has been completed. Regardless, researchers begin with an initial problem statement to guide their activities.

PROBLEM FORMULATION IN QUANTITATIVE RESEARCH

Asking questions about a general topic is the starting point for defining a research problem. Then, the problem is narrowed to specific research questions or hypotheses. For example, the topic of educational policy-making might focus on school board policies, and that broad topic might be narrowed to certain policies, such as fiscal, student, or personnel. The topic can be focused even more: Is the interest in the antecedents to the policies, the process of policy-making, or the consequences of the policies for whom? From one general topic, a number of questions can thus be generated. Suppose the selected topic is instruction. Again, one could ask similar questions: What kind of instruction? Is the focus on the antecedents, the process, or the consequences? Is the interest in students of specific ages or with certain characteristics?

If the problem is too general, then the results will be difficult to interpret. Ultimately, the researcher has to make decisions about the selection of variables, the population, and the *logic for the problem*. This means that the initial problem statement is usually revised many times. The logic of quantitative problems is illustrated in Figure 3.1.

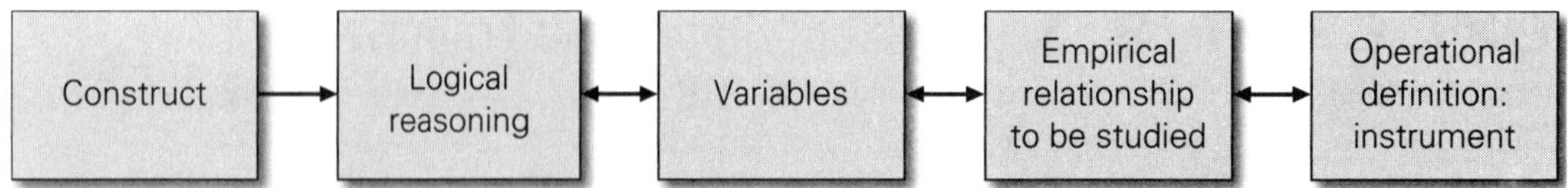

FIGURE 3.1 **Quantitative Research: The Logic of Constructs, Variables, and Operational Definitions**

The Logic of Constructs, Variables, and Operational Definitions

To formulate a problem, researchers begin with an abstract construct, logically link that construct to a set of variables, and then decide the operational definition for each variable. The reasoning process moves from an abstract construct to less abstract variables to a selected instrument. The arrows in Figure 3.1 indicate that several decisions are made and reviewed *before* data are collected.

Constructs In research, an abstract concept is called a **construct.** Often derived from theory, a construct expresses the idea behind a set of particulars. Examples of constructs are motivation, intelligence, thinking, anxiety, self-concept, achievement, and aptitude. Another way to define a construct is to say that it is created by combining variables in a meaningful pattern. Such variables as visual perception, sight/sound discrimination, audio acuity, and left-to-right orientation are meaningfully combined to suggest the construct of reading readiness.

Variables A **variable** is an *attribute* or *level* that expresses a construct and has different values, depending on how it is used in a particular study. There are several kinds of variables. A variable used to separate subjects or entities into two or more attributes is a **categorical variable.** Categorical variables may have only two attributes (e.g., male/female, married/single, and pass/fail) or more than two levels (e.g., income level, educational attainment, religious affiliation). A **continuous** or **measured variable** is one in which the attribute or level of an entity is measured and can assume an infinite number of values within a range (e.g., socioeconomic status, test score, and age). Each variable should be a separate and distinct phenomenon. Educational research investigates many factors as variables: classroom variables (e.g., teaching styles, interaction patterns, cognitive levels of questions); environmental variables (e.g., parental educational level, social class, family structure); and personal variables (e.g., age, gender, intelligence, motivation, self-concept).

Types of Variables In experimental research, one variable precedes another, either logically or in time. The variable that comes first and influences or predicts is called the **independent, manipulated,** or **experimental variable**—that is, the variable that is manipulated or changed by the researcher to investigate the effect on a dependent variable. The second variable, which is affected or predicted by the independent variable, is the **dependent variable** (see Excerpt 3.2). The independent variable is the *antecedent;* the dependent variable is the *consequence*. The dependent variable is labeled as such because its value depends on and varies with the value of the independent variable. Suppose a researcher wants to see the effect of the timing of a review on social studies achievement. The researcher will manipulate the timing of the review—immediate and delayed—and then measure the effects on social studies achievement.

In nonexperimental research, the independent variable *cannot* be manipulated. For example, a study of the effect of school size (independent variable) on achievement (dependent variable) may use large, medium, and small schools (levels of the independent variable). Obviously, the researcher will not manipulate the sizes of the selected schools but will choose the schools from enrollment records. In some correlational research, the antecedent variable is called the **predictor variable** and the predicted variable is called the **criterion variable.** In a study that examines the relationship of scores on the Scholas-

EXCERPT 3.2 Experimental Research: Independent and Dependent Variables

Research questions to examine the effects of teaching a lesson of emotionally charged issues on achievement, attitude, . . . [using Multisensory Instructional Packages {MIP}]:

1. Will there be significantly higher student achievement test gains when the Holocaust is taught using the MIP as opposed to when it is taught traditionally?
2. Will there be significantly higher student attitude test scores toward instruction methods when the Holocaust is taught with the MIP as opposed to when it is taught traditionally? (p. 43)

Source: From Farkas, R. D. (2003). Effects of traditional versus learning-styles instructional methods on middle school students. *Journal of Educational Research, 97*(1), 42–51.

tic Aptitude Test (SAT) to success in college, the predictor variable is the SAT scores and the criterion variable is college success. In other correlational studies, there is no obvious antecedent variable; such is the case in considering the relationship between self-concept and achievement. The researcher here is not interested in prediction but in determining the strength and direction of the relationship between the variables (see Excerpt 3.3). Some researchers use the terms *independent* and *dependent* with correlational and other non-experimental research when it is clear that one variable precedes the other variable or that categories have been created to allow comparisons.

In most descriptive research and some survey research, there is only one variable of interest. For instance, a study that describes the reading achievement of second-graders or a survey of parental attitudes toward a school policy contains only one variable of interest (see Excerpt 3.4).

EXCERPT 3.3 Correlational Research: Predictor and Criterion Variables

The present study has two main purposes: (1) to develop a comprehensive set of kindergarten prereading tasks that would predict reading achievement at the end of first and second grade, and (2) to determine at what point in the kindergarten year—beginning, middle, or end—the various tasks would exert maximum predictive power. (p. 95)

Source: From Morris, D., Bloodgood, J., & Perney, J. (2003). Kindergarten predictors of first- and second-grade reading achievement. *The Elementary School Journal, 104*(2), 93–110.

EXCERPT 3.4 Survey Research: Variable of Interest

To obtain information about low-income parents' beliefs about their role that could help guide future efforts to increase . . . their participation. . . . (1) How much parents from diverse backgrounds value involvement in their children's schooling; (2) what factors are associated with differences among parents in the belief about involvement; and (3) what parents say, in their own words, they should be doing to help their children succeed in school. (pp. 200–201)

Source: From Drummon, K. V., & Stipek, D. (2004). Low-income parents' beliefs about their role in children's academic learning. *The Elementary School Journal, 104*(3), 197–214.

TABLE 3.1 Examples of Variables and Constitutive versus Operational Definitions

Variable	Constitutive Definition	Operational Definition
Self-concept	Characteristics used to describe oneself	Scores on the Coopersmith *Self-Esteem Inventory*
Intelligence	Ability to think abstractly	Scores on the Stanford-Binet
Teacher with-it-ness	Awareness of student involvement and behavior	Results of the *Robinson Scale Teacher With-It-Ness*

A variable may be independent in one study and dependent in another; a variable also may be a predictor or a criterion variable. How the variable functions (e.g., as independent, dependent, predictor, criterion or as the only variable of interest) in a given study depends on the purpose, logic, and design of the study. The problem statement is phrased to indicate the function of the variable(s) in the proposed study and thus implies the design.

Operational Definitions Each variable in a quantitative study must be defined operationally and subsequently categorized, measured, or manipulated. A constitutive (i.e., dictionary) definition defines a word by using other terms, such as defining *anxiety* as "apprehension or vague fear." In contrast, the researcher uses an **operational definition,** which assigns meaning to a variable by specifying the activities or operations necessary to measure, categorize, or manipulate that variable. An operational definition tells the researcher and the reader what is necessary to answer the question or test the hypothesis. Variables frequently can be defined operationally in several ways, and some operations may be more valid for certain research problems than others. The operational definition for a variable is often not as valid as the researcher desires. To conduct an evidence-based inquiry, however, one must define each variable operationally.

Table 3.1 provides some examples of variables, each described with a constitutive definition and an operational definition.

Problem Formulation

A useful procedure for transforming a general topic into a manageable problem is to identify the population, the variables, and the logic of the problem. Suppose a supervisor is interested in determining whether organizing programs for gifted elementary students in different ways will affect student creativity. The gifted programs are organized as: (1) special programs, in which students remain together for a comprehensive program; (2) pullout programs, in which students attend regular classes except for two hours' daily instruction by selected teachers; and (3) enrichment programs, in which students complete enrichment activities as an extension of their regular instruction. The research question is, Is there a difference in creativity (the dependent variable) among gifted elementary students (the population) who participate in a special program, a pullout program, or an enrichment program (three levels of one independent variable)? This question is narrowed to the degree that it identifies the population and the two variables. The logic behind the question is clear because the relationship between the independent and dependent variable can be identified.

A question phrased as Does mainstreaming do any good? is too broad and has neither a population nor variables. The researcher must narrow the problem to be more specific:

Is there a difference between high school students' (the population) attitudes toward students with disabilities (the dependent variable) who participated in a six-weeks mainstreamed class and the attitudes of those students who did not participate in the class (two levels of the independent variable)? Now the question is focused. In addition, it implies an experimental design, and the logic behind the problem is explicit.

By identifying the types of variables and the population, the researcher clarifies the focus and logic of the problem. This process is not easy; it requires rewriting and reconceptualizing the problem. Reading literature, brainstorming with others, and talking with experienced researchers all can help in clarifying a problem. Once the idea is clearly in mind, the researcher can write a formal problem statement.

ALERT! It is better to do the preliminary work necessary to write a problem statement that has a specific purpose than to proceed with a broad statement and purpose.

Specific Research Questions and Hypotheses

In a quantitative study, the research problem may be stated as a question or a hypothesis. The question format is often preferred because it is simple and direct. Psychologically, it orients the researcher to the immediate task: to develop a design to answer the question. Research questions may be descriptive questions, relationship questions, or difference questions. Each type of question implies a different design (see Figure 3.2).

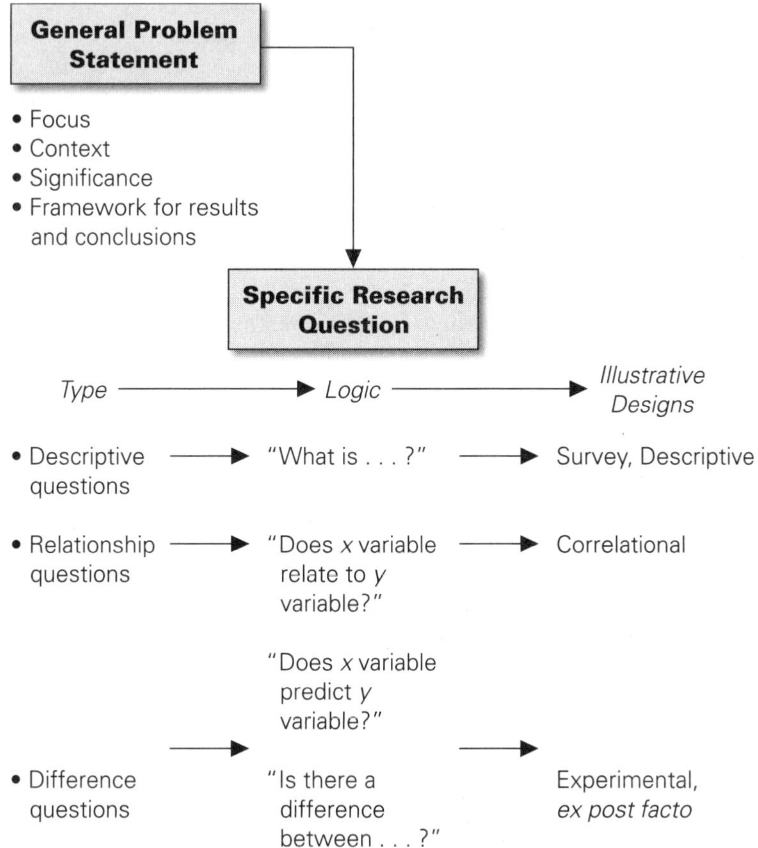

FIGURE 3.2 **Logic of Quantitative Problem Statements and Specific Research Questions**

EXCERPT 3.5 Descriptive Problem—Survey Research

In the present study, we examine the degree to which exemplar teachers reported using cooperative learning versus the degree to which they would prefer to use this method, as well as the relative use of each element of cooperative learning. (p. 234)

Source: From Lopata, C., Miller, K. A., & Miller, R. H. (2003). Survey of actual and preferred use of cooperative learning among exemplar teachers. *Journal of Educational Research, 96*(4), 232–239.

Descriptive Research Questions Descriptive research questions typically ask What is? and imply a survey research design. These terms, however, are not always used in the wording of the research question. For example, a research question may be What is the achievement level of our fourth-grade students on the Iowa Test of Basic Skills? Evaluation research often investigates the perceptions of groups concerned with a practice, such as What are the administrators' opinions of a program? Which of the alternative bus routes do our pupils' parents prefer? and What does the staff perceive as our most important instructional needs? (see Excerpt 3.5).

Relationship Questions A relationship question asks, What is the relationship between two or more variables? and implies a correlational design. For example, Does self-concept relate to achievement? asks a question about the relationship between one variable (self-concept) and another (achievement). Studies that determine the best predictors for a variable, such as predictors of college success, imply relationship questions between the possible predictor variables—such as high school grade-point average and class rank, recommendations, and participation in extracurricular activities—and the dependent variable, college success. Excerpt 3.6 illustrates a problem statement that implies a relationship question between selected long-range predictors and children's social adjustment. The problem statement also suggests the design for the study.

Difference Questions A difference question typically asks Is there a difference between two groups or two or more treatments? This type of question is used when the study compares two or more observations. Asking Is there a difference? rather than Is there a relationship? between two or more observations clarifies the underlying logic of the study. Questions such as Is there a difference between pretest and posttest scores? are more useful than those phrased Is there a relationship between pretest and posttest scores? (see Excerpt 3.7).

If the researchers firmly believe that in addition to predicting a difference between two or more variables, they can predict the direction in which the difference lies, then the direction should be stated in the research question. The question Is there a difference in pretest and posttest scores? may thus be stated Is there greater mastery of reading comprehension on the posttest than on the pretest?

EXCERPT 3.6 Relationship Problem—Correlational Research

In this study, I examined variables that predict how African American parents and guardians of school-aged children rate their children's elementary and secondary school teachers, and the public school system as a whole. (p. 279)

Source: From Thompson, G. L. (2003). Predicting African American parents' and guardians' satisfaction with teachers and public schools. *Journal of Educational Research, 96*(5), 277–285.

EXCERPT 3.7 Difference Questions—Experimental Research

RQ 1: Are there significant differences in student affective learning between traditional classroom instruction and instruction through a game/simulation?

RQ 2: Are there significant differences in student cognitive learning between traditional classroom instruction and instruction through a game/simulation?

RQ 3: Are there significant differences in student motivation between traditional classroom instruction and instruction through a game/simulation? (p. 38)

Source: From Garard, D. L., Hunt, S. K., Lippert, L., & Raynton, S. T. (1998). Alternative to traditional instruction: Using games and simulation to increase student learning and motivation. *Communication Research Reports, 15*(1), 36–44.

Research questions are *not* statistical questions stated for data analysis. A statistical question may be phrased Is there a statistically significant difference between A and B variables? or Is there a statistically significant relationship between A variable and B variable? Statistical questions are stated in the Methodology section of a study. Research questions are stated in the Introduction and suggest the design.

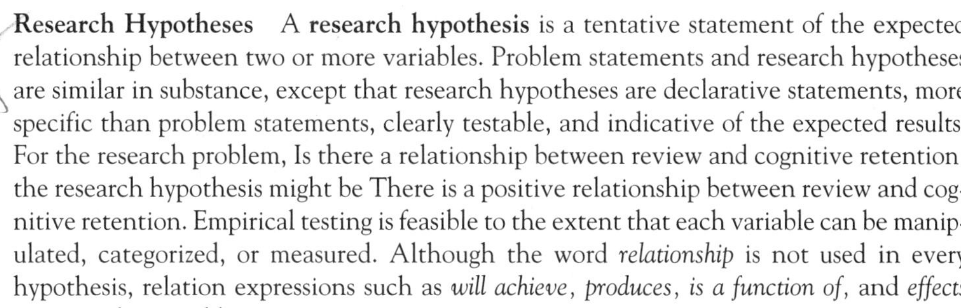

Research Hypotheses A **research hypothesis** is a tentative statement of the expected relationship between two or more variables. Problem statements and research hypotheses are similar in substance, except that research hypotheses are declarative statements, more specific than problem statements, clearly testable, and indicative of the expected results. For the research problem, Is there a relationship between review and cognitive retention? the research hypothesis might be There is a positive relationship between review and cognitive retention. Empirical testing is feasible to the extent that each variable can be manipulated, categorized, or measured. Although the word *relationship* is not used in every hypothesis, relation expressions such as *will achieve*, *produces*, *is a function of*, and *effects* connect the variables.

A hypothesis implies an if/then logic. Most hypotheses can be put into an if/then form to indicate the relationship between variables—for example, If perceived student differences, then greater differences in teaching behavior; If a remedial course, then higher reading comprehension; and If democratic leadership style, then faculty satisfaction. The logic is similar for a hypothesis with more than two variables.

A hypothesis is a conjectural explanation of phenomena that is accepted or rejected by empirical evidence. In the preceeding examples, a remedial reading course explains higher achievement and a democratic leadership style explains faculty satisfaction.

To be useful in research, a hypothesis should meet several standards:

1. ***The hypothesis should state the direction of the relationship.*** A statement such as If teacher feedback, then student science achievement implies a relationship but is not a hypothesis. The directional hypothesis might state Teacher feedback will relate positively to student science achievement or There is a positive relationship between teacher feedback and student science achievement. When a treatment is administered to one group of subjects but not another, researchers should hypothesize directional differences—for example, Fifth-grade students who receive microcomputer-assisted instruction will have higher math achievement than comparable students who did not receive microcomputer-assisted instruction.

2. ***A hypothesis should be testable.*** A testable hypothesis is verifiable; one can draw conclusions from empirical data that indicate whether the hypothesized consequences did or did not occur. To be testable, a hypothesis must include variables that can be measured or categorized by some objective procedure (see Excerpts 3.8 and 3.9). For example, because one can classify first-grade students as having attended preschool or not into two levels, a hypothesis might state Children who attend preschool will have higher scores on a scale of social maturity than children who do not attend preschool.

EXCERPT 3.8 Research Hypothesis

Boys and girls who attend single-sex Catholic secondary schools score higher on tests of academic achievement and self concept than their counterparts who attend coeducational Catholic secondary schools. (p. 493)

Source: From LePore, P. C., & Warren, J. R. (1997). A comparison of single-sex and coeducational catholic secondary schooling: From the national educational longitudinal study of 1988. *American Educational Research Journal, 34,* 485–511.

EXCERPT 3.9 Research Hypothesis

The foregoing literature review suggests that parents who attend school meetings or conferences and interact with school personnel are likely to have children who demonstrate higher levels of achievement at school than children of parents who fail to participate in their child's school program. (p. 92)

Source: From Shaver, A. V., & Walls, R. T. (1998). Effect of Title 1 parent involvement on student reading and mathematics achievement. *Journal of Research and Development in Education, 31,* 90–97.

3. ***A hypothesis should offer a tentative explanation based on theory or previous research.*** A well-grounded hypothesis indicates that there is sufficient research or theory for considering the hypothesis important enough to test. A research hypothesis usually is stated after a literature review, at which point the researcher has knowledge of the previous work or theory. In many areas of education, however, there is little conclusive evidence, and only some educational research can serve as a basis for the research hypothesis.

MISCONCEPTION Girls achieve less than boys in mathematics in primary school, and few girls pursue math- and science-related majors in college even though their SAT scores are similar to those of boys.

EVIDENCE After changing the research problem, it was found that fewer girls than boys took advanced high school mathematics courses to prepare for math- and science-related college majors.

4. ***A hypothesis should be concise and lucid.*** In its simplest form, a hypothesis should have logical coherence and a clear order of arrangement. Brief statements aid both the reader and the researcher in interpreting the results. A general rule is to state only one relationship per hypothesis. Although a researcher may have one general hypothesis, it is better to rephrase it into more specific hypotheses for clarity.

PROBLEM FORMULATION IN QUALITATIVE RESEARCH

Problem formulation in qualitative research begins with selecting a general topic and a mode of inquiry (i.e., interactive or noninteractive). The topic and methodology are *interrelated* and selected almost simultaneously, rather than in separate research steps. For example, an early research decision is whether to examine ongoing or past events. Suppose that a study of current phenomena requires the researcher to have access to a site or to a group of people who shared some social experience, such as working in the same school system or participating in a special project or a class. A study of past events will require that archival collections of primary documents be made available to the researcher. These considerations will begin to shape and influence the selection of a general topic.

Qualitative researchers begin by narrowing a general topic to a more definitive topic. A principal may notice that a growing number of African American women are seeking promotions in a large urban district. The researcher will begin to wonder What experiences have veteran African American women principals had that may provide useful directions to future administrators? As another example, suppose that a researcher notices that deaf children and their hearing peers in a public school often fail to communicate. The researcher might ask How does this failure affect the children's cognitive and social development?

Many qualitative research interests come from personal experience—a long-time concern or interest in a topic developed from opportunities in one's current biography and personal background. Prior experience gives the researcher physical and/or psychological access to present or past social settings. In other words, research problems lie in many personal situations and experiences, as well as in general reading, which need only to be recognized as potential research problems. Thinking further, puzzling, and being aware of qualitative research traditions enable researchers to establish the logic behind the problem.

The Logic of Qualitative Field Records, Descriptions, and Abstractions

Qualitative research, in contrast to quantitative research, employs primarily *inductive reasoning* but deductive reasoning is used at selected times. The problem is most clearly stated after much data collection and preliminary analysis. The researcher obtains comprehensive field records of a present or past situation, which give detailed descriptions of people's perceptions and social realities, and then forms abstractions from these descriptions to explain the phenomenon. Inductive reasoning allows one to explore and discover with an emerging research design, rather than test deductions using theories from a predetermined design. The research problem is typically reformulated during data collection so that the data closely represent the reality of the shared social experiences.

Problem formulation begins with the selection of a particular case for in-depth study. The inductive process is schematically represented in Figure 3.3. Note that the arrows in

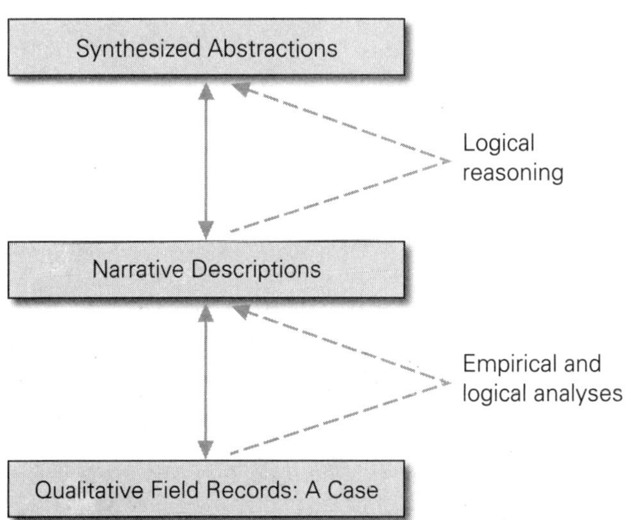

FIGURE 3.3 The Logic of Qualitative Research: Field Records, Descriptions, and Abstractions

the center of the figure go in two directions (i.e., from the bottom upward and from the top downward) to illustrate the use of both inductive and deductive reasoning.

Qualitative Field Records: A Case Researchers select a specific case for in-depth study. A **case** is a particular social situation chosen by the researcher in which some phenomenon will be described by participants' perceptions. The researcher also decides on a primary qualitative methodology (e.g., participant observations, in-depth interviews, or analysis of documents). In selecting a case, the researcher limits the research problem to a particular context, such as foreign-born teachers in a school district who speak English as a second language, informal mentors working with native Mexican adolescents in an urban setting, or teachers implementing a mathematics curricular reform. Thus, the researcher selects a particular case, rather than variables, to gain an understanding of a broader phenomenon. The broader phenomenon in Excerpt 3.10 is leadership in policy implementation and school change.

Qualitative field records, which are obtained over a lengthy time period, include data such as participant observation field notes, interview tapes, and researcher notes about historical documents. Each field note, transcript, or document note contains the date of occurrence and the context, such as the social scene, situation, and participants. The field data collected initially may lead to collecting data from other people, sites, and archive collections, as the researcher discovers more aspects about the selected case. In other words, the term *case* does not refer to one person or one archival collection or one locale but to the *social situation* examined. Data collection strategies are adjusted to obtain a holistic view of the phenomena and then to study certain aspects in depth.

Narrative Descriptions Researchers construct from the data **narrative descriptions,** or detailed accounts of the people, incidents, and processes. The entire narrative description is completed after data collection because of the discovery orientation of the research. To inductively generate a descriptive narration, certain kinds of data must be in the field notes, transcripts, or notes of historical documents.

Descriptive narrations, sometimes called "rich" or "thick" description told in "loving detail," contain at least four elements: people, incidents, participants' language, and participants' "meanings":

1. *Participants* are described as individuals who have different personal histories and display different physical, emotional, and intellectual characteristics in various situations.
2. *Incidents* form a narration about the social scenes, similar to telling a story.
3. Descriptions emphasize the *participants' language*, not that of researchers or of social science. For instance, participants' names for incidents, locations, objects, special events, and processes are all noted. Language refers to many forms of communication such as verbal and nonverbal expressions, drawings, cartoons, symbols, and the like.
4. Descriptions emphasize *participant "meanings,"* which are people's views of reality or how they perceive their world. These meanings are conveyed when a person states *why* or *because* an event happened.

EXCERPT 3.10 Understanding a Case of Policy Implementation

The purpose [is] . . . to explicate the concept of transition leadership and its centrality to understanding policy implementation and school change through a case study of one district and its school principals. . . . This study rests with understanding the actions principals define for themselves during an extreme state of transition. Specifically, our research questions explore, How do principals define leadership in transition? Where do they see leadership possibilities? What are their leadership priorities? (pp. 473–474)

Source: From Goldring, E., Crowson, R., Laird, D., & Berk, R. (2003). Transition leadership in a shifting policy environment. *Educational Evaluation and Policy Analysis, 25*(4), 473–488.

Synthesized Abstractions Researchers generate abstract summaries from the data to produce **synethesized abstractions** or summary generalizations and explanations of the major research findings of a study. Synethesized abstractions may take different formats, such as a list of narrative themes, "lessons learned," the essence of a shared experience, a delineated concept, or an assertion or propositional statement. The researcher constructs a picture that takes shape as he or she collects data and examines the parts. The subtle meanings of the phenomenon can be understood more clearly by the readers.

Problem Reformulation

A qualitative research problem is reformulated several times *after* the researcher has begun data collection. The research problem is stated initially in planning for the study, reformulated during early data collection, and reformulated as necessary throughout data collection. The continuing reformulation of the research problem reflects an emergent design. Reformulation relates to changing data collection strategies to acquire the totality of the phenomena and then to study some aspect in greater depth. The specific research problem evolves and is condensed toward the end of data collection. In most publications, the condensed version of the research problem often is not the same problem that initiated the research (see Excerpt 3.11).

Foreshadowed Problems Qualitative researchers begin with **foreshadowed problems,** or anticipated research problems that will be reformulated during data collection. The statement of foreshadowed problems depends to some extent on prior knowledge of the events and processes at a site, of the people to be interviewed, and of archival collection documents. Thus, foreshadowed problems are not directly derived from an exhaustive literature review but rather from the researcher's initial experiences in planning the study. A preliminary literature review, however, aids the researcher in phrasing the foreshadowed problems.

Foreshadowed problems are usually phrased as broad, general questions, focusing on the What? How? and Why? of the situation. The What? refers to who, when, where, and which social scenes occur. The How? refers to the processes to be examined and what influenced them (see Excerpt 3.12). The Why? refers to participant "meanings," or people's explanations for the incidents and social scenes observed. Each of these questions is deliberately broad to allow for discovery and development of an emergent design.

Condensed Problem Statements A condensed problem statement may be written any time during or after data collection. It is usually the selected major research question that will focus the entire report. The title, literature review, and discussion often use abstract terms of qualitative scholars; however, the research problem may or may not be phrased in descriptive terms (see Excerpt 3.13).

EXCERPT 3.11 Initial Problem and Reformulation from the Sites

[Initially] show how teachers and their administrators were attempting to come to terms with top-down, . . . [state], and district mandates to make more and better use of computer technologies in teaching and learning. . . .

How are existing power relations in schools reinforced and/or reorganized by the introduction of computer technologies? How do these new technologies change the work of teaching and how do these changes undermine or encourage the teacher's . . . sense of control and ownership? . . . These questions emerged from a series of conversations and experiences we had with individual teachers . . . [who] consistently raised issues of gender inequities both in the context of schooling and in relation to the technology itself. . . . *[We] did not set out to study gender.* (pp. 170, 171)

Source: From Jenson, J., & Rose, C. B. (2003). Women@work: Listening to gendered relations of power in teachers' talk about new technologies. *Gender and Education, 15*(2), 169–181.

EXCERPT 3.12 Ethnographic Problem Statement and Research Questions

Social relationships for people with disabilities have been a central concern . . . for many years. So too have sibling relationships. Specifically, we will report the findings of a case study of the sibling relationships of Raul, a young man with Down syndrome. . . . We focused on the following questions:

1. What are the predominant types of interactions between the siblings and Raul?
2. How does Raul participate in these interactions?
3. How do the observed sibling interactions compare to findings about Raul's interactions with nondisabled peers at school? (pp. 289, 291)

Source: From Harry, B., Day, M., & Quist, F. (1998). "He Can't Really Play": An ethnographic study of sibling acceptance and interaction. *JASH: Journal of the Association for Persons with Severe Handicaps, 23*(4), 289–299.

EXCERPT 3.13 Qualitative Problem Statement

Working as a principal in any large, urban school today can be both a difficult and dangerous assignment. However, a growing number of African American women administrators are seeking promotional opportunities to lead in schools. . . . Listening to and recording veteran African American women principals' experiences may provide useful direction to future administrators who aspire. (p. 339)

Source: From Bloom, C. M., & Erlandson, D. A. (2003). African American women principals in urban schools: Realities, (re)constructions, and resolutions. *Educational Administration Quarterly, 39*(3), 339–369.

Statements of Qualitative Research Purposes and Questions

Qualitative studies contain statements of research purposes and questions that imply the inductive logic for the problem at hand. The statement of research purpose is the final condensed version of the initial problem statement. Specific research questions may be stated or implied. The statement of purpose implies the chosen qualitative mode of inquiry: interactive or noninteractive research.

Qualitative Problem Statements and Questions The qualitative research traditions of ethnography, phenomenology, case study, grounded theory, and critical study focus on current phenomena for which data can be obtained through interacting with the participants in a selected social situation (see Excerpt 3.14).

Historical Problem Statements and Questions Historical research problems focus on past events and often require access to documents in historical archives. A historical study

EXCERPT 3.14 Qualitative Problem Statement

The following questions are addressed: . . .

In what ways do foreign-born ESL teachers draw on their experiences as foreign-born residents living in the United States to open or close new social networks for their students?

How can these practices be seen as a way of breaking down the power differentials between minority and majority groups? (p. 128)

Source: From Case, R. E. (2004). Forging ahead into new social networks and looking back to past social identities: A case study of a foreign-born English as a second language teacher in the United States. *Urban Education, 39*(2), 125–148.

EXCERPT 3.15 Historical Problem Statement

By the century's end, vacation schools offering summer recreation and industrial education to the children of the urban, immigrant poor became yet another philanthropic program to enter the public school domain. What happened to vacation schools in New York City as a consequence of public administration is the focus of this article. (p. 18)

Source: From Gold, K. M. (2002). From vacation to summer school: The transformation of summer education in New York City, 1894–1915. *History of Education Quarterly, 42*(1), 18–48.

may begin when archival documents are made available to scholars. Such a study may also begin when only a few people remain of those who experienced the event, such as a labor strike over the right of married women teachers to be tenured (see Excerpt 3.15). Because back issues of major newspapers and journals are often stored on data disks and available on the Internet, more historical research can be done today than in the past, when only bound collections of information existed. In addition, many public agencies now keep their permanent records in easily accessible formats.

PROBLEM FORMULATION IN MIXED-METHOD RESEARCH

Like a study that is either completely quantitative or qualitative, a mixed-method investigation begins with identification of a general problem, which provides a context and background. Identifying the general problem is followed by indicating a more specific purpose for the study. At this point, the researcher could indicate that a mixed-method design will be used and write specific quantitative research questions and foreshadowed problems. In addition, some researchers present more specific questions and problems after their review of the literature.

Since a good research problem implies the design, the research questions and foreshadowed problems should be presented in a way that is consistent with how the methods will be used. The *relative importance* of how each method functions in the study should be communicated (e.g., whether a quantitative or qualitative approach is emphasized or both are given equal weight) along with the overall purpose of the research. Knowing the relative importance of each method used in the study helps determine the type of mixed-method design.

Equal Priority to All Questions When a variety of questions are asked and all are equally important, then both quantitative and qualitative data are collected at about the same time. The research questions and foreshadowed problems are usually presented together. Doing so communicates that both kinds of data have equal priority. Suppose a researcher is interested in studying beginning teachers and has formulated this general problem: What kinds of help are most important in ensuring the success of beginning elementary teachers? The following questions are more specific:

1. To what extent have several kinds of help been received by beginning elementary teachers? (quantitative)
2. How do beginning elementary school teachers rate the helpfulness of the assistance received? (quantitative)
3. How does the elementary school principal rate the helpfulness of assistance provided to beginning teachers? (quantitative)
4. Why have certain kinds of assistance proven most helpful? (qualitative)
5. How does the context of the teaching situation influence the need for different kinds of assistance? (qualitative)

The first three quantitative questions could be addressed with an instrument that lists the types of assistance received (e.g., from a mentor, principal, other teacher) and provides a rating scale for evaluating the extent of helpfulness. The qualitative questions (items 4 and 5) could be answered by conducting interviews with teachers and principals at about the same time that the surveys are being completed. Findings from both kinds of data would be analyzed and interpreted to determine if similar results are obtained. The questions imply a *triangulation design* because using both methods provides a more complete result.

Measured Results Explained by Qualitative Data Suppose these research questions were being considered: Are there differences in the amounts of helpful assistance that beginning teachers receive? If so, how do beginning teachers explain why some types of assistance are helpful and others are not? Researchers must see the results of the first question to decide if they need further data to explain the findings. A survey could be used to identify individual teachers who have received the greatest amount of effective assistance and those teachers who have received the least amount of assistance. Once those individuals have been identified, qualitative interviews could be conducted with a small sample from each group. The interviews could explore reasons that particular kinds of assistance were helpful or not helpful. The research design could be represented like this:

Quantitative		Qualitative
Which elementary teachers have received the greatest amount of assistance? Which elementary teachers have received the least amount of assistance?	→	What explanations do teachers have about why some kinds of assistance are helpful and other kinds are not?

When data are collected sequentially—quantitative first, qualitative second—the quantitative phase provides general results that are then explained with qualitative data. When data are collected sequentially, an *explanatory design* is implied.

Qualitative Questions, Then Quantitative Questions When there is little prior research on a topic or a practice is new, qualitative methods may be used first to investigate the scope of the phenomenon, followed by quantitative methods. The data identified in the qualitative phase will then be investigated in a more structured way using quantitative approaches. For example, in a study of beginning teacher assistance, it may be necessary to explore the types of assistance received before measuring the relationship among the types. The quantitative results extend what is found in the qualitative phase. The following research design could be used:

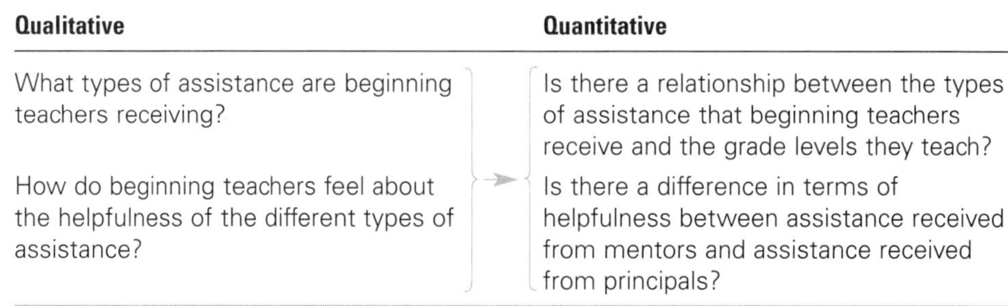

Qualitative		Quantitative
What types of assistance are beginning teachers receiving? How do beginning teachers feel about the helpfulness of the different types of assistance?	→	Is there a relationship between the types of assistance that beginning teachers receive and the grade levels they teach? Is there a difference in terms of helpfulness between assistance received from mentors and assistance received from principals?

When qualitative methods initiate the inquiry and are then followed by quantitative techniques, the problem implies an *exploratory design*. Exploratory designs are often used to develop instruments. A topic will be studied in depth to clarify all important dimensions, and then these dimensions will be used as a framework for developing a questionnaire. For instance, a researcher could spend considerable time in a school observing the nature of school climate and then use that information to develop an objectively scored instrument that captures all aspects of school climate.

THE SIGNIFICANCE OF PROBLEM SELECTION

The **significance of the problem** is the rationale for a study. It justifies why an evidence-based inquiry is important and indicates the reasons for the researcher's choice of a particular problem. Because research requires knowledge, skills, planning, time, and fiscal resources, the problem to be investigated should be important. In other words, the study should have a potential payoff.

A research problem is significant when it aids in developing theory, knowledge, or practice. That significance increases when several reasons can be provided to justify the inquiry. Justifications may be based on one or more of the following criteria: whether the study provides knowledge about an enduring practice, tests a theory, is generalizable, extends understanding of a broader phenomenon, advances methodology, is related to a current issue, evaluates a specific practice at a given site, or is an exploratory study.

Knowledge of an Enduring Practice The study may provide knowledge about an enduring educational practice. Perhaps previous research on the practice has been done, but this particular research problem has not been investigated. The practice being studied may be common to many schools but not necessarily found in every school. The study will add knowledge about an enduring common practice (see Excerpt 3.16).

Theory Testing The study may be significant because it tests an existing theory with a verification design. The focus may be on social science theories of child or adult development, organizational development, conflict, and so on. Educational theories may focus on curricula, instructional models, staff development, learning styles, teaching strategies, or the like. By testing a theory in different situations or on different populations, the researcher may modify or verify it.

Generalizability The study may be designed so the results will be generalizable to different populations or practices. A study may replicate or include other variables not investigated in previous research, or it may call for using a different population than the original research to enhance generalizability (see Excerpt 3.17).

Extensions of Understanding Many qualitative studies conducted in the phenomenological tradition extend understanding, rather than generalizability. By describing a selected case of a social situation in detail, such a study provides an understanding of the

EXCERPT 3.16 Significance: Add to Knowledge of an Enduring Practice

The study adds to parent involvement research by examining parents' beliefs about involvement in different domains. (p. 201)

Source: From Drummon, K. V., & Stipek, D. (2004). Low-income parents' beliefs about their role in children's academic learning. *The Elementary School Journal, 104*(3), 197–214.

EXCERPT 3.17 Justification: Replication and Generalization

Thus, the objective of the present inquiry was to replicate and extend the work of Witcher, et. al. (2001). Specifically our purpose was to investigate what preservice teachers view as important characteristics of effective teachers. (p. 118)

Source: From Minor, L. C., Onwuegbuzie, A., Witcher, A. E., & James, T. L. (2002). Preservice teachers' educational beliefs and their perceptions of characteristics of effective teachers. *Journal of Educational Research, 96*(2), 116–127.

phenomena observed. That understanding provides an image or configuration of reasonable expectations that might be useful in similar situations.

Methodological Advancement The study may be significant because it increases the validity and reliability of an instrument or uses a methodology different from the methodologies used in previous studies. Much of the research on educational measurement investigates questions related to assessment, such as testing procedures, the order of the items on an instrument, the item format or response set, and the information processes of the respondent. Another study may develop a statistical or methodological technique and elaborate on its usefulness for research.

Current Issues The study may focus on a social issue of immediate concern. As mentioned previously, organized political movements such as those for women's rights and civil rights have generated educational research. Public recognition of social problems has frequently led to assessment of their educational effects. The increasing prevalence of single-parent families, for example, has raised questions about the impact of single parenting on student self-concept and achievement. Similarly, studies on the instructional effects of students having laptops and Internet access have originated from social concerns about living in a highly technological society (see Excerpt 3.18).

Evaluation of a Specific Practice or Policy at a Given Site The study may evaluate a specific practice or policy for decision makers at a given site or for external groups. Evaluation research determines worth: Does the practice need improvement? Is it effective? Should its usage be expanded? Similar questions are addressed in policy studies. Such research supplies information for immediate use in site decision making, which may be at

EXCERPT 3.18 Justification: Current Issue

[Being aware of] the No Child Left Behind Act . . . can enable educators to get a head start not only on hearing the concerns of African American parents but also on improving their relations with these parents and seeking effective ways to improve the quality of education that they offer to African American students. (pp. 277, 279)

Source: From Thompson, G. L. (2003). Predicting African American parents' and guardians' satisfaction with teachers and public schools. *Journal of Educational Research, 96*(5), 277–285.

the local, state, or national level. While the study is not concerned initially with generalizability or theory development, it may have implications for developing such knowledge (see Excerpt 3.19).

Exploratory Research Exploratory research is usually conducted in new areas of inquiry, and such studies may be quantitative or qualitative. For example, a study might field test a particular assessment format to determine whether it can be used by sixth-grade students and if it discriminates against any particular student groups. Qualitative exploratory studies often examine phenomena that have not been studied previously. Some exploratory studies develop theory or components of a concept (see Excerpts 3.20 and 3.21).

EXCERPT 3.19 Justification: Evaluation of a New Program at a Site

[For] our research project, "The Effects of Standards-Based Assessments on School and Classrooms," [we] selected Washington because of the newness of its reform effort. We decided to study implementation at the local level, persuaded by the generally accepted belief that large-scale reforms succeed or fail based on issues of local implementation. (pp. 171–172)

Source: From Borko, H., Wolf, S. A., Simone, G., & Uchiyama, K. P. (2003). Schools in transition: Reform efforts and school capacity in Washington state. *Educational Evaluation and Policy Analysis, 25*(2), 171–201.

EXCERPT 3.20 Significance: To Develop Components of a Concept

The purpose [is] . . . to begin the process of fleshing out the construct of leadership content knowledge, [that is] . . . how and why subject matter knowledge matters in educational leadership; . . . [to] analyze three cases of instructional leadership [principal, associate superintendent, and central office team], . . . and [to] examine each for evidence of leadership content knowledge in use. (p. 424)

Source: From Stein, M. K., & Nelson, B. S. (2003). Leadership content knowledge. *Educational Evaluation and Policy Analysis, 25*(4), 423–448.

EXCERPT 3.21 Justification: Explore to Develop Theory

Several objectives guided this study. Specifically . . . to (1) identify and explore (and ultimately develop a conceptual framework for) the various domains of discomfort that teachers face; (2) explore dimensions within these various discomfort domains that define whether moments of discomfort for students and teachers become debilitating or educative; (3) explore the impact of discomfort on teacher's beliefs and pedagogical practices; and (4) explore the notion of teaching *toward* discomfort. (p. 130)

Source: From Frykholm, J. (2004). Teachers' tolerance for discomfort: Implications for curricular reform in mathematics. *Journal of Curriculum and Supervision, 19*(2), 125–149.

STANDARDS OF ADEQUACY FOR PROBLEM STATEMENTS

Research problems are critically evaluated on the three elements discussed in this chapter: the statement of the general research problem, the significance of the problem, and the specific research purpose, question, or hypothesis. In addition, other criteria may be applied.

General Research Problem The following questions appraise the general statement of the problem:

1. Does the statement of the general research problem imply the possibility of empirical investigation?
2. Does the problem statement restrict the scope of the study?
3. Does the problem statement give the educational context in which the problem lies?

Significance of the Problem Readers assess the significance of the problem in terms of one or more of the following criteria:

- Develops knowledge of an enduring practice
- Develops theory
- Generalizable—that is, expands knowledge or theory
- Provides extension of understandings
- Advances methodology
- Is related to a current social or political issue
- Evaluates a specific practice or policy at a given site
- Is exploratory research

Specific Research Question or Hypothesis Different criteria are applied in the evaluation of quantitative, qualitative, and mixed-methods research questions.

Quantitative

1. Does the specific research purpose, question, or hypothesis state concisely what is to be determined?
2. Does the level of specificity indicate that the question or hypothesis is researchable, or do the variables seem amenable to operational definitions?
3. Is the logic of the research question or hypothesis clear? Are the independent and dependent variables identified?
4. Does the research question or hypothesis indicate the framework for reporting the results?

Qualitative

1. Do the research questions, foreshadowed problems, and condensed problem statement indicate the particular case of some phenomena to be examined?
2. Is the qualitative methodology appropriate for the description of present or past events?
3. Is the logic of the research reasonably explicit?
4. Does the research purpose indicate the framework for reporting the findings?

Mixed-Method

1. Is the relative emphasis of each method made explicit?
2. Is the order in which quantitative and qualitative data are collected clear (e.g., how each type of data will be used in the study)?

Other Criteria for Standards of Adequacy Before conducting a study, the researcher, a possible funding agency, review committees, and other groups also evaluate the problem according to additional criteria. These criteria concern the ability of the researcher to conduct the study and the feasibility and ethics of the research design. Typical questions asked include the following:

1. Is the problem one in which the researcher has a vital interest and a topic in which the researcher has both knowledge and experience?
2. Are the problem and the design feasible in terms of measurement, access to the case, sample, or population, permission to use documents, time frame for completion, financial resources, and the like?
3. Does the researcher have the skills to conduct the proposed research and to analyze and interpret the results?
4. Does the proposed research ensure the protection of human subjects from physical or mental discomfort or harm? Is the right of informed consent of subjects provided? Will ethical research practices be followed?

SUMMARY

This chapter has examined the major aspects of research problem statements, problem formulation in quantitative and qualitative research, the significance of the problem, and standards of adequacy for a problem statement. The primary concepts can be summarized as follows:

1. A research problem implies the possibility of empirical investigation.
2. Sources for research problems are casual observations, theory, literature, current issues, practical situations, and personal insights.
3. A research problem statement specifies the focus, educational context, importance, and framework for reporting the findings.
4. In quantitative research, deductive logic is employed in selecting the construct, variables, and operational definitions.
5. A construct is a complex abstraction and as such is not directly observable. A variable is an event, category, behavior, or attribute that expresses a construct and has different values, depending on how it is used in a study.
6. Variables may be categorical or continuous. Variables may be dependent, independent, manipulated, experimental, predictor, or criterion variables in different designs.
7. An operational definition assigns meaning to a variable by specifying the activities or operations necessary to measure, categorize, or manipulate the variable.
8. To formulate a quantitative problem, the researcher decides the variables, the population, and the logic of the design.
9. Specific quantitative research problems may ask descriptive, relationship, or difference questions or state a hypothesis.
10. In qualitative research, the general topic, the case, and the methodology are interrelated and selected interactively, rather than in separate research steps.
11. A case is a particular situation selected by the researcher in which some phenomenon will be described by participants' "meanings" of events and processes.
12. A qualitative study employs logic to use field records to generate a descriptive narration and to develop abstractions from that narration.
13. Qualitative field records, obtained over a lengthy time, are recorded as participant observation notes, transcripts of in-depth interviews, and researchers' notes of historical documents.
14. Qualitative descriptions are detailed narrations of people, incidents, and processes that emphasize participants' "meanings."
15. Qualitative research problems are reformulated several times during data collection, while quantitative research problems are stated before data collection begins.
16. Mixed-method problem statements indicate the relative importance of quantitative and qualitative data (i.e., how the method will function in the design).
17. A research problem is significant if it provides knowledge about an enduring practice, tests a theory, increases generalizability, extends empirical understanding, advances methodology, focuses on a current issue, evaluates a specific practice, or is an exploratory study.
18. Problem statements are judged by the criteria for statement of a research problem, the problem significance, the specific research questions or hypotheses, and the appropriate logic and feasibility.

CHECK YOURSELF

Multiple-choice review items, with answers, are available on the Companion Website for this book.

www.ablongman.com/mcmillanschumacher6e

APPLICATION PROBLEMS

1. The following are examples of research topics. Indicate the decisions necessary in order to conduct the study, and restate each as a useful research question.
   a. Effects of different ways of learning social studies
   b. Effects of cooperative versus competitive instruction on attitudes toward learning
   c. Opinions of parents toward education
   d. Family characteristics and school attendance
   e. Validity of the Wechsler Intelligence Scale for Children (WISC) for school performance
2. Write a directional hypothesis for the following problem statement, and identify the type of variables in the hypothesis: Low-achieving students frequently respond positively to behavior modification programs. Is there any relationship between the type of reward (tangible or intangible) and the amount of learning?
3. State a hypothesis based on each of the following research questions:
   a. What is the effect of individualized and structured social studies on high school students?
   b. Are there any differences in students' engagement in tasks when a teacher uses a positive introduction and when a teacher uses a neutral introduction to tasks?
   c. Does nonpromotion of elementary pupils improve their social adjustment?
   d. Do teachers' perceptions of job stress differ among teachers of mildly retarded, moderately retarded, and nonretarded children?
4. In the following qualitative problem statements, identify the case to be studied:
   a. This study describes and analyzes how women faculty members at an urban university perceive their professional and personal lives and how they integrate their lives.
   b. School board records of a suburban school system were analyzed for the ideologies articulated by various school board members to legitimize systemwide curriculum policies from 1950 to 1980.
   c. The research problem is to describe how Sue Olson, a first-year elementary school teacher, learns a professional role with students, faculty, administrators, and parents and how she develops meaning for teacher professionalism.
   d. The research problem is to describe and analyze a faculty social system in the implementation of an innovative middle school program for grounded theory.

Read the following full-text studies.

5. Box, J. A., & Little, D. C. (2003). Cooperative small-group instruction combined with advanced organizers and their relationship to self-concept and social studies achievement of elementary school students. *Journal of Instructional Psychology, 30*(4), 284–287. Accession Number: 12010631.
   a. What is the operational definition for each dependent variable?
   b. Is each operational definition valid for the study? Why?
   c. Could the operational definitions influence the varied results?
6. Ukrainetz, T. A., & Fresuez, E. F. (2003). "What isn't language?": A qualitative study of the role of the school speech-language pathologist. *Language, Speech, and Hearing Services in School, 34*(4), 285–299. Accession Number: 11021893.
   a. What is the selected case?
   b. How many people and settings constitute the case?
   c. Who are the ancillary participants?

7. Denner, P. R., Richards, J. P., & Albanese, A. J. (2003). The effect of story impressions preview on learning from narrative text. *Journal of Experimental Education, 71*(4), 313–333. Accession Number: 11453638.
   a. What are the independent and dependent variables?
   b. What is the operational definition for each level of the independent variable?
   c. Why was a second experiment done?
8. Cho, S., Singer, G. H., & Brenner, M. (2000). Adaptation and accommodation of young children with disabilities: A comparison of Korean and Korean American parents. *Topics in Early Childhood Special Education, 20*(4), 236–250. Accession Number: 3933327.
   a. How many people and locations constituted the case for this article?
   b. What does the word *comparison* mean in this study?
   c. What is the topic of each specific research question?
   d. Are the findings organized by the specific research questions?

CHAPTER

4 Literature Review

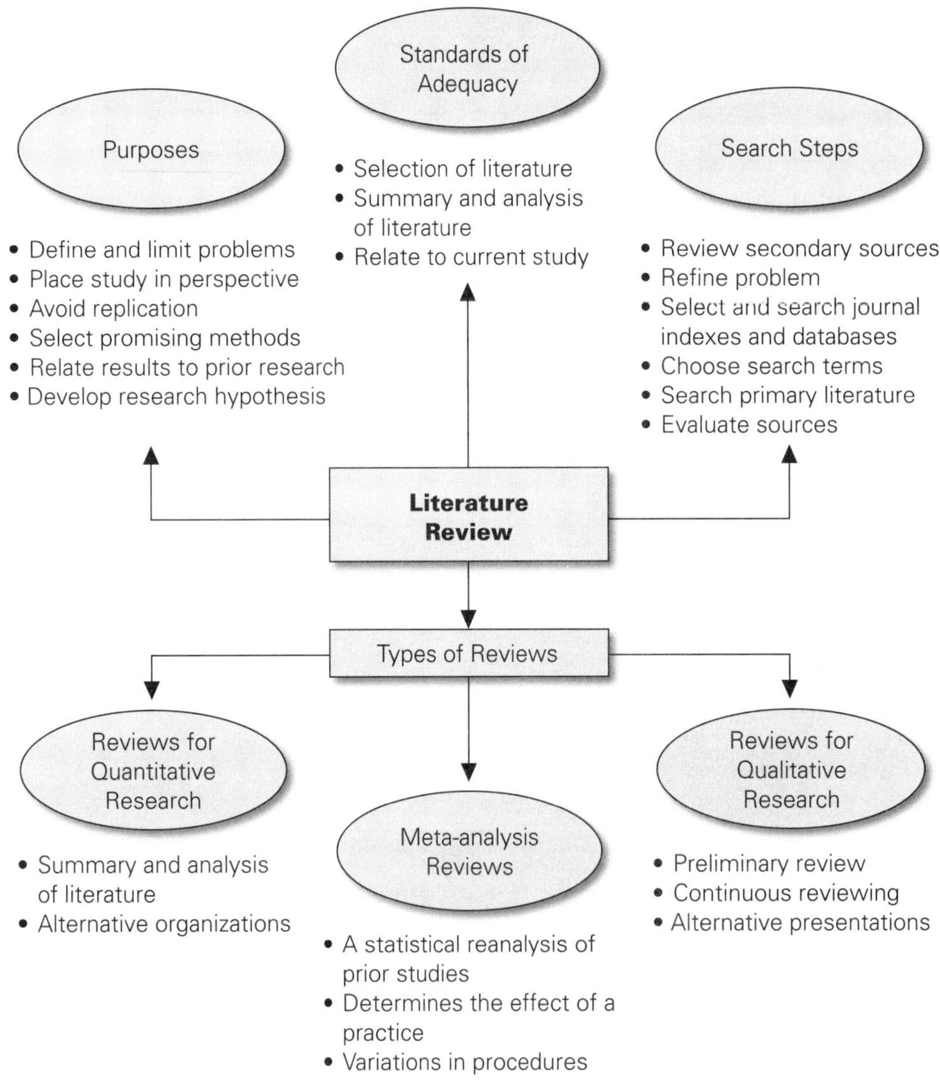

KEY TERMS

literature review
electronic resources
related literature
secondary literature
primary literature
ERIC
ERIC digests
report literature
preliminary search
exhaustive search
thesaurus
refereed
meta-analysis

A literature review, if conducted carefully and presented well, will add much to an understanding of the research problem and help place the results of a study in a historical perspective. Without conducting a review of the literature, it is difficult to build a body of scientific knowledge about educational phenomena.

During the last three decades, the landscape of literature searches has changed dramatically. Once done manually, such searches are now done electronically, whether on the Internet with a computer, or by accessing the many electronic databases available. Because of the accessibility of so much literature, the reviewer must be an *active decision maker* at every step of the process. Otherwise, he or she may be lulled into letting the computer do the selecting of relevant literature, rather than being extremely discerning in making his or her own choices.

This chapter explains the purposes of the literature review and the steps involved in searching for relevant secondary and primary literature. Most literature reviews comprise a narrative, interpretive criticism of the existing research. Literature reviews for quantitative and qualitative research are described. Later in the chapter, the discussion turns to meta-analysis, a literature review that statistically summarizes the results of prior research. Finally, standards are provided for evaluating narrative literature reviews. Because use of the Internet is now essential in reviewing the literature, some Internet resources are examined in this chapter.

FUNCTIONS OF A REVIEW OF RELATED LITERATURE

An interpretive review of the literature is exactly that—a summary and analysis of the relevant literature about a research problem. A **literature review** illuminates the related literature to enable a reader to gain further insights from the study.[1]

Literature includes many types of sources: professional journals, scholarly books and monographs, government documents, dissertations, and electronic resources. **Electronic resources** include various types of literature published on the Internet, a global network of computer databases. Some refereed journals and conference proceedings are published only electronically.

Related literature is that which is directly relevant to the problem, such as previous research investigating the same variables or a similar question, a theory and the testing of the theory, and studies of similar practices. Thoroughly researched topics in education usually have sufficient research pertinent to the problem. New and little-researched topics usually require a review of any literature that is related in some essential way to the problem.

Purposes of a Literature Review

A review of the literature serves several purposes in research. The knowledge gained from the literature aids in stating the significance of the problem, developing the research design, and relating the results of the study to prior knowledge. A review of the literature enables the researcher to do the following:

1. ***Define and limit the problem.*** Most studies that add to education knowledge investigate only one aspect of a larger topic. By becoming familiar with the major works on that topic and the possible breadth of that topic, the researcher can refine his or her general idea to a specific problem.

2. ***Place the study in a historical perspective.*** To add to the knowledge in any subfield, researchers analyze how their study relates to existing literature. A researcher may state that the research of A, B, and C has added a certain amount to the body of current knowledge, that the work of D and E has further added to that knowledge; and that this study extends knowledge by investigating the stated question.

3. ***Avoid unintentional and unnecessary replication.*** Conducting a thorough search of the literature enables the researcher to avoid unintentional and unneeded replication. The researcher, however, may deliberately replicate a study for verification.

4. ***Select promising methods and measures.*** As researchers sort out the knowledge on a subject, they assess the research methods that have been used to establish that knowledge. Analysis of instruments, sampling, and methods of prior research may lead to a more sophisticated design, the use of a different instrument, a more appropriate data analysis procedure, or an improved methodology for studying the problem.

5. ***Relate the findings to previous knowledge and suggest further research.*** The results of a study are contrasted to the findings of previous research in order to determine how the study adds new knowledge. Most researchers suggest directions for further research based on insights gained from conducting their studies.

6. ***Develop research hypotheses.*** In some quantitative studies, researchers use the literature to justify the formulation of specific research hypotheses. Previous studies may suggest certain results, and the hypotheses should be consistent with those studies. Sometimes, researchers use theories, rather than empirical studies, to justify research hypotheses.

Steps in Writing a Review of the Literature

The review of the literature is usually done in broad, sequential steps. Researchers often return to prior steps, however, as they gain understanding of the topic or restate the problem. The general steps for reviewing the literature include the following:

1. ***Analyze the problem statement*** to identify concepts and variables that suggest topic areas and key terms to search.

2. ***Read secondary literature*** to define the problem in more precise terms and to locate primary literature.

3. ***Decide the search strategy for primary literature*** such as deciding if this is a preliminary search or an exhaustive search.

4. ***Transform the problem statement into search language and conduct a search.*** The key terms appropriate for searching databases may be used in different combinations.

5. ***Evaluate the pertinent primary literature*** for inclusion in the review.

6. ***Organize and logically group selected literature.*** Empirical studies may be classified in several ways: by the variables, by the populations, by historical order, by similar results, or by designs and methods.

7. ***Write the review*** to provide readers with an understanding of the problem and the need for or importance of the research.

SOURCES FOR A LITERATURE REVIEW

Although a review emphasizes primary literature, secondary literature is also useful. **Secondary literature** reviews prior research and gives a quick overview of empirical studies on the topic. This literature eliminates much of the technical information about the original study but cites extensive references. Research and theoretical reviews may be found in monographs, encyclopedia articles, and journals that contain reviews.

Primary literature is the original research study or writing by a theorist or a researcher. Primary literature contains the full text of a research report or a theory and thus is more detailed and technical. These materials are published in journals, research reports, monographs of single studies, and dissertations and are also placed in databases.

Primary and secondary literature provide different information and are used in different ways in the search process. Secondary literature provides general background information and gives clues for searching primary literature. Primary sources provide detailed information of current research, theories, and methods used to investigate the problem.

ALERT! Recent primary literature, not secondary literature, is the essence of a review!

Sources for Secondary Literature

Recognized authorities write reviews of original studies when sufficient work has been done to enable a critical assessment of the stature of the knowledge. The topics for reviews are usually selected by a committee of researchers and scholars who are aware of current issues and research. When work on a topic is ongoing, conducting a thorough review may not be warranted for several years. Thus, some reviews may appear dated yet provide useful information.

There are several advantages to starting with secondary literature instead of primary literature. First, secondary literature gives the researcher knowledge of the research on the topic to the date of publication. Second, these sources can help refine a problem to a more specific research question. Third, secondary literature helps identify primary literature through the bibliography. Last, secondary literature can provide a cluster of key terms about the topic to use in a search. The following sections describe the usefulness of some of the secondary sources listed in Table 4.1 (see Excerpt 4.1).

Quarterly and Annual Reviews General references provide reviews on topics selected from the entire field of education. Quarterly and annually published reviews give detailed syntheses of narrow topics along with exhaustive references. Usually, the author has a conceptual framework, which provides the criteria for selecting the reviewed study.

Professional Books Professional books, including some textbooks, give detailed analyses of broad fields from particular perspectives. The subject index of *Books in Print*, which cites *all* currently published books, is available online in most libraries.

Encyclopedias Reading the short, authoritative summary of a topic in an encyclopedia is helpful in the early stages of a review. The *Encyclopedia of Educational Research*, with over 250 articles and extensive bibliographies, represents a comprehensive analysis of 15 or more fields of educational research. There are also more specialized encyclopedias, which

EXCERPT 4.1 Review in a Secondary Source

Results of the analyses showed no significant differences on any of the student participation variables as a result of class size. . . . Observations were made in Grades 4 and 5 rather than in earlier grades and students had only attended small classes for 1 year and then changed to larger classes. Patterns of engagement behavior may be relatively stable by this time and difficult to change. (p. 326)

Source: From Finn, J. D., Pannozzo, G. M., & Achilles, C. M. (2003). The "why's" of class size: Student behavior in small classes. *Review of Educational Research, 73*(3), 321–368.

TABLE 4.1 Selected Sources for Reviews of Secondary Literature

General References

Review of Educational Research (1931–present, journal)
Review of Research in Education (1973–present, annual book)
Educational Psychology Review (1989–present, journal)
Yearbook of the National Society for the Study of Education (1902–present, annual)
Encyclopedia of Educational Research, 6th ed. (1992)
Books in Print

Specialized References

Handbook of Educational Psychology (1996)
Handbook of Qualitative Research in Education, Second Edition (2000)
Handbook of Reading Research (2002)
Handbook of Research on Curriculum (1996)
Handbook of Research on Educational Administration (1999)
Handbook of Research on Mathematics Teaching and Learning (1992)
Handbook on Research on Multicultural Education (2001)
Handbook of Research on Music Teaching and Learning (2003)
Handbook of Research on School Supervision (1998)
Handbook of Research on Social Studies Teaching and Learning (1991)
Handbook of Research on Teacher Education (1996)
Handbook of Research on Teaching, 4th ed. (2001)
Handbook of Research on Teaching the English Language Arts (2003)
Handbook of Research on the Education of Young Children (1993)
Handbook of Schooling in Urban America (1993)
Handbook of Research on Science Teaching and Learning (1994)
Handbook of Special and Remedial Education: Research and Practice (1995)
Handbook of Sport Psychology (2001)
Yearbook of Adult and Continuing Education (1976–present)
Yearbook of Special Education (1976–present)
The Second Handbook on Parent Education (1989)
International Handbook of Bilingualism and Bilingual Education (1998)
International Handbook of Early Childhood Education (1992)
International Handbook of Women's Education (1990)

contain articles about certain topics, such as early childhood education, special education, school administration and supervision, teaching and teacher education, and so on.

Specialized Handbooks and Yearbooks Handbooks and yearbooks that specialize in certain areas of practice and research are similar to encyclopedias, with several exceptions. The authoritative chapters in specialized handbooks and yearbooks are usually more comprehensive and longer than those in encyclopedias but also more narrowly focused. If a handbook or yearbook exists on the topic one wishes to review, that would be a better place to start. One example is the *Annual Review of Research for School Leaders*.

Other Specialized References Other handbooks and encyclopedias, primarily from social science disciplines, may serve as secondary sources for literature reviews. Specialized references, for example, are available in anthropology, social psychology, aging, child psychology, adolescent children, organization management, political science, and other disciplines.

Databases and Indexes Another approach is to locate secondary sources from databases and indexes, which are typically used for locating primary sources. For example, in addition to primary materials, the Education Resources Information Center, or **ERIC,** provides citations to books, book chapters, literature reviews, guides, and opinion papers.

One of the most helpful secondary sources included in ERIC is the collection of **ERIC digests,** short reports that synthesize research and ideas about contemporary educational issues. There are more than 2,400 full-text digests in the ERIC database. In general, many of the indexes listed in Table 4.2 also provide online access to some secondary literature. By using various search options, which are often found in the "Advanced Search" section within a database, a search can be limited by type of publication.

Online Library Catalogs Most libraries have online catalogs of their books, which allow you to conduct different types of searches. Not only can you search by author or title, but you can also search by additional commands that allow you to target a specific topic or field of study. (This is explained in the section on conducting a search.)

Each library will have somewhat different procedures for searching its catalogs and accessing its different databases. And so while the basics will be very similar for all libraries, you will need to become acquainted with the specific searching procedures of the library in which you are working.

Sources for Primary Literature

Primary literature includes empirical studies, research reports, government documents, and scholarly monographs. Indexes identify primary published literature, giving the location of each source and an abstract. Selected sources for a review of primary literature are listed in Table 4.2. Most of these are available on the World Wide Web.

The most thorough indexing and abstracting service for education periodicals is provided by ERIC (Education Resources Information Center). ERIC has established a database of literature since 1966. This database contains 1.1 million bibliographic citations to a broad collection of education-related resources. In 2004 ERIC instituted a new process for obtaining and selecting documents and journals to include in the database. The standards and criteria now used are provided on the ERIC website (www.eric.ed.gov). This means that some journals that were included in ERIC prior to 2004 may not be included after 2004.

Current Index to Journals in Education (CIJE) *CIJE* abstracts from over 1,000 education journals and periodicals, from 1969–2004. It also indexes educationally relevant articles from such periodicals as the *Personnel Journal* and the *Journal of Family Counseling*.

Resources in Education (RIE) *RIE* indexes and abstracts from 1969–2004 non-journal documents or what is called **report literature,** documents other than journals, which include speeches and presentations made at professional meetings, monographs, final reports of federally funded research, state education department documents, final reports of school district projects, and the like. *RIE* documents from 1969–2004 are in the ERIC Document Microfiche Collection, which is available in universities, state departments of education, and many public school systems. Beginning in 2004 non-journal documents from 1993 to the present are available online at no cost.

ALERT! For many educational topics, *CIJE* or *RIE* is the best place to start searching for the most recent relevant sources.

TABLE 4.2 Selected Indexes for Primary Literature

Type of Source	Related Index/Indexes
Educational journals	*Current Index to Journals in Education (CIJE)*
Report literature	*Resources in Education (RIE)*
General and educational periodicals and monographs	*Education Index* (1929–present)
Selected abstracts and indexes in specialized areas	*Psychological Abstracts* (PsycINFO) (1887–present) *Sociological Abstracts* (1953–present) *Exceptional Child Education Resources* (1966–present) *Physical Education Index* (1970–present) *State Education Journal Index* (1963–present) *Educational Administration Abstracts* (1966–present) *Higher Education Abstracts* (1965–present) *Sociology of Education Abstracts* (1965–present)
Government documents	*Monthly Catalog of U.S. Government Publications* (1895–present) *Digest of Educational Statistics* (1962–present) *American Statistics Index* (1973–present)
Dissertations and theses	*Dissertation Abstracts International* (1861–present)
Citation indexes	*Arts and Humanities Citation Index* (1975–present) *Science Citation Index (SCI)* (1945–present) *Social Science Citation Index (SSCI)* (1956–present)

Educational Index The *Educational Index* primarily references educational periodicals, yearbooks, and monographs. It indexes more than 300 journals but does not provide annotations and abstracts. If an exhaustive search is required, the *Educational Index* is useful because it provides coverage since 1929. Most reviewers use CIJE from 1969 to date but use the *Educational Index* for enduring topics.

ALERT! Because the *Educational Index* is not limited to scholarly journals, key term searches can retrieve information from educational articles in nonrefereed journals, such as *School Shop* and *Library Talk.*

PsycINFO PsycINFO, sponsored by the American Psychological Association (APA), covers all types of scholarly documents, including journal articles, books, book chapters, technical reports, and dissertations. References are provided to studies in cognitive, social, and moral development; learning processes; and classroom, peer, and teacher effects on learning. The articles have been carefully selected for behavioral relevance from education-related journals. Retrospective coverage of literature, updated monthly, is available as far back as 1887.

Selected Abstracts and Indexes in Subjects Related to Education The sources discussed thus far have very broad coverage for most problems in educational research. Several other abstracts and indexes, however, have more narrow coverage, focusing on single subjects related to education. If a research problem is limited to a specific topic, a thorough search would include the more specialized reference, including the following:

- *Psychological Abstracts*, published in print format monthly by the APA since 1927, indexes and abstracts more than 950 journals, technical reports, monographs, and other scientific documents in psychology and related disciplines. *Psychological Abstracts* usually provides more thorough coverage than *CIJE* of educational problems related to psychological topics such as human development, counseling, exceptional children, and learning.
- *Sociological Abstracts*, which is similar to *Psychological Abstracts*, has been published five times a year since 1953. Because its subject index uses single terms, the reviewer must check the abstract to determine the article's relevance.
- *Exceptional Child Education Resources (ECER)*, published since 1969, uses a format similar to that of *CIJE*. Many of the 200 or more journals it covers are not listed in *CIJE*.
- The *Physical Education Index*, published quarterly since 1970, provides a subject index on educational topics and specific sports. It also indexes sports medicine.
- The *State Education Journal Index*, published twice a year since 1963, is a subject and bibliographic index on articles from about 100 state education journals. These journals cover a broad range of topics and are useful primarily for such state-level issues as federal aid, collective bargaining, and teacher certification.
- *Educational Administration Abstracts*, published since 1966, abstracts articles from about 100 journals. The references section classifies abstracts into 42 subjects and provides author and journal indexes but not a subject index.

Government Documents Indexes The *Monthly Catalogue of United States Government Publications* indexes books, pamphlets, maps, and periodicals of all types—over 15,000 per year. All of the publications are organized alphabetically by department and bureau with monthly and annual indexes by author, title, and subject and by series/report numbers. The *Digest of Educational Statistics*, published annually, contains demographic statistics and some longitudinal analyses of enrollment, staffing, student retention rates, and educational achievement at all levels of education. The *American Statistics Index*, published monthly and annually, cites publications of departments and agencies other than the U.S. Department of Education. For example, information on vocational education, emolument, and specialized training programs, welfare recipients with children in school, and drug abuse may be collected by the U.S. Departments of Agriculture, Commerce, Health and Welfare, and Justice.

Dissertation Abstracts International This resource abstracts dissertations that have been accepted by more than 375 institutions in the United States and Canada. Most dissertations and theses are original and unpublished studies and thus primary research.

Citation Indexes Citation indexes enable a researcher to determine the impact of a key study or theory on the works of other scholars and researchers. This is particularly important if the first work was controversial, began a subfield, or initiated a series of studies. The *Science Citation Index (SCI)* and the *Social Science Citation Index (SSCI)* provide bibliographic information for all the references that cited the earlier work. Psychology citations are indexed in *SCI*, and education and psychology are indexed in *SSCI*.

STEPS IN CONDUCTING AN ELECTRONIC SEARCH

Before conducting any search of the literature, you should become thoroughly familiar with the library you plan to use. It is best to have someone orient you to the library, showing you where reference materials, microfiche collections, and journal indexes are located.

Most important, you need to understand the computer software that is used. If a reference librarian or an instructional technology specialist is assigned to or knows about educational literature, he or she will be especially helpful, and you should feel free to ask questions. Searching the literature can be quite time consuming, and the librarians are there to help you. Many students are surprised at how long it takes to do a review. It is not unusual to do a number of different searches as you increase your understanding of your research question and its ramifications.

The steps that are summarized in the sections that follow begin with secondary sources. However, because the use of computers and accessing databases via the Internet have made searching for primary sources more efficient, many researchers start with them instead (Step 3). This can be done if the researcher has already done considerable reading in the topic being investigated or if the proposed study is one of many on the same topic. Regardless, when initially investigating the topic, it is still best to start with *secondary* sources. By following a set of sequential steps, you will increase the quality of the search and be able to locate the most appropriate studies more quickly (see Figure 4.1).

Step 1: Use Secondary Sources to Locate Reviews and Related Literature

Libraries have computerized catalogs of their books, which allows you to conduct different types of searches. Not only can you search by author or title, but you can also search by using additional commands that allow you to target a specific topic or field of study. The most commonly used commands are *subject* and *keyword,* and both are used with logical connectors such as *and, or,* and *not.*

Keyword searching with connectors will result in a precise retrieval. Such a search is used when you have incomplete information about an author or title and the subject headings are too broad. If the keywords *cooperative learning* and *achievement* are connected with *and,* the search will be narrowed to records that contain both of these terms. Using *not* as a connector will also narrow the search by including records with one term but not the other. For instance, searching on *cooperative learning not achievement* will exclude any record that contains the term *achievement* even if *cooperative learning* is in the record. If the *or* connector is used, the search will be broadened to records that have either term.

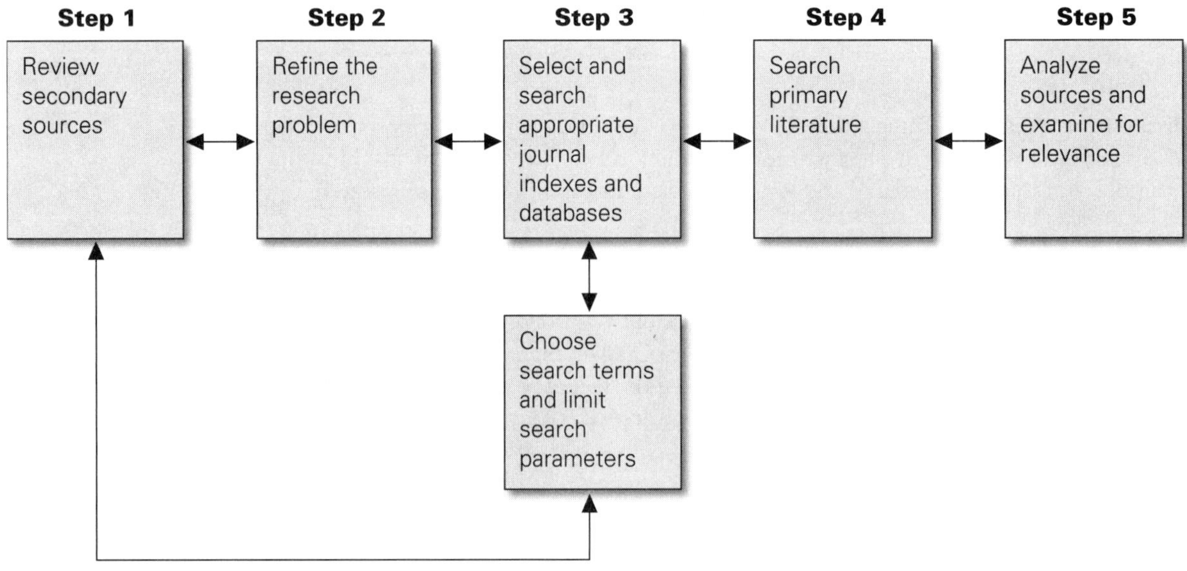

FIGURE 4.1 **The Literature Search Process**

Another approach to identify secondary sources is to use one of the databases that can be accessed through a search engine on the World Wide Web such as *Ovid* or *FirstSearch*. FirstSearch allows you to electronically search Education Abstracts Information, a database that contains English-language periodicals and yearbooks. Subjects include administration, teaching methods and curriculum, literacy, government funding, and more.

ALERT! FirstSearch may be used for an initial search. However, it contains limited sources to educational literature compared to the ERIC system, which retrieves only educational sources.

An additional approach to identify secondary sources is to use indexes and databases that are more typically used for locating primary sources. For example, besides indexing primary sources, ERIC provides citations to books, book chapters, literature reviews, and opinion papers. As noted earlier, the ERIC digests are among the most helpful secondary sources included in ERIC. In general, many of the indexes listed in Table 4.2 also provide online access to some secondary literature. By using various search options which are often found in an "Advanced Search" section, you can usually limit your search by type of publication.

Again, each library will have somewhat different searching procedures for both its catalogs and its online materials. Although the basics are similar for all libraries, you will need to become acquainted with the specific search procedures in the library in which you will be working.

Step 2: Refine the Research Problem for Key Concepts

The initial research problem is often general and somewhat tentative. At this stage, the researcher thinks that the problem may be adequate but that it needs to be more specific and limited. By reviewing secondary literature and related primary literature, he or she will learn how others have defined the problem in more specific ways. The researcher will find ideas and examples to help delimit the problem, and concepts and variables will be clarified as he or she finds operational definitions. Most important at this time is to identify the key concepts that will help you select the appropriate journal indexes and specialized indexes for use in searching for primary literature (see Table 4.3).

The process of refining a research problem can be frustrating. Typically, an initial problem that seems to have merit will be revised as the researcher reviews previous studies. A new problem will be formulated, and often it too will be revised as further literature is reviewed. This pattern of reviewing and revising may be repeated many times.

In addition, the researcher must decide the type of search to be done: a preliminary search to select a research problem; an exhaustive review for a thesis, dissertation, or major study; or an update of a previous literature review. A **preliminary search** to refine a problem usually examines about 10 of the most recent references from one or two databases. The search is limited by the numbers of years and databases. An **exhaustive search** of the literature is done for a narrowly focused problem and examines more than 10 years of materials and perhaps multiple databases. However, doing a keyword search with an Internet search engine for either type of search will not be sufficient; the researcher will eventually have to go to specialized indexes, abstracts, and databases to obtain quality primary sources.

Using the term *recent* to describe the literature obtained in a search is somewhat misleading. It usually takes six months to a year for a manuscript that has been accepted for publication to actually be published. It may take as long as two years for a book or a collection of chapters written by different authors to be published. *Recent* is therefore a relative term in this context.

TABLE 4.3 Selected Indexes, Abstracts, and Databases

ERIC
Exceptional Children Educational Resources
PsycINFO [Psychological Abstracts]
PsycARTICLES
Books in Print
Social SCISEARCH and Backfiles [*Social Science Citation Indexes*]
GPO Monthly Catalogue [*Monthly Catalogue of U.S. Government Documents*]
Public Affairs Information Service [PAIS]
Legal Resources Index [LAWS]
Sociological Abstracts
Family Resources [NCFR]
Ageline [AARP]
National Rehabilitation Information Center [NRIC]
National Institute of Mental Health Database [MCMH]
Resources in Vocational Education
Sport Database
Bilingual Education Database
Dissertation Abstracts On-line
National Newspaper Index

Step 3: Select and Search Appropriate Journal Indexes and Databases

Many indexes can be used to locate research in education. By selecting an index, you are choosing a database and, consequently, the sources to be searched. Each database has its own search procedures and options. Although there is much overlap of sources between some databases, some sources are unique to certain databases. In addition, different indexes provide a range of aids to the reviewer, such as annotations, abstracts, and different searchable fields to refine a search. Figure 4.2 shows an annotated sample ERIC journal entry.

The PsycINFO database, also mentioned earlier, contains bibliographic sources from the literature in psychology and related disciplines (including education), and the citations are available in computerized and print formats. The entire PsycINFO database is online at most libraries (www.psyinfo.com). PsycINFO contains abstracts of articles from more than 1,800 journals, as well as abstracts of books, book chapters, dissertations, reports, and other documents. PsycARTICLES (www.psycinfo.com/psycarticles) contains the full text of 49 APA journals and also covers over 165 education and education-related journals. Sample topics include learning, students, teachers, educational testing and measurement,[2] counseling and guidance, family issues, social processes, and social behavior.

Both the ERIC and the PsycINFO databases can be accessed via the Internet. This allows students and other researchers to conduct their searches of these databases from any location with Internet access.

Once the database has been selected, then the proper search terms and search parameters must be decided. Indexes organize the literature by subject, title, key terms, and author. To select the most appropriate key terms for a topic, you should use a **thesaurus** of terms for that database. For most searches of educational literature, it is best to use the *Thesaurus of ERIC Descriptors*. The *Thesaurus of ERIC Descriptors* is essentially a list of terms, or *controlled vocabulary,* by which ERIC citations are indexed. It organizes the terms alphabetically and defines each one so that the researcher can match his or her definition

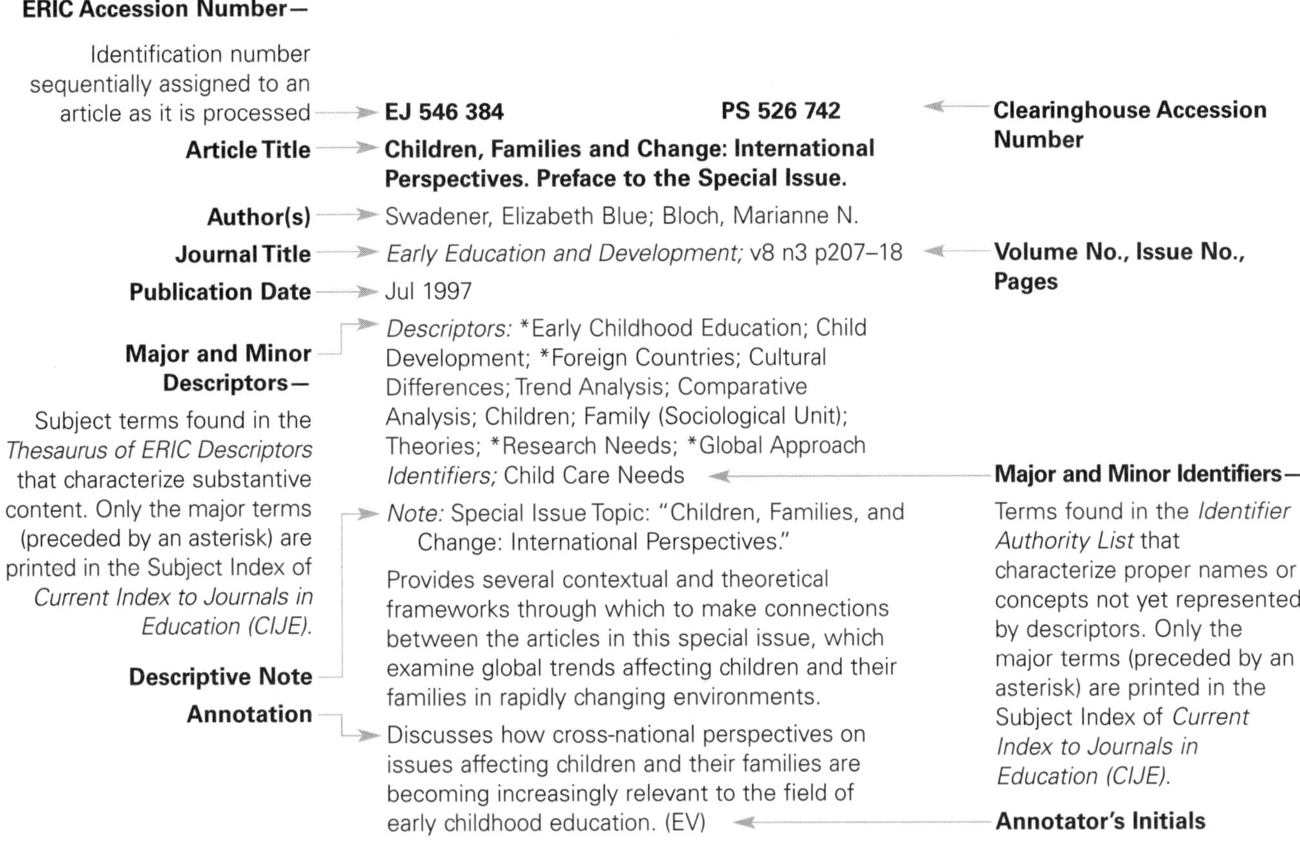

FIGURE 4.2 **Sample ERIC Journal Article Entry**

to the one used in the indexes. Once the researcher has identified the best thesaurus descriptors, he or she uses them to continue the search. The thesaurus also indicates terms that are closely related to the descriptors, both more broad and more narrow terms. For example, suppose you are searching for sources about this research problem: What is the effect of teaching style on student achievement? The key terms are *teaching styles* and *student achievement*. Figure 4.3 shows the entry for *teaching styles* in a recent ERIC *thesaurus*. Note that this term has been used as an ERIC descriptor since 1966. It is wise to look at the definitions of the related terms because one of them may be closer to what you mean by *teaching styles* than the definition in the ERIC system. Related terms are also used in conducting an exhaustive search of the literature. The only way to learn if a descriptor will be useful in identifying literature related to your research problem is to use it to locate articles and reports and then to examine the titles and abstracts. If the materials seem promising, it makes sense to use that descriptor. If you find a research article that matches almost exactly what you mean by *teaching styles*, then you should note the descriptors (sometimes called *key terms* listed by the authors or editors on the first page of the article or the descriptors assigned to it in the index). These key terms may be useful in identifying the most relevant studies.

To research a problem that is psychologically oriented and that involves searching the psychological literature, you should consult the *Thesaurus of Psychological Index Terms* before searching the PsycINFO database. The terms in this index are different from those in ERIC.

The search begins when you go online and access the page of the database website that allows you to enter appropriate terms. The first choice you will make is which terms to use in your search. Before starting to search, you should limit your search parameters to locate

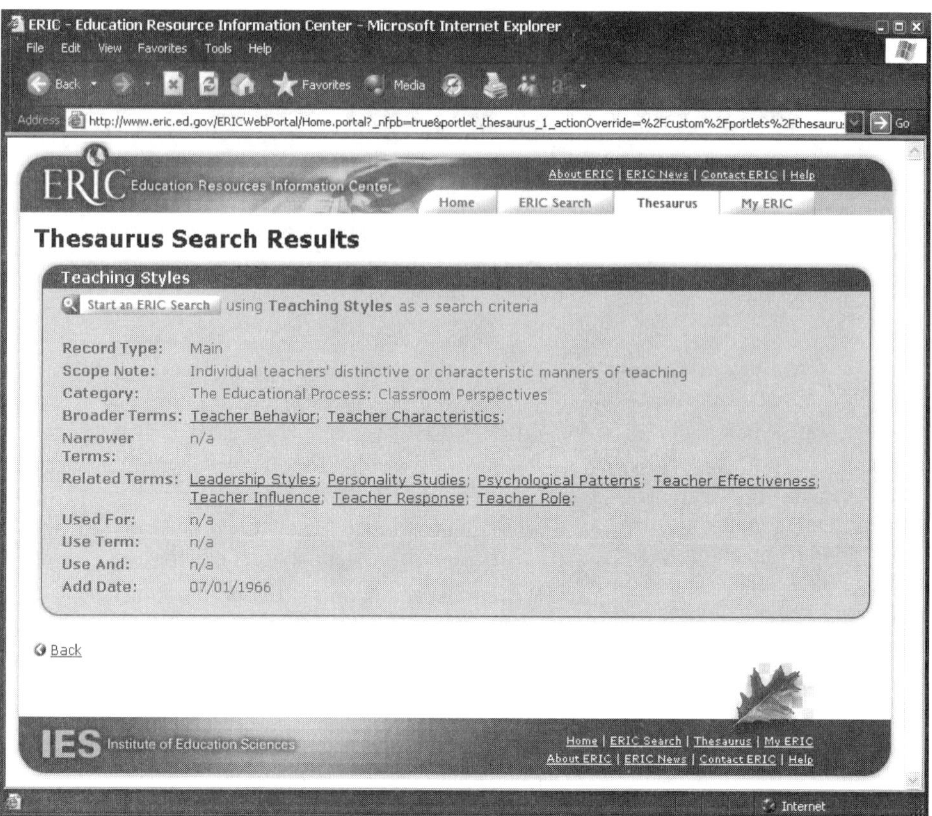

FIGURE 4.3 **Sample Thesaurus Entry**

the literature most relevant to your problem. These parameters are very important and must be attended to *before* submitting your search. Figure 4.4 shows a recent ERIC webpage.

ALERT! The ERIC website and database are periodically redesigned by a U.S. Department of Education contractor. The current webpage may look different and provide different options depending on the search engine. Check with a reference librarian at your library for the current status of ERIC.

This webpage offers the choice to narrow your search by specifying the type of publication. By using the pull-down menus, you can limit your search exactly. For example, to conduct an initial search, it is usually wise to limit your search to journal articles published over the last 10 years. When the sources are displayed, you can review each in greater detail by clicking on its title to reveal the full abstract and bibliographic information.

Step 4: Search Primary and/or Secondary Literature

Most searches must be tailored even further to identify a reasonable number of sources that appear to be closely related to the research problem at hand. The most common way of delineating the search is with the logical connector *and*. Using *and* will reduce the search because the computer will look only for entries that are categorized by all the descriptors indicated. For example, a search of *teaching styles* ***and*** *elementary education* would have fewer "hits" than using only *teaching styles*. (*Teaching styles* alone would include elementary, middle, and high schools, as well as colleges and universities.) If a third descriptor,

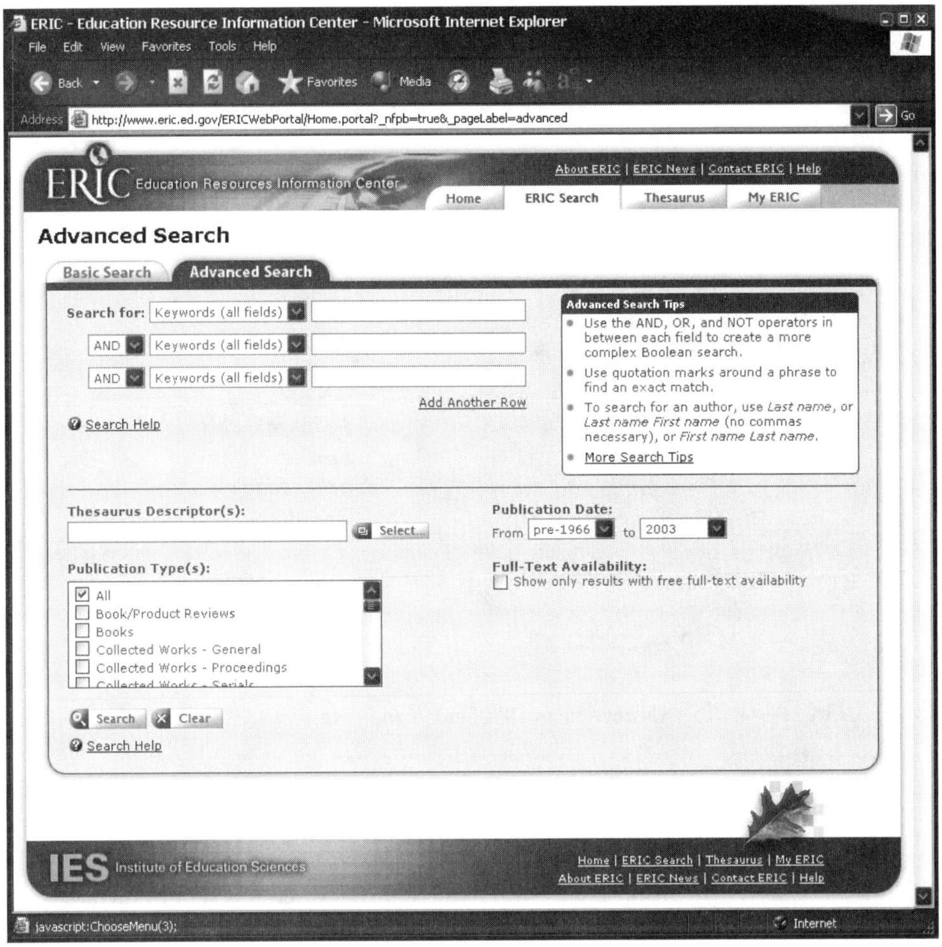

FIGURE 4.4 **Sample Limits for ERIC Searching**

achievement, were added, the search would be even further refined. This process of narrowing the search is illustrated in Figure 4.5. (The numbers of entries were retrieved in March 2003 and are those entered between 1993 and 2003.)

If your search produces very few "hits," then you should try using other major descriptors or related descriptors in your search. Each entry in ERIC can have up to six major descriptors. You can also broaden your search by using the connector *or*. For example, a search of *teaching styles* ***or*** *teaching behaviors* ***and*** *elementary education* ***and*** *achievement* would locate articles that contain either *teaching styles* or *behaviors* and both of the other two descriptors.

Once you have limited your search to a workable number of title entries, then you should examine each source in greater detail to determine if it would be beneficial to obtain the entire article. The more detailed information on the screen will indicate whether the record is in *CIJE* or *RIE* (i.e., *CIJE* entries have *EJ* accession numbers and *RIE* entries have *ED* accession numbers). In addition, it will include complete bibliographic information and an abstract. After reading the abstract on screen, many researchers initially rank each citation by degree of potential usefulness, such as 3 for "most important," 2 for "possible use," and 1 for "irrelevant." Most libraries have the capability to print out information from the screen or to save it to your own diskette.

Primary sources are reported in a wide variety of journals. In fact, there are hundreds of them that differ greatly in quality. Journals that submit all of the manuscripts sent to them to a *blind review process* are considered to have more articles of quality. (In a blind

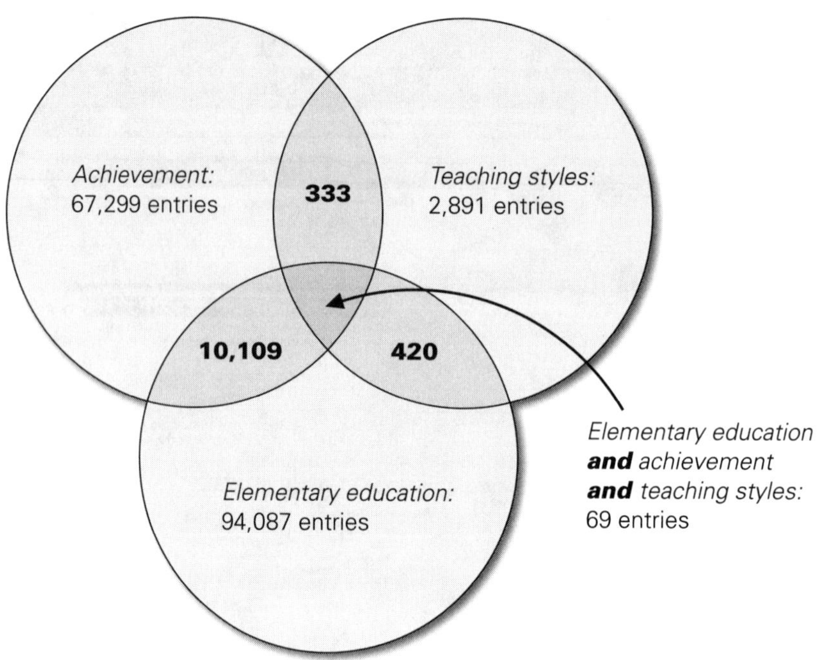

FIGURE 4.5 **Narrowing an ERIC Search with *and***

review, the names of the manuscript's authors are omitted when it is sent to reviewers for the purpose of reducing reviewer bias.) Two or three reviewers, all experts on the topic investigated, will comment on the significance of the problem, methodology, data analysis, contribution of the findings and conclusion, and other aspects of the manuscript. Usually, reviewers are asked to recommend whether the manuscript should be published as submitted, revised and resubmitted, or rejected. Rarely do reviewers recommend to publish something as submitted. Indeed, a journal's rejection rate is often used (and justifiably so) as a barometer of its quality. A journal is said to be **refereed** if this review procedure is followed. Conversely, a journal is nonrefereed if it does not use external reviewers to evaluate manuscripts. Regardless, just because a study is published, that does not mean that it contains good research, so you may want to learn which journals in your area are regarded as high-quality publications.

Step 5: Analyze Sources and Examine for Relevance

To locate a specific source, you must know how your library is organized and especially how it provides access to journals. Journals may be found in a variety of formats, including online, print, and microform.

Sources that are not available locally or by Internet may be obtained through interlibrary loan or by obtaining a photocopy from another library. Some database services, such as *Psychological Abstracts*, provide the author's address. By conducting an Internet search or using a directory of membership for the American Education Research Association or the American Psychological Association, you could locate and write the author for a reprint of an article or paper. The source also might be available for purchase through a service such as Infotrieve (www4.infotrieve.com) or Ingenta (www.ingenta.com) or at the journal publisher's website. No article reproduction service covers all of the ERIC-indexed journal titles, however.

After obtaining copies of the articles that seemed most important based on reading the abstract and considering the journal's reputation, your next task is to read the study to see if it will be useful in one's review. At this stage, you will probably reject some of the articles as not pertinent. Usually, researchers continue searching until they have 15 to 30 articles. You will always locate and read more studies than you will eventually use in a review.

A *mediated online search* is used when the reviewer has found insufficient literature by searching the library-mounted databases and now needs to search distant indexed databases. This type of search is conducted by a search analyst or librarian. The cost is based on how long the analyst or librarian is connected to a database and how many citations are saved. To minimize the cost, it is important to work with the search analyst to select the appropriate descriptors before going online.

EVALUATE, SUMMARIZE, AND ANALYZE PRIMARY SOURCES

The first requirement of conducting a good review is to select good studies to summarize and analyze. Use these three criteria to evaluate your primary studies:

1. ***Credibility*** Does the study appear objective, are the conclusions reasonable, and was the methodology appropriate for the investigation? (Many of these issues are discussed in later chapters.) Other indicators of credibility center on the author, his or her prior research, if the study was supported by external grants or funds, and if it is one of a line of inquiry by the author.
2. ***Journal reputation*** Is the journal refereed or not? Journals sponsored by national associations tend to have excellent reputations and use a blind review process.
3. ***Relevance*** Each study should be clearly related to the research problem or provide background or a historical perspective. Because one cannot include every study in a review, recent, well-done, and representative studies should be selected for review.

As you read each study, it is useful to record your notes electronically or on index cards (e.g., 5" ˘ 8" size), which can be easily organized in different ways. You should begin by reading the abstract of the article, if there is one, and the purpose or research problem. Next, you should read the results and decide if it is worthwhile to read the article more carefully and take notes on it. At this point, you may have to discard some of the articles as not useful.

If you decide to use the article, then you should begin taking notes by writing down the complete bibliographic information, by summarizing the research problem as briefly as possible, and by underlining or circling the independent and dependent variables. Next, you should indicate in outline form the design (i.e., subjects, instruments, procedures) and then summarize the results and conclusions. On the back of the index card, you should record interesting and insightful quotations, weaknesses or limitations in the methodology, analysis of the data and conclusions; and how the study may be related to the research problem. You can use a code to indicate your overall judgment of the article. If you find it closely related to your research problem and highly credible, you might rate the article as an A (see Excerpt 4.2); if somewhat related and credible, a B; and so on.

It is also helpful to develop a code that indicates the major focus of the study by topic. For example, in reviewing studies on student engagement, you may find that some studies examine the effect of engagement on student achievement, that some focus on strategies to improve student engagement, and that others emphasize different approaches to student engagement depending on the type of students. Each of these could be identified using a code or notation on the card, such as "Effect on ach.," "Improv. engage.," and "Approaches."

EXCERPT 4.2 Analysis of a Prior Study

In another study addressing the utility of portfolios, Wolf, Lichtenstein, Bartlett, and Hartman (1996) investigated the first-year results of the . . . school district's teacher evaluation system in which teacher portfolios figured heavily in pay-for-performance decisions. They found that, of 829 teachers eligible to participate in the program, 266 submitted portfolios. Of the 266 teacher portfolio participants, 236 or approximately 90% of these who applied, were awarded an outstanding designation and a $1000 cash bonus. "As measured by the general reaction of teachers, administrators, and the public, the overall pay-for-performance program was a success" (Wolf et al., 1966, pp. 284–285).

Source: From Tucker, P. D., Stronge, J. H., Gareis, C. R., & Beers, C. S. (2003). The efficacy of portfolios for teacher evaluation and professional development: Do they make a difference? *Educational Administration Quarterly, 39*(5), 572–603.

ORGANIZING AND WRITING A LITERATURE REVIEW

The nature of the written review of literature will depend on whether the study is quantitative or qualitative. Quantitative reviews are often detailed and found in the beginning sections of articles. Qualitative reviews tend to be brief in the beginning but more integrated throughout the complete articles.

Quantitative Reviews of Literature

The review of the literature can be organized in several ways, but the most common approach is to group studies that investigate similar topics or subtopics. This can be done more easily if you coded the studies as you read them. Index cards about articles with one code can be put in one pile, those with another code in a second pile, and so forth. The cards or articles then can be put in order, usually with articles related to the problem in a more general way first and those more specifically related to the problem last. Within each article topic, it may be possible to organize the studies by date, with the most recent studies last. This arrangement provides a sense of the development of the research over time. Studies that are only generally related to the research problem should be summarized briefly. If several studies have similar results, they should be grouped and their findings summarized as such—for example, "Several studies found that teachers' expectations are related to student achievement (Jones, 1978; Smith, 1984; Watson, 1982)."

ALERT! A literature review should *not* be organized by study, with each paragraph in the review dealing with a different study.

The following steps will be useful for reviewing studies that are closely related to the research problem:

1. Provide a brief summary of the article.
2. Analyze the study. The analysis is important because it demonstrates that one is not accepting the study as credible without critically examining the methodology of the research to evaluate the contributions of the results.
3. State explicitly how the reviewed study is related to the research problem. A critical examination shows the relationship of the proposed study or current study to previous literature. This step is essential for ensuring that the results contribute to the current body of knowledge and for generating ideas for future research.

For a few studies, then, specifically those that are closely related to the problem, the review should include three elements: a *summary* of the study, an *analysis* of the study, and a statement of how the study *relates* to the research problem (see Excerpt 4.3). The review should not contain long quotations or use the same wording in discussing different studies.

Quotations, in general, should be used sparingly and only when a special or critical meaning cannot be indicated using your own words. You should use short sentences, as well as transitional sentences, to provide a logical progression of ideas and sections.

Some reviews are organized in alternative ways, depending on the type of study and the topic researched. For instance, reviews may be organized by (a) variables, (b) treatments, (c) research designs and methods, (d) different results from investigations of the same problem, or (e) any combination of these (see Excerpt 4.4). A study that is better designed than the previous research emphasizes methodological criticism (see Excerpt 4.5).

The length of the review depends on the type of study, its purpose (e.g., class paper, thesis or dissertation, manuscript for publication, etc.), and the topic. The literature review

EXCERPT 4.3 Relating Prior Research to Current Study

It would seem, however, that studies on the relationship between families and Black college students are more limited. The present study was designed to examine this gap in the literature on Blacks in higher education. The purpose of this study was to explore the role of family in the life of African American college students. (p. 494)

Source: From Herndon, M. K., & Hirt, J. B. (2004). Black students and their families: What leads to success in college. *Journal of Black Studies, 34*(4), 489–513.

EXCERPT 4.4 Organizing Previous Studies by Similar Conclusions

Despite more than 30 years of extant scholarship, . . . the myth remains that the ideal leader for most schools conforms to a White, masculine stereotype, especially at the secondary level (Brunner & Peyton-Caire, 2000; Murtadha & Larson, 1999; Shakeshaft, 1989). The educational literature offers limited knowledge construction based on data gathered from African American women principals (Alston, 2000; K. W. Collins & Lightsey, 2001; Henry, 2001; Lomotey, 1989). (p. 346)

Source: From Bloom, C. M., & Erlandson, D. A. (2003). African American women principals in urban schools: Realities, (re)constructions, and resolutions. *Educational Administration Quarterly, 39*(3), 339–369.

EXCERPT 4.5 Methodological Criticism

Although results supported the effectiveness of cooperative learning, school favorableness toward cooperative learning might have created a selection bias that threatened the validity of the results. Specifically, schools whose faculty agreed to implement the structured model of cooperative leaning were included in the treatment group. Despite this weakness, Stevens and Slavin (1995) contended that cooperative learning positively affected academic achievement. (p. 233)

Source: From Lopata, C., Miller, K. A., & Miller, R. H. (2003). Survey of actual and preferred use of cooperative learning among exemplar teachers. *Journal of Educational Research, 96*(4), 232–239.

for an exploratory study may not be very long, whereas that in a thesis or dissertation may be 30 or 40 typed pages. A lengthy review requires structuring with major and minor headings and periodic summaries. Excerpt 4.6 is an example of a quantitative research literature review.

Qualitative Reviews of Literature

Similar to a review of quantitative research literature, a review of literature in qualitative research is used to document the importance of the topic. Otherwise, the literature is used

EXCERPT 4.6 Quantitative Research Literature Review

Often, African American and Hispanic parents do not attend school functions. Consequently, there is a widely held belief among educators in poor and urban schools that those parents do not care about their children's education (Delpit, 1995; Flores, Tefft-Cousin, & Diaz, 1991; Poplin & Weeres, 1992; Thompson, 2002). Moreover, in its Schools and Staffing Surveys for 1990–1991 and 1993–1994, *The Digest of Education Statistics* (U.S. Department of Education, 1999) reported that lack of parent involvement was a great concern for many public school teachers.

Summary

Some researchers have found that there is a mismatch between teachers' perceptions of parent and guardian involvement and reality (Flores et al., 1991; Poplin & Weeres, 1992). For example, Thompson (2002) conducted a study of the K–12 schooling experiences of nearly 300 African American students in a southern California region that had many underperforming schools. Although there was a widespread assumption among educators in the region that the parents and guardians of most children of color were apathetic about their children's formal education, Thompson found that when the African American students in her study were asked to rate the level of their parents' involvement, the majority of students rated it as excellent or good. The students' ratings were compared later with data from African American parents in the same region. The overwhelming majority of the parents also rated their involvement in their children's education as excellent or good (Thompson, 2003). Furthermore, in their examination of the National Education Longitudinal Study data, Cook and Ludwig (1998) found that African American parents were as involved in their children's education as were White parents from similar socioeconomic backgrounds. These findings are similar to those of other researchers who found that educators are not always the most reliable judges of parent involvement (Flores et al., 1991; Poplin & Weeres, 1992).

Furthermore, some researchers have specifically described the positive correlation between parent involvement and the schooling experiences of African American students. . . . Floyd (1995) examined variables that contributed to the academic success of a group of lower socioeconomic status (SES) African American high school students. She found that good parental relationships or positive relationships with other adults played an important role in the students' academic success. Wilson and Allen (1987) studied African American adults to identify links between educational attainment and family practices. They concluded that parents play a significant role in their children's education. Clark (1983) studied the home environments of high- and low-achieving poor African American high school seniors and found that parents of high achievers used regular routines to assist their children academically. Conversely, the parents of low achievers were so overwhelmed by adversity that they made few positive contributions to their children's formal schooling. . . .

Analysis

A logical first step is for educators to begin to listen to the voices of parents in order to hear their concerns. In an effort to begin this discussion, I sought to provide educators with feedback from African American parents about their children's schooling experiences. In this study, I examined variables that predict how African American parents and guardians of school-aged children rate their children's elementary and secondary school teachers, and the public school system as a whole. (pp. 278–279)

Related to current study

Source: From Thompson, G. L. (2003). Predicting African American parents' and guardians' satisfaction with teachers and public schools. *Journal of Educational Research, 96*(5), 277–285.

EXCERPT 4.7 Providing a Conceptual Framework and Relating to Current Research

Building on the work of Weedon (1987), Peirce (1995) developed a concept of *social identity* . . . as 'the conscious and unconscious thoughts and emotions of the individual, her sense of herself and her ways of understanding her relation to the world' (p. 32, quoted in Peirce, 1995). In opposition to the Western notion of identity as centered, singular, and unitary, [social identity] takes on three characteristics. . . . This article uses Peirce's (1995) conception of social identity as a means to identify the unique qualities that the foreign-born ESL teacher brings to instruction and curriculum. (pp. 126–128)

Source: From Case, R. E. (2004). Forging ahead into new social networks and looking back to past social identities: A case study of a foreign-born English as a second language teacher in the United States. *Urban Education, 39*(2), 125–148.

differently in qualitative research. Rather than provide a detailed analysis of the literature prior to the methods section, the review is a preliminary one. A qualitative review simply introduces the purpose of the study and the initial broad questions that will be reformulated during data collection. Qualitative researchers usually provide the conceptual framework that they began with, as well (see Excerpt 4.7).

Unlike a quantitative researcher, a qualitative researcher conducts a continuing literature search during data collection and analysis. This approach to reviewing the literature merely reflects the discovery orientation typical of qualitative research. A continuing literature review is done because the exact research focus and questions evolve as the research progresses. Using this approach, the researcher can better understand what he or she is actually observing and hearing. The literature may provide meaningful analogies, a scholarly language to synthesize descriptions, or additional conceptual frameworks to better organize the findings. As with quantitative research, the literature review in qualitative research is integrated with the discussion and conclusion sections of the article or report. At this point, additional new literature may be introduced to better explain and interpret the findings. Thus, by the completion of a study, the researchers have done an extensive literature review (see Excerpt 4.8).

The literature review in a qualitative study is (a) presented as separate discussion and/or (b) integrated within the text. Seldom is an entire section of a journal article or an entire chapter in a report called a "Literature Review." The literature is found in the introduction and the more detailed discussion is located in the concluding interpretations of the study. Given the format required by some journals, a "Literature Review" header may be provided for readers.

META-ANALYSIS LITERATURE REVIEWS

Unlike a narrative criticism of the literature, a **meta-analysis** is a review that uses statistical techniques to summarize the results of prior studies that have been independently conducted. Because this type of review has only recently been published, there are some concerns about its credibility. The ERIC digest *Meta-Analysis in Educational Research* and the spring 2001 issue of the *Review of Educational Research* both discuss the relative merit of different meta-analyses. These sources illustrate the strengths and limitations of meta-analysis and show how researcher judgment is always an important influence in interpreting data. (For a more detailed discussion, see J. E. Hunter [2004] *Methods of meta-analysis: Correcting error and bias in research findings* [2nd ed.].)

Statisticians have long noted that in many applied fields, the treatment effects are small and therefore difficult to detect in a single study. A natural question is whether the

EXCERPT 4.8 Qualitative Research Literature Review

Background

The interrelationships among gender, higher education, and inequality in the workplace have been examined from diverse theoretical perspectives and through a number of different disciplines. Probably the most influential idea to account for women college students' lower career aspirations and their resignation to accepting lower-paying, less prestigious careers has been that institutions of higher education discourage or discriminate against women (Astin 1978; Dweck et al. 1978; Hall and Sandler 1982; Holmstrom and Holmstrom 1974; Sadker and Sadker 1994; Stacey et al. 1974; Sternglanz, and Lyber-Beck 1977). . . .

Summary

Holland and Eisenhart's [1990] long-term study of women students on two southern campuses moves away from social reproduction theory to a theory of "cultural production." Their approach allows us to see students as active agents who construct "systems of meaning" through which they relate to and act within their world. The most important construction that Holland and Eisenhart uncover in their study is a "culture of romance" that privileges males and is generated within student peer groups. Some women students fall into the "culture of romance" as they become discouraged in their studies. . . .

The Holland and Eisenhart study provides rich material on women students' ideas about romance and marriage, but, curiously, it does not touch on students' ideas about motherhood or how these ideas might be related to students' decisions about their careers.

Summary of major study

By contrast, Anne Machung's (1989) study of Berkeley students, conducted at about the same time, indicates that senior women students planned to interrupt their careers for child rearing. Likewise our study reveals that a "culture of motherhood" rather than a "culture of romance" may lie behind women students' lower career aspirations.

Analysis of second major study

Granted, this difference between our findings and those of Holland and Eisenhart may be partly because of the different foci and methods of these two studies. The Holland and Eisenhart research focused only on women students, whereas our study compared women and men. This allows us to highlight those views of women students that stood out in strong contrast to those of men, in particular their contrasting views about the compatibility between their careers and their roles as parents. Another difference is that our study looked at students only over one academic year, whereas Holland and Eisenhart followed a group of women students over several years during and after college. This allowed them to document the women's lowering aspirations and their increasing involvement in romantic relationships over time, whereas our methods could not detect major shifts in students' interests and involvements. Yet we were able to uncover something that may have been missed in the Holland and Eisenhart study. Our study shows that a perceived incompatibility between motherhood and full-time careers is a central theme in students', especially women students', discussions of their futures. (pp. 68–70)

Analysis and relationship to current research

Source: From Stone, L., & McKee, N. P. (2000). Gendered futures: student visions of career and family on a college campus. *Anthropology and Education Quarterly, 31*(1), 67–89.

aggregate of studies might not have statistical and practical significance even though no single study does. Thus, meta-analysis determines the size of the effect of educational practices investigated in a number of individual studies.

A key concept in any synthesis is *pattern*. The distinction between primary analysis and meta-analysis may be analogous to the distinction between taking observations at ground level and taking observations from the air. As one rises in an airplane, the precision achieved at ground level lessens and is replaced by a greater recognition of patterns. Thus, the pattern of skyscrapers that is indiscernible when driving into a large city becomes more evident from a higher-elevation vantage point. Second, the conclusions based on a meta-analysis can be stronger than those of the component studies because pooling of data generally increases statistical power of the *effect size*.[3]

The Research Process

The steps to conduct integrative research reviews are similar to the tasks of original research. Cooper (1998) characterized rigorous research synthesis as having five phases: problem formulation, data collection, data evaluation, analysis and interpretation, and public presentation. Each phase of the review involves methodological issues and requires subjective decisions that can lead to procedural variations which can profoundly affect the outcome of the review. Obviously, the validity of the conclusions of research or research reviews depends on the decisions made in each phase. Each of these phases is summarized in the following list from the viewpoint of helping readers evaluate a research synthesis:

1. ***Problem formulation*** To formulate a research synthesis problem, the reviewer decides what questions or hypotheses to address and what evidence should be included in the review. Meta-analysis procedures are primarily used to integrate research results and are seldom applied to theoretical or methodological literature.

2. ***Data collection*** This phase involves the specification of procedures to be used in finding relevant reviews. Whereas the primary researcher samples individuals, the reviewer, in a sense, retrieves researchers. In reality, reviewers are not trying to draw representative samples of studies from the literature, but they are attempting to retrieve an *entire population* of studies. This goal is rarely achieved, but it is more feasible in a review than in primary research. The investigator hopes the review will cover all previous research on the problem.

To minimize bias in data collection, a reviewer should use more than one major database, informal communications, and the bibliographies of past researchers or reviews. Reviewers should be explicit about how studies were gathered, providing information on sources, years, and keywords used in the search, and they should present whatever indices of potential retrieval bias are known to them. Characteristics of individuals used in the separate studies should be summarized.

3. ***Data evaluation*** The data evaluation phase involves specifications about decisions concerning evidence that will be included in the review. Both primary researchers and research reviewers examine their data sets for extreme values, errors in recording, and other unreliable measurements. In addition, the research reviewer should discard data because of questionable research design validity. In other words, the reviewer makes either a discrete decision—whether to include or exclude the data in the review—or a continuous decision—whether to weigh studies dependent on their relative degree of trustworthiness. Most social scientists agree that methodological quality should be the primary criterion for inclusion.

4. ***Data analysis and interpretation*** In contrast to primary study reviewers, meta-analysis reviewers interpret data using rules of inference that build on standard statistical techniques. Analysis and interpretation methods are frequently idiosyncratic to the particular reviewer. This leads to criticisms of subjectivity and a concern that a variety of methods have been introduced into the reviewing process. Further, quantitative reviewing is based on certain premises. The basic premise is that a series of studies was selected that address an identical conceptual hypothesis.

Methods for data analysis range from simple vote-counting methods to sophisticated statistical techniques to obtain indices of the effect size. Either the results or the raw data of each component study can be integrated. Reviewers should be careful to distinguish between study- and review-generated evidence.

5. ***Public presentation*** The presentation of a meta-analysis involves decisions about what information should be included in the final report. Two primary threats to validity are the omission of details on how the review was conducted and the omission of evidence about variables and moderators of relations that other inquirers may find (or will be) important to the hypothesis. Slavin (1984) suggests that the effect size for each study should be included and that the coding of studies on various criteria should be presented.

STANDARDS OF ADEQUACY

The adequacy of a narrative literature review is judged by three criteria: the selection of the sources, summary and analysis of the literature, and the relevance of the literature to the current study.

Selection of Literature

1. Is the purpose of the review (preliminary or exhaustive) indicated?
2. Are the parameters of the review reasonable? Why were certain bodies of literature included in the search and others excluded?
3. Is primary literature emphasized in the review and secondary literature, if cited, used selectively?
4. Are most of the sources from reputable, refereed journals?
5. Are recent developments in the literature emphasized in the review?
6. Is the literature relevant to the problem?
7. Are complete bibliographic data provided for each source cited?

Summary and Analysis of Literature

1. Is the review organized by topics or ideas, not by author?
2. Is the review organized logically?
3. Are major studies discussed in detail and the actual findings cited?
4. Are minor studies with similar results or limitations summarized as a group?
5. Is there adequate analysis or critique of the methodologies of important studies so that the reader can determine the quality of previous research?
6. Are studies compared and contrasted and conflicting or inclusive results noted?
7. For some basic and applied studies and qualitative research, is the conceptual framework or theory that guides the study explained?

Relationship to Current Study

1. Does the summary provide an overall interpretation and understanding of prior research?
2. Does the review of major studies relate explicitly to the research problem and methods?
3. Do the methodological analyses provide a rationale for the design to follow?
4. Does the review of the literature help establish the significance of the research?

A literature review is not judged by its length or by the number of references it includes. Rather, it is judged in the context of the proposal or the completed study. The problem, the significance of the study, and the research problem all influence the type of literature review.

SUMMARY

This chapter summarized the reasons for conducting a literature review, the nature of the search process, literature reviews in quantitative and qualitative studies, and meta-analysis. In summary:

1. Literature for review is taken from journals, reports, monographs, government documents, dissertations, and electronic resources.
2. Reviewing the literature enables the researcher to define and limit the problem, to place the study in historical perspective, to avoid unnecessary replication, to elect promising methods, to relate the findings to prior research, and to suggest research hypotheses.
3. Primary literature is essential in a review; secondary literature, however, provides useful information to get started.
4. The process of reviewing the literature is as follows: analyze the problem, read secondary sources, decide on a search strategy, transform the problem into search language, conduct the search, evaluate obtained sources, organize notes, and write the review.
5. Secondary literature is a synthesis of original work and usually consists of articles in general and specialized educational journals, annuals, yearbooks, handbooks, encyclopedias, and books.

6. Primary literature is the original empirical study or writings of a researcher, which is found by using indexes, abstracts, and databases.
7. Steps in conducting a search are to review secondary sources, to refine the research problem, to select and search appropriate indexes and/or databases, to search primary literature, and to analyze sources for relevance.
8. A reviewer reads each source that was obtained, summarizes and analyzes it using notes on index cards, and then organizes the cards according to a classification system of merit or worth.
9. Sources are evaluated by three criteria: credibility, journal reputation (i.e., refereed or nonrefereed journal), and relevance to the current research.
10. The steps in writing a review are to provide a summary and analyze the studies, stating explicitly how the reviewed study is related to the research problem.
11. In quantitative research, the literature review is usually organized by topic: summarizing the minor studies as a group, analyzing the major studies individually, and usually proceeding from the most general topic to the most related topic. There are alternative ways to present the literature in quantitative research.
12. In qualitative research, a preliminary literature review suggests the need for the study and the conceptual framework employed, but the literature search continues during data collection and analysis. Literature is presented in the introductory discussion and integrated within the text.
13. A meta-analysis uses statistical techniques to summarize the results of prior studies that were independently conducted.

CHECK YOURSELF

Multiple choice review items with answers are available on the Companion Website for this book.

www.ablongman.com/mcmillanschumacher6e

APPLICATION PROBLEMS

1. Suppose that a supervisor wants to locate mathematics curriculum guidelines and evaluation studies of mathematics programs formulated under Title I of the Elementary and Secondary Education Act and those most recently done through Chapter 1. Which database and type of search would be most efficient?
2. Below is a problem statement and descriptors for each concept. The descriptors are listed in order of importance to a literature search.

   How do teacher-questioning techniques affect fourth-grade students' learning in social studies?

   A. questioning techniques
   B. questioning
   C. questioning behavior
   D. questions
   E. achievement
   F. skills
   G. recall
   H. social studies
   I. history
   J. upper elementary
   K. elementary education

   a. Direct a narrow search to obtain pertinent literature using *and* to join the descriptors from A through K that most closely match the research question.
   b. Direct a more thorough search using *or* to join the different key terms for the same concept and using *and* to connect the descriptors A through K.
3. A reviewer has classified his or her relevant sources in the following manner:

   A. evaluations of behavior modification programs: effects on instructional approach, teacher questioning style
   B. descriptions of behavior modification programs and management implications
   C. evaluations of behavior modification programs and management implications

D. theories of stimulus-response learning
E. studies of operant conditioning on animals

Organize these in order for a literature review on the problem of "evaluation of instruction, student behavior, and learning in a behavior modification program."

NOTES

1. The authors greatly appreciate the assistance of James Ghaphery, Virginia Commonwealth University Reference Specialist, in preparing this chapter.
2. References for measurement are cited in Chapter 5.
3. Effect size (ES) is, in principle, the difference on a criterion measure between an experimental and a control group divided by the control group's standard deviation.

PART

II

QUANTITATIVE RESEARCH DESIGNS AND METHODS

Part II presents the designs and methods of quantitative research. Chapter 5 presents fundamental principles of sampling, measurement, and research design. Basic terminology and statistical procedures are presented to enable a reader to interpret the results sections of quantitative research and a researcher to select appropriate statistical procedures, based on the design of the study.

CHAPTER

5 Designing Quantitative Research

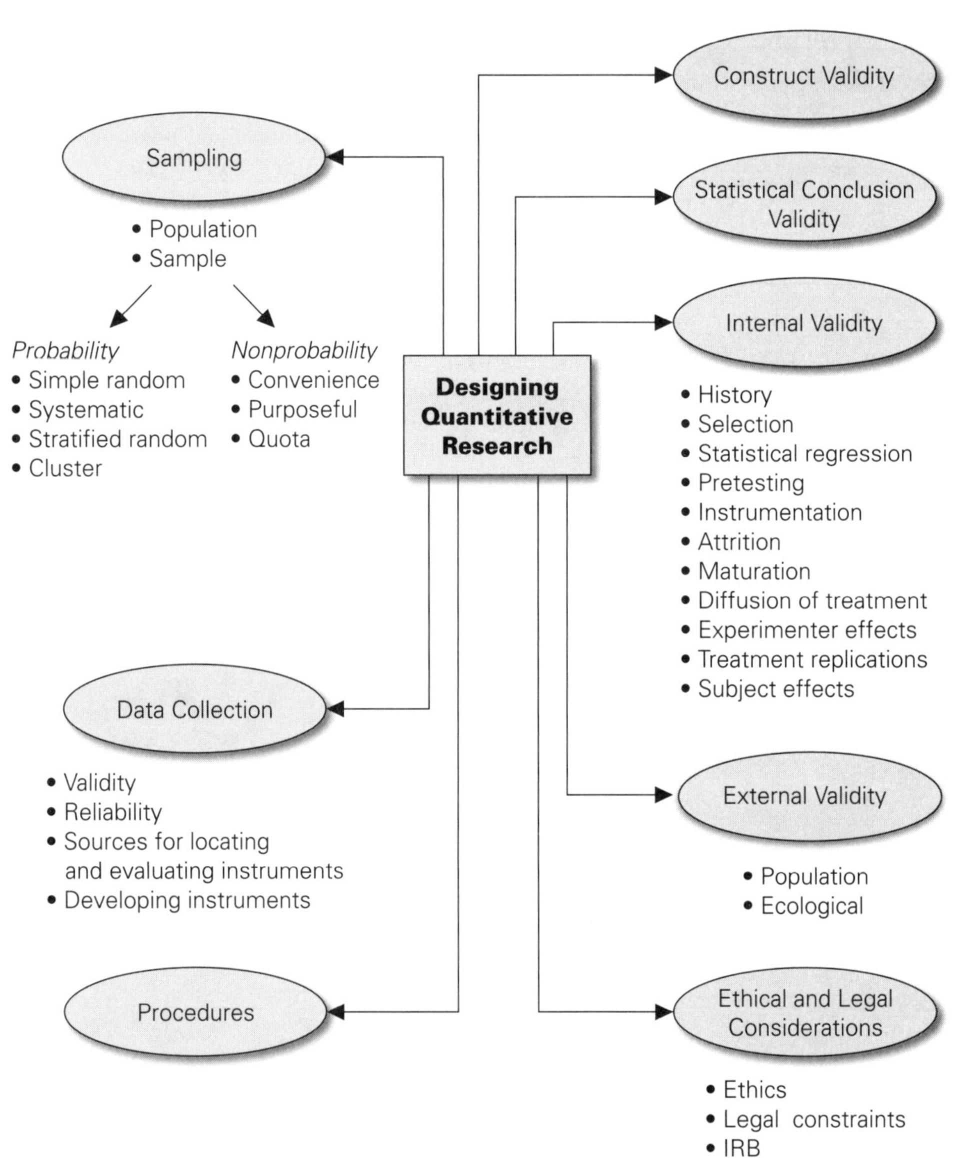

KEY TERMS

research design
credibility
variability
sources of variability
MAXMINCON
subjects
participants
sample
population
probability sampling
random sampling
simple random sampling
systematic sampling
stratified random sampling
proportional sampling
nonproportional sampling
cluster sampling
multistage cluster sampling
nonprobability sampling
convenience sampling
purposeful sampling
quota sampling
instrument validity
instrument reliability
statistical conclusion validity
internal validity
construct validity
external validity
plausible rival hypotheses
history
selection
statistical regression
pretesting
instrumentation
attrition
maturation
diffusion of treatment
experimenter effects
treatment replications
subject effects
demand characteristics
inadequate explication of the constructs
mono-operation bias
mono-method bias
population external validity
ecological external validity
Hawthorne effect
informed consent
internal review board (IRB)

Designing quantitative research involves choosing subjects, data collection techniques (e.g., questionnaires, observations, or interviews), procedures for gathering the data, and procedures for implementing treatments. Together, these components constitute the methods part of the study. The essential elements of designing quantitative research will be discussed in this chapter, with an emphasis on important principles for conceptualizing and planning a study. Each of these components will be discussed, with attention to principles in each component that enhance the quality of the research. Important ethical and legal considerations in planning and conducting research will be discussed, as well.

THE PURPOSE OF RESEARCH DESIGN

As introduced in Chapter 2, the term **research design** refers to a plan for selecting subjects, research sites, and data collection procedures to answer the research question(s). The design shows which individuals will be studied and when, where, and under which circumstances they will be studied. The goal of a sound research design is to provide results that are judged to be *credible*. **Credibility** refers to the extent to which the results approximate reality and are judged to be accurate, trustworthy, and reasonable. Credibility is enhanced when the research design takes into account potential sources of error that may undermine the quality of the research and may distort the findings and conclusions. By carefully designing the study, the researcher can eliminate or at least reduce sources of error. Not every potential source of error can be controlled completely in research conducted in field settings, such as schools, but there are principles for planning research to minimize such influences.

In quantitative research, researchers consider different *sources of variability*. **Variability** refers to how much observations of something take on different values. For example, we know that our mood varies day to day, just as we know that a student's academic performance will not be the same each time he or she completes a test.

From the standpoint of design, it is important to recognize and control three **sources of variability:** systematic, error, and extraneous. *Systematic variance* is related to the variables that are being investigated. What you want is a design that will *maximize* this kind of variation. For instance, when studying the relationship between engaged time and achievement, you would want to design the research so that the two variables of interest, engagement and achievement, both have high variability. If, say, all the students received the same or very similar achievement scores, then you would not be able to demonstrate the relationship.

Similarly, in an experiment, you want to maximize the variance of the dependent variable when comparing the groups. This is often accomplished by making sure that the treatments in the study will potentially produce quite different results. For example, systematic variance is likely to be greater in a study comparing individualized instruction with small-group discussion than comparing two kinds of small-group discussion formats.

Error variance is something to be minimized. It includes sampling and measurement error and other kinds of random events that make it difficult to show relationships. *Extraneous variance* needs to be controlled. This kind of variability affects relationships directly, rather than in a random fashion. For instance, in examining the relationship between test scores and class size, the socioeconomic status of the students would be a variable that would need to be controlled. That is, you would get a better estimate of the relationship if the effect socioeconomic status, which is related to achievement, were removed statistically.

It is helpful to use the following acronym to remember the three sources of variability in designing and evaluating research: **MAXMINCON.** Quantitative research needs to MAXimize systematic variance, MINimize error variance, and CONtrol extraneous variance. Methods to achieve these goals are summarized in Table 5.1 and will be discussed in further detail in later chapters.

TABLE 5.1 Principle of MAXMINCON

MAXimize Systematic Variance	MINimize Error Variance	CONtrol Extraneous Variance
1. Use design measures that provide sufficient variability. 2. Use a sample to provide sufficient variability. 3. Use design interventions that are very different.	1. Standardize measurement procedures. 2. Use measures with high reliability. 3. Aggregate individual scores into group scores. 4. Use large samples. 5. Assure standardization in implementing the intervention in an experiment.	1. Make potential confounding variables constant. 2. Use random assignment; matching, if random assignment is not possible. 3. Build a possible confounding variable into the design as another independent variable. 4. Use statistical adjustment procedures to help control the effects of confounding variables.

SUBJECTS: POPULATIONS AND SAMPLES

One of the first steps in designing quantitative research is to choose the subjects. **Subjects** (abbreviated as S) are the individuals who participate in the study, and from whom data are collected. In an experiment, for instance, each person who is given an intervention and whose response is measured is a subject. In a nonexperimental study, individuals whose present or past behavior is used as data are considered subjects. For example, a researcher might use 2004 tenth-grade test scores; each tenth-grader who provided scores would be considered a subject. In some studies, the term **participants** is used rather than subjects.

Collectively, the group of subjects or participants from whom the data are collected is referred to as the **sample.** The sample can be selected from a larger group of persons, identified as the population, or simply refer to the group of subjects from whom data are collected (even though the subjects are not selected from the population). The nature of the sampling procedure used in a particular study is usually described by one or more adjectives, such as *random sampling, convenience sampling,* or *stratified sampling.* This describes the technique used to form the sample.

We will consider two major categories of different sampling techniques: probability and nonprobability. First, though, some further discussion of *population* is needed.

What Is a Population?

A **population** is a group of elements or cases, whether individuals, objects, or events, that conform to specific criteria and to which we intend to generalize the results of the research. This group is also referred to as the *target population* or *universe*. The target population is often different from the list of elements from which the sample is actually selected, which is termed the *survey population* or *sampling frame*. For example, in a study of beginning teachers, the target population may be first-year teachers across the United States in all types of schools. The survey population may be a list of first-year teachers from 24 states. Thus, although the intent of the research is to generalize to all beginning teachers, the sampling frame places some limitations on such generalizations.

It is important for researchers to carefully and completely define both the target population and the sampling frame. This begins with the research problem and review of literature, through which a population is described conceptually or in broad terms. A more specific definition is then needed based on demographic characteristics such as age, gender, location, grade level, position, and time of year. These characteristics are sometimes referred to as *delimiting variables*. For example, in a study of rural first-grade minority students, there are four delimiting variables: rural, students, first-grade, and minority. A complete description is then included in the subjects section of the report.

Probability Sampling

In **probability sampling** subjects are drawn from a larger population in such a way that the probability of selecting each member of the population is known. This type of sampling is conducted to efficiently provide estimates of what is true for a population from a smaller group of subjects (sample). That is, what is described in a sample will also be true, with some degree of error, of the population. When probability sampling is done correctly, a very small percentage of the population can be selected. This saves time and money without sacrificing accuracy. In fact, in most social science and educational research, it is both impractical and unnecessary to measure all elements of the population of interest.

Several methods of probability sampling can be used to draw representative, or *unbiased,* samples from a population. Each method involves some type of **random sampling,** in which each member of the population as a whole, or of subgroups of the population, has the same chance of being selected as other members in the same group. Bias is avoided with random sampling because there is a high probability that all the population characteristics will be represented in the sample. If the correct procedures are not followed, though, what may seem to be random sampling will actually produce a biased sample (biased in the sense that certain population characteristics are over- or under-represented). For example, you may think that you can obtain a random sample of college students by standing by a busy corner and selecting every third or fourth student. However, you may not be able to keep an accurate count, and you may inadvertently select more males or females or more older or younger students. Such a procedure would result in a biased sample.

ALERT! A very common mistake is for researchers to generalize their results far beyond the characteristics of their sample. Using probability samples enhances the credibility of researchers' generalizations.

The concept of inferring what is probably true for the population from a sample is very important. As illustrated in Figure 5.1, once the sample has been selected, it is used to make inferences about the population. This always involves some degree of error. The degree of error is inversely related to the sample size—that is, the larger the sample size, the less the likelihood of error in making inferences about what is true for the population.

Simple Random Sampling In **simple random sampling,** subjects are selected from the population so that all members have the same probability of being chosen. This method is often used when the population is small. For example, a common type of simple random sampling is drawing names out of a hat.

With a large population, it is necessary to use a more precise procedure. One such procedure is to use a table of random numbers, which is a set of randomly assorted digits. Suppose, for example, that a researcher has a population of 100 third-graders and wants to select 20 by simple random sampling. First, each third-grader in the population is assigned a number from 001 to 100. (It could be 00 to 99.) Second, the researcher randomly selects a starting point in a table of random numbers. Then he or she reads all three-digit numbers, moving either across rows or down columns. The researcher follows the three-digit rows or columns while selecting 20 three-digit numbers between 000 and 100. Table 5.2 contains an example of simple random sampling. Five of the 20 subjects chosen to be included in the sample are circled, beginning with the top left and moving down each column.

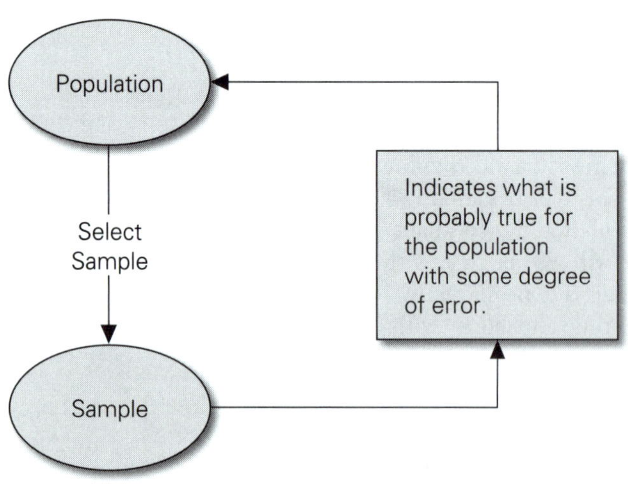

FIGURE 5.1 **Relationship of Sample to Population**

TABLE 5.2 **Randomly Assorted Digits**

46614	20002	17918
16249	05217	54102
91530	62481	05374
62800	62660	20186
10089	96488	59058
47361	73443	11859
45690	71058	53634
50423	53342	71710
89292	32114	83942
23410	41943	33278
59844	81871	18710
98795	87894	00510
86085	03164	26333
37390	60137	93842
28420	10704	89412

EXCERPT 5.1 Simple Random Sampling

The sample (n = 600) was randomly drawn from the enrolled population of University of Florida (UF) undergraduates (30,866) who were 18 years of age or older and holding a free computing account. . . . Because other population characteristics were not considered relevant to the research questions for this preliminary investigation, we chose not to draw a stratified sample.

Source: From Pealer, L. N., Weiler, R. M., Piggs, Jr., R. M., Miller, D., & Dorman, S. M. (2001). The feasibility of a web-based surveillance system to collect health risk behavior data from college students. *Health Education and Behavior, 28,* 547–559.

A more efficient and increasingly popular way to draw a simple random sample is by using an appropriate computer software program, such as SPSS. This is especially easy and effective if the sampling frame is in an electronic format. Excerpt 5.1 provides an example of simple random sampling.

Systematic Sampling In **systematic sampling,** every *n*th element is selected from a list of all elements in the population, beginning with a randomly selected element. Suppose there is a need to draw a 10 percent sample from a population of 100. A number from 1 to 10 is randomly selected as the starting point. If 5 is selected, every tenth name on the list will then be selected: 5, 15, 25, 35, and so on. This approach can be used only when the researcher has a sequential list of all the subjects in the population, but it is easier than simple random sampling because not every member of the population needs to be numbered.

Systematic sampling is illustrated in Figure 5.2. From among 60 students, we need to select 6 to be in our sample (10 percent). We would randomly select a number from 1 to 20 (say, 2), and then select every twelfth student for our sample.

There is a possible weakness in systematic sampling if the list of cases in the population is arranged in a systematic pattern that is related to what is being investigated. For

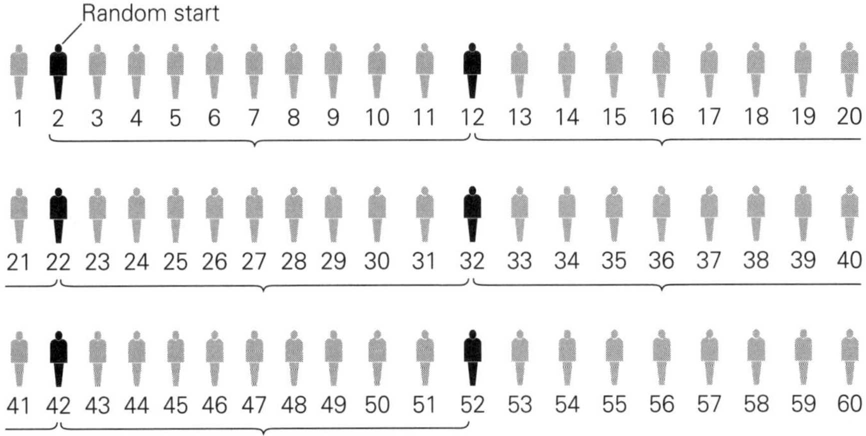

10 percent sample (every 10th student):

FIGURE 5.2 **Systematic Sampling**
Source: Adapted from Babbie, 1998.

EXCERPT 5.2 Systematic Sampling

Three samples were drawn from this study. They were samples of (a) practicing teachers, (b) college sophomores beginning a teacher education program, and (c) college seniors completing a teacher education program (but prior to student teaching). For the first sample, survey forms were mailed in a rural western state to 700 teachers randomly selected from the State Department of Education list of all licensed educators.

Source: From Green, K. E. (1992). Differing opinions on testing between preservice and inservice teachers. *Journal of Educational Research, 86,* 37–42. Reprinted by permission.

example, suppose we are sampling teachers from many schools and the list obtained from each school is rank ordered in terms of length of service. If this cyclical pattern (referred to as *periodicity*) is related to every *n*th subject, the sample would systematically exclude teachers with certain ages and not represent the population. Alphabetical lists do not usually create periodicity and are suitable for choosing subjects systematically.

An advantage to systematic sampling is that if the population is rank ordered on a variable that is related to the dependent variable, this ordering has the effect of stratifying and making sure that the sample is represented by each level of that variable. For instance, if the population list is ordered by aptitude test scores (highest scores first, followed by lower scores), when we then select every *n*th subject we will be assured that all levels of aptitude will be represented in the sample. Systematic sampling is illustrated in Excerpt 5.2. In this study, the first of three samples, practicing teachers, is selected randomly from a list.

Stratified Random Sampling A common variation of simple random sampling is called **stratified random sampling.** In this procedure, the population is divided into subgroups, or strata, on the basis of a variable chosen by the researcher, such as gender, age, location, or level of education. Once the population has been divided, samples are drawn randomly from each subgroup. The number of subjects drawn is either *proportional* or *nonproportional*. **Proportional sampling** is based on the percentage of subjects in the population that is present in each stratum. Thus, if 40 percent of the subjects in the population are represented in the first stratum, then 40 percent of the final sample should be from that stratum. In **nonproportional** (or disproportionate) **sampling,** the researcher selects the same number of subjects to be in each stratum of the sample.

Whether proportional or nonproportional, stratified random sampling is often more efficient than simple random sampling because a smaller number of subjects needs to be used. As long as the characteristic used to create the strata is related to the dependent variable, then using a stratified sample will result in less sampling error. Dividing the population into subgroups also allows the researcher to compare subgroup results.

Excerpts 5.3, 5.4, and 5.5 illustrate the use of stratified random sampling. In Excerpt 5.5, for example, the researchers have stratified the teacher population on the basis of grade level and scores on the EFT (Embedded Figures Test) and the student population by class-

EXCERPT 5.3 Stratified Random Sampling

The samples of telephone numbers used in telephone interview surveys are based on a random digit stratified probability design. The sampling procedure involves stratifying the continental U.S. into 4 time zones and 3 city-size strata within each time to yield a total of 12 unique strata.

Source: From Saad, L. (2000). Most working women deny gender discrimination in their pay. *Gallup Poll Monthly,* 413, 35–36.

EXCERPT 5.4 Stratified Random Sampling

A stratified random sample of schools was selected across population density (i.e., urban, suburban, and rural), enrollment (i.e, 0–599, 600–999, 1000 and greater), and school levels (i.e., middle school and high school). Percentages of schools across population density and enrollment [and level] were established to maintain a sample consistent with the overall make-up of schools in Maryland.

Source: From Maccini, P., & Gagnon, J. C. (2002). Perceptions and application of NCTM standards by special and general education teachers. *Exceptional Children, 68*(3), 325–344.

room. The sampling is diagrammed in Figure 5.3. To ensure that the final sample has a sufficient number of subjects in each group, nonproportional sampling is used.

Cluster Sampling Cluster sampling is similar to stratified random sampling in that groups of individuals are identified from the population and subjects are drawn from these groups. In **cluster sampling,** however, the researcher identifies convenient, naturally occurring groups, such as neighborhoods, schools, districts, and regions, not individual subjects, and then randomly selects some of these units for the study. Once the units have been selected, individuals are selected from each one.

Cluster sampling is needed in studies in which the researcher cannot obtain a complete list of all members of the population but can identify groups, or clusters, of subjects. For example, it would be very unusual to have a single list of all of the individuals participating in adult literacy programs in a state. However, all of the literacy centers in the state (which are known) could be sampled and then individuals could be sampled from the lists provided by the selected centers.

Thus, cluster sampling consists of at least two stages. Using more than two stages (e.g., school districts, schools within districts, classrooms within schools, students within classrooms) would be called **multistage cluster sampling.** We could begin by sampling 40 of 150 school districts, then 6 classrooms in each of the 40 districts, and then 10 students in each classroom (or all students in each classroom), using simple random or systematic sampling. Multistage cluster sampling is often used in states using geographic designations or districts as units that are initially selected, with schools selected from the geographic areas or districts. Cluster sampling usually results in a less representative sample of the population than either simple or stratified random sampling. See Figure 5.4, which illustrates different sampling procedures.

EXCERPT 5.5 Stratified Random Sampling Participants

Thirty-six female elementary school teachers were randomly selected from a volunteer pool in a southern school district. The sample consisted of 18 second-grade teachers and 18 fifth-grade teachers and was restricted to female teachers, since there were few male teachers in the school district at the primary level. Based on the EFT* scores, 9 teachers at each grade level were randomly selected from those who were field independent, and 9 others were selected from those who were field dependent. There were 12 students (6 males and 6 females) who were selected randomly from each teacher's classroom for purposes of testing. The second-grade children ranged in age from 7 years to 7 years 11 months, whereas the fifth-grade children ranged in age from 10 years to 10 years 11 months.

*EFT refers to the Embedded Figures Test.

Source: From Saracho, O. N., & Dayton, C. M. (1980). Relationship of teachers' cognitive styles to pupils' academic achievement gains. *Journal of Educational Psychology, 72,* 544–549.

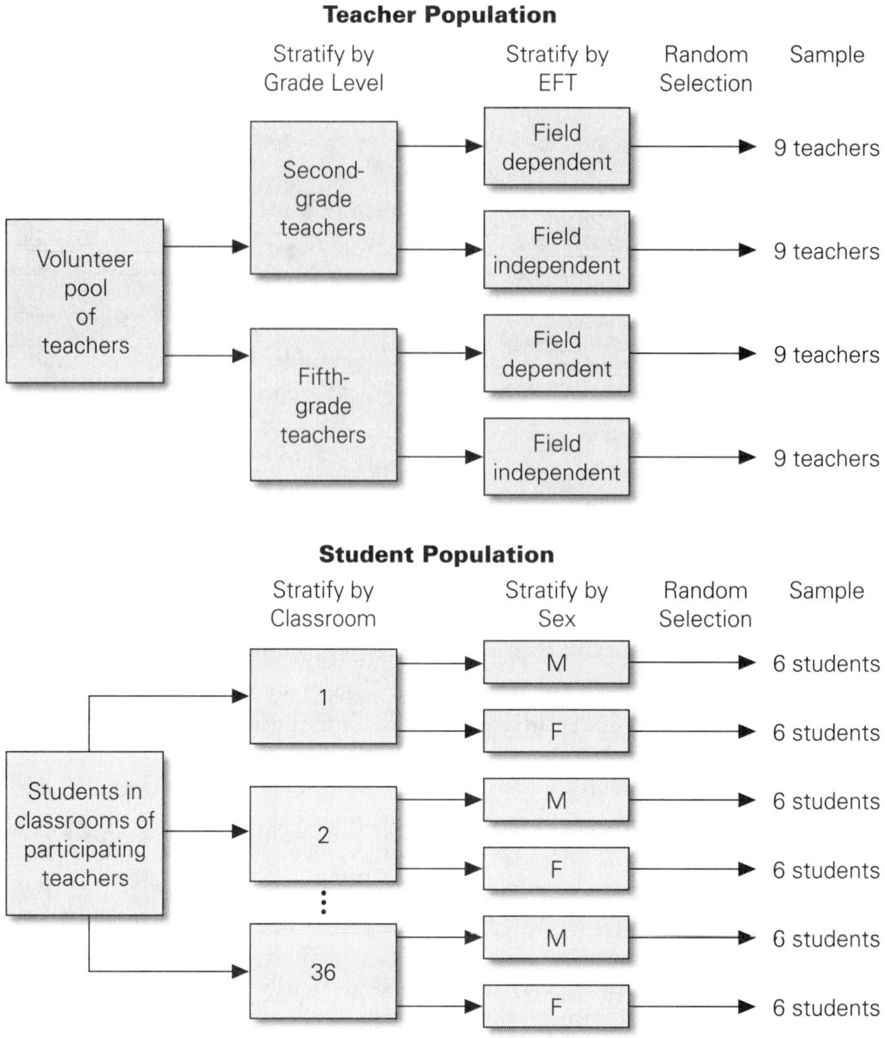

Teacher Population
Stratify by Grade Level
Stratify by EFT
Random Selection
Sample
Volunteer pool of teachers
Second-grade teachers
Fifth-grade teachers
Field dependent
Field independent
Field dependent
Field independent
9 teachers
9 teachers
9 teachers
9 teachers
Student Population
Stratify by Classroom
Stratify by Sex
Random Selection
Sample
Students in classrooms of participating teachers
1
2
36
M
F
M
F
M
F
6 students
6 students
6 students
6 students
6 students
6 students

FIGURE 5.3 **Stratified Random Selection of Subjects for Saracho and Dayton Study**

Probability sampling
Simple random sampling
Systematic random sampling
Stratified random sampling
Cluster sampling
Proportional sampling
Nonproportional sampling
Nonprobability sampling
Convenience sampling
Purposeful sampling
Quota sampling

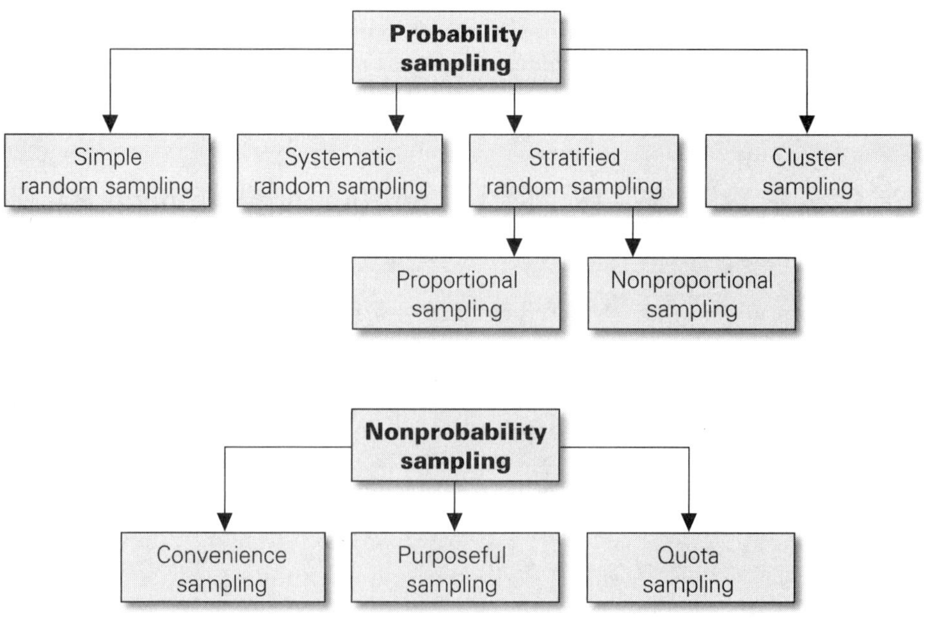

FIGURE 5.4 **Types of Sampling Procedures**

Nonprobability Sampling

In many educational studies, particularly experimental and quasi-experimental investigations, probability samples are not required or appropriate, or it may be impossible or unfeasible to select subjects from a larger group. Rather, **nonprobability sampling** is used. In fact, this form of sampling is the most common type in educational research. Nonprobability sampling does not include any type of random selection from a population. Rather, the researcher uses subjects who happen to be accessible or who may represent certain types of characteristics. For example, this could be a class of students or group gathered for a meeting. Many circumstances bring people together in situations that are efficiently and inexpensively tapped for research.

We will consider three types of nonprobability sampling: convenience sampling, purposeful sampling, and quota sampling. Additional nonprobability sampling techniques are covered in Chapter 6 for qualitative designs.

Convenience Sampling In **convenience sampling** (also called *available sampling*) a group of subjects is selected on the basis of being accessible or expedient. It is convenient to use the group as subjects. This could be a university class of a professor who is doing research on college student learning styles, classrooms of teachers enrolled in a graduate class, school principals who participate in a workshop or conference, people who decide to go to the mall on Saturday, or people who respond to an advertisement for subjects. While this type of sample makes it easier to conduct the research, there is no precise way of generalizing from the sample to any type of population. This means that the generalizability of the findings will be limited to the characteristics of the subjects. This does not mean that the findings are not useful; it simply means that caution is needed in generalizing. Often, researchers will describe convenient samples carefully to show that although they were not able to employ random selection, the characteristics of the subjects matched those of the population or a substantial portion of the population.

Although we need to be very wary of convenience samples, they often provide the only possibility for research. Also, the primary purpose of the research may not be to generalize but to better understand relationships that may exist. In such a case, it may not be necessary to use probability sampling. Suppose a researcher is studying the relationship between creativity and intelligence, and the only possible sample consists of children in an elementary school in his town. The study is completed, and the results indicate a moderate relationship: Children who are more intelligent tend to be more creative. Because there is no probability sampling, should we ignore the findings or suggest that the results are not credible or useful? That decision seems overly harsh. It is more reasonable to interpret the results as valid for children similar to those studied. If the school serves a low socioeconomic area, the results will not be as useful as they would be if the school represented all socioeconomic areas. The decision is not to dismiss the findings but to limit them to the type of subjects in the sample. As more and more research accumulates with different convenient samples, the overall credibility of the results will be enhanced. Excerpt 5.6 is an example of using a convenient sample.

EXCERPT 5.6 Convenience Sampling

During the fall of 2002, the researcher surveyed the population of interest (specifically inservice teachers) with respect to their assessment literacy. The group of inservice teachers consisted of 197 teachers, representing nearly every district in a three-county area surrounding the researchers' institution. The schools were selected based on convenience due to their geographic location.

Source: From Mertler, C. A. (2003). Patterns of response and nonresponse from teachers to traditional and web surveys. *Practical Assessment, Research, & Evaluation, 8*(22). Retrieved May 10, 2004, from http://PAREonline.net/getvn.asp?v=8&n=22.

EXCERPT 5.7 Purposeful Sampling

Participants were chosen from three pullout resource room programs for students with mild disabilities. Participants met the following criteria:

1. They were identified as having LD under the 1986 Oregon administrative rules;
2. They were participants in special education programs;
3. They had an active Individualized Education Program (IEP) in reading; and
4. They had parent permission and gave their own permission to participate in the study.

Source: From DiCecco, V. M., & Gleason, M. M. (2002). Using graphic organizers to attain relational knowledge from expository text. *Journal of Learning Disabilities, 35*(4), 306–320.

Purposeful Sampling In **purposeful sampling** (sometimes called *purposive, judgment,* or *judgmental sampling*), the researcher selects particular elements from the population that will be representative or informative about the topic of interest. On the basis of the researcher's knowledge of the population, a judgment is made about which subjects should be selected to provide the best information to address the purpose of the research. For example, in research on effective teaching, it may be most informative to observe expert or master teachers, rather than a sample of all teachers. To study school effectiveness, it may be most informative to interview key personnel, rather than a random sample of the staff.

As we will see in Chapter 6, there are several types of purposeful sampling procedures for qualitative investigations. In quantitative studies, the emphasis is more on relying on the judgment of the researcher to select a sample that is representative of the population or that includes subjects with needed characteristics. That is, the emphasis tends to be on representativeness, while qualitative researchers are more interested in selecting cases that are "information rich." Excerpts 5.7 and 5.8 are examples of using a purposeful sampling procedure in a quantitative study.

Quota Sampling **Quota sampling** is used when the researcher is unable to take a probability sample but is still able to select subjects on the basis of characteristics of the population. Certain quotas are established so that the sample represents the population according to these characteristics. Different composite profiles of major groups in the population are identified, and then subjects are selected, nonrandomly, to represent each group. For example, it is typical to establish quotas for such characteristics as gender, race/ethnicity, age, grade level, position, and geographic location. The advantage of this type of sampling is that it is more representative of the population than is a purposeful or convenience sample, but there is still great reliance on the judgment of the researcher to select the subjects.

Nonprobability sampling has two major limitations. First, the sample is not representative of a larger population, so generalizing is more restricted. The generalizability of the findings will be limited to the characteristics of the subjects. This does not suggest that the findings are not useful; it simply means that greater caution is necessary in

EXCERPT 5.8 Purposeful Sampling

Data for the study were collected in 16 high schools in California and Michigan. The 16 schools were chosen purposefully to guarantee diversity in secondary-school teaching contexts in terms of state policies, district resources, school organization, and student composition.

Source: From Raudenbush, S. W., Rowan, B., & Cheong, Y. F. (1993). Higher order instructional goals in secondary schools: Class, teacher, and school influences. *American Educational Research Journal, 30,* 523–553.

generalizing the results. Often, researchers will describe the subjects carefully to show that although they were not selected randomly from a larger population, the characteristics of the subjects appear representative of much of the population.

A second limitation is that a nonprobability sample may be biased. This is particularly true for *volunteer samples*, in which subjects volunteer to participate in the research. Studies indicate that volunteers differ from nonvolunteers in important ways. Volunteers tend to be better educated, of higher social class, more intelligent, more sociable, more unconventional, less authoritarian, less conforming, more altruistic, and more extroverted than nonvolunteers. These characteristics could obviously affect the results, leading to conclusions that would be different if a probability sample were used. For example, suppose a researcher wants to survey students on their attitudes toward the college they attended. Letters are sent to the graduated class of 500; 25 agree to come back to campus for interviews. Is it reasonable to conclude that the attitudes of these 25 volunteer students are representative of the class?

MISCONCEPTION Some would argue that North Dakota and Minnesota have the strongest high schools because students in these states score highest on the SAT. However, this finding is a reflection of sampling.

EVIDENCE Most students in these states take the ACT; only the best students need to take the SAT and actually do so. As a result, these students' scores are very high. In sum, the SAT scores of students in Minnesota and North Dakota are not truly representative when compared to the scores of students in other states, where almost all students applying to college take the SAT.

In deciding on a sampling procedure, it is helpful to keep in mind the strengths and weaknesses of the different procedures, as summarized in Table 5.3. The final choice of procedure will depend on your purpose, availability of subjects, and financial resources.

Sample Size

The number of subjects in a study is called the *sample size*, represented by the letter *n* or *N*. The general rule in determining sample size is to obtain a sufficient number to provide a credible result. This usually means obtaining as many as possible. However, in situations in which a random sample is selected from a large population, a sample size that is only a small percentage of the population can approximate the characteristics of the population satisfactorily. Rowntree (1941) illustrated this point many years ago in a study of the percentage of income that was spent on rent by five categories of working-class families in England. Data were collected for the entire population and compared with the data that would have been reported by different sizes of random samples. As indicated in Table 5.4, there was little difference between a sample size of 2 percent (1 in 50) and 10 percent (1 in 10).

There are essentially two approaches to determining adequate sample size. One uses published tables or sample size calculators (easily found on the Internet), based on established formulas. The tables and calculators use information provided by the researcher to determine what size of sample is needed for a given level of precision. This works well for some studies, but often the information needed is not readily available. A second approach uses various rules of thumb or general guidelines. It turns out that these more informal procedures are used most in educational research. For example, when a population is very large—say, greater than 10,000—the size of the sample needed will usually range from 1,000 to 1,200. A 5 percent sample from a population of 2,000 (i.e., 100) would be insufficient. A 5 percent sample for a population of 40,000 is twice as many as needed.

TABLE 5.3 Strengths and Weaknesses of Sampling Methods

Sampling Method	Strengths	Weaknesses
	Probability	
Simple random	Easy to understand Little knowledge of population needed Free of subject classification error Easy to analyze and interpret results	Requires numbering each element in the population Larger sampling error than in stratified sampling for same sample size
Systematic	Simplicity of drawing sample Easy to understand Free of subject classification error Easy to analyze and interpret results Subjects do not need to be numbered	Larger sampling error than in stratified sampling for same sample size Periodicity in list of population elements
Proportional stratified	Allows easy subgroup comparisons Usually more representative than simple random or systematic Fewer subjects needed if strata are related to the dependent variable Results represent population without weighting	Requires subgroup identification of each population element Requires knowledge of the proportion of each subgroup in the population May be costly and difficult to prepare lists of population elements in each subgroup
Nonproportional stratified	Allows easy subgroup comparisons Usually more representative than simple random or systematic Fewer subjects needed if strata are related to the dependent variable Assures adequate numbers of elements in each subgroup	Requires subgroup identification of each population element May be costly and difficult to prepare lists of population elements in each subgroup Requires weighting of subgroups to represent population
Cluster	Low cost Efficient with large populations Permits analysis of individual clusters	Less accurate than simple random, systematic, or stratified May be difficult to collect data from elements in a cluster Requires that each population element be assigned to only one cluster
	Nonprobability	
Convenience	Less costly and time consuming Ease of administration Usually assures high participation rate Generalization possible to similar subjects	Difficult to generalize to other subjects Less representative of an identified population Results dependent on unique characteristics of the sample Greater likelihood of error due to experimenter or subject bias
Purposeful	Less costly and time consuming Ease of administration Usually assures high participation rate Generalization possible to similar subjects Assures receipt of needed information	Difficult to generalize to other subjects Less representative of an identified population Results dependent on unique characteristics of the sample Greater likelihood of error due to experimenter or subject bias

TABLE 5.3 *(continued)*

Sampling Method	Strengths	Weaknesses
Quota	Less costly and time consuming Ease of administration Usually assures high participation rate Generalization possible to similar subjects Tends to provide more representative samples than convenience or purposeful	Requires identification information on each subject Difficult to generalize to other subjects Less representative of an identified population Results dependent on unique characteristics of the sample Greater likelihood of error due to experimenter or subject bias More time consuming than convenient or purposeful

Further informal criteria are summarized in the following list:

1. ***The type of research*** Correlational research should have a minimum of 30 subjects, and in research comparing groups, there should be at least 15 subjects in each group. (Some highly controlled experiments will contain as few as 8 to 10 subjects in each group.) In survey research studies, there should be about 100 subjects for each major subgroup that is analyzed and 20 to 50 subjects in minor subgroups.
2. ***Research hypotheses*** If the researcher expects to find small differences or relationships, it is desirable to have as large a sample as possible. For example, the effect of coaching courses on standardized test scores will produce relatively small but important practical differences. This effect would be generally undetectable in studies with small numbers of subjects.
3. ***Financial constraints*** Obviously, the cost of conducting a study will limit the number of subjects included in the sample. It is best to estimate these costs before beginning the study.
4. ***Importance of results*** In exploratory research, a smaller sample size is acceptable because the researcher is willing to tolerate a larger margin of error in the results. In research that will result in the placement of children in programs or in the

TABLE 5.4 Percentage of Income Spent on Rent

Income Class	Number of Families	Population Data	Sample Size			
			1 in 10	1 in 20	1 in 30	1 in 50
A	1748	26.5	26.6	25.9	28.3	27.1
B	2477	22.7	22.9	23.5	22.3	22.6
C	2514	19.8	18.1	17.2	17.2	18.0
D	1676	15.8	16.0	14.4	17.1	16.9
E	3740	11.3	11.0	10.1	11.2	11.5

Source: From *Poverty and Progress: A Second Social Survey of York,* by B. S. Rowntree, 1941, London: Longman, Green. Reprinted by permission of The Joseph Rowntree Charitable Trust.

expenditure of a large amount of money, however, it is imperative for the researcher to attain a sample large enough to minimize error.

5. ***Number of variables studied*** A larger sample is needed for a study that has many independent or dependent variables or for a study in which many uncontrollable variables are present.
6. ***Methods of data collection*** If methods of collecting information are not highly accurate or consistent, a larger sample will be needed to offset the error inherent in the data collection.
7. ***Accuracy needed*** The accuracy of the results (i.e., the degree of confidence that can be placed in a statement that the sample data are the same as for the population) is greater as the sample size increases. As the study by Rowntree (1941) demonstrates, however, a point of diminishing returns is reached as the sample size increases to a certain percentage of the population.
8. ***Size of the population*** As the size of the population increases, the researcher can take a progressively smaller percentage of subjects from the population.

ALERT! In small sample studies, finding "no difference" or "no relationship" usually means that the conclusions that follow from the results are not credible.

DATA COLLECTION TECHNIQUES

Research involves gathering information about the variables in the study. The researcher chooses from a wide range of techniques and approaches for collecting data from the subjects. Each method has advantages and disadvantages, and the specific approach adopted should be the best one for answering the research question.

At this point it is important to understand two basic principles of measurement that are common for all methods: validity and reliability. Knowledge of these principles is used both to choose instruments and to evaluate the adequacy of data collection reported in research studies.

Instrument Validity

Instrument validity is the extent to which inferences and uses made on the basis of scores from an instrument are reasonable and appropriate. Validity is a judgment of the appropriateness of a measure for specific inferences, decisions, consequences, and uses that result from the scores that are generated. In other words, validity is a situation-specific concept; it is dependent on the purpose, population, and situational factors in which measurement takes place. The results of a test, questionnaire, or other measure can therefore be valid in one situation and invalid in another.

This definition has important implications for designing and evaluating research, since findings are directly related to the measure that is used. The investigator who is designing research should first clearly define the inferences, uses, or decisions that will be made from the results. Then an instrument should be selected that provides good evidence that making such inferences or decisions is valid.

Instrument Reliability

Instrument reliability refers to the consistency of measurement, or the extent to which the scores are similar over different forms of the same instrument or occasions of data collection. The goal of developing reliable scores is to minimize the influence on the scores of chance and other variables unrelated to the intent of the measure.

EXCERPT 5.9 Instruments Section

Future Career Preference

Girls rated the probability of entering each of 19 potential job or career categories on a 7-point scale ranging from "very unlikely" to "very likely." Each category was presented with a label, followed by a brief description (e.g., food service, like waiter, waitress, cook, food preparation). The categories that involved science were (a) health paraprofessional, (b) health professional with a bachelor's degree, (c) science- or math-related professional with a bachelor's degree, (d) health professional with an advanced degree, and (e) science professional with an advanced degree. Examples and degree qualifications were given for each category. Ratings for all five categories were averaged to create a single score for a science career (alpha = .78); ratings for categories (b) and (d) were averaged to create a health professional score (alpha = .81); and ratings for categories (c) and (e) were averaged to create a physical science professional score (alpha = .77).

Source: From Jacobs, J. E., Finken, L. L., Griffin, N. L., & Wright, J. D. (1998). The career plans of science—talented rural adolescent girls. *American Educational Research Journal, 35*(4), 681–704.

Designers and readers of research should interpret reliability in much the same way as validity, looking for evidence that sufficient reliability of each score is documented. Also, many studies fail to support their hypotheses because of significant errors in measuring the variables. (With more reliable measures, the hypotheses might be supported.)

In reading the instruments section of a study or in designing data collection, there are a few questions to keep in mind:

1. Are the scores reliable for the subjects of the particular research?
2. Are the characteristics of the subjects used to establish validity and reliability similar to the characteristics of the subjects in the study?
3. Are the instruments used the best ones? Would others be more reliable and provide more valid results?
4. Why did the researcher choose these instruments?
5. Are the instruments described well enough or referenced to allow another researcher to replicate the research?

Excerpt 5.9 is from the instruments section of a study. The extent of the description provided is about what is expected in reporting most types of research.

Sources for Locating and Evaluating Existing Instruments

In conducting research, the researcher should choose an instrument that has established the reliability and validity he or she needs and that will provide sufficient variability of scores. Although reliability and validity are the most important considerations in selecting an instrument, there are other considerations, such as purchasing costs, availability, simplicity of administration and scoring, copyright limitations, level of difficulty, and appropriateness of norms.

While it is often difficult to find an instrument that will meet all of the criteria a researcher might have, there are thousands of instruments, and it is probable that one is available that can be used intact or modified to meet a specific purpose. The easiest way to locate existing instruments is to use sources that summarize information on several measures. The sources in the following list are widely used and accessible:

Tests in Print, Volume 6, published periodically by the Buros Institute of Mental Measurement (Murphy, Plake, Impara, & Spies, 2002): Provides a summary of tests reviewed in all preceding mental measurement yearbooks.

Handbook of Research Design and Social Measurement, 6th edition (Miller & Salkind, 2002): Reviews and critiques popular social science measures.

Index to Tests Used in Educational Dissertations (Fabiano, 1989): Describes tests and test populations used in dissertations from 1938 to 1980; keyed by title and selected descriptors.

Commissioned Reviews of 250 Psychological Tests (Maltby, Lewis, & Hill, 2000): Contains brief reviews of tests published in the 1990s. Provides variable measured, description, sample tested, reliability, validity, where test can be found, and evaluative comments.

Directory of Unpublished Experimental Mental Measures, Volume 8 (Goldman & Mitchell, 2002): Describes nearly 1,700 experimental mental measures that are not commercially available. Includes references, source, and purpose on topics ranging from educational adjustment and motivation to personality and perception.

ETS Test Collection and *Testlink Test Collection Database:* The Educational Testing Service (ETS) has developed several sources that describe more than 20,000 tests and instruments. The database covers published and unpublished measures in several areas, including achievement, attitudes and interests, personality, special populations, and vocation/occupation. Each of over 200 separate bibliographies describes instruments and appropriate uses and can be ordered from ETS. *Tests in Microfiche* lists unpublished research instruments, also in a wide variety of areas.

Tests: A Comprehensive Reference for Assessments in Psychology, Education, and Business, 10th ed. (Maddox, 2003): Provides descriptions of over 3,100 published tests, including purpose, cost, scoring, and publisher.

Test Critiques, Volumes 1–10 (Keyser & Sweetland, 1984–1994): Gives in-depth evaluations for widely used, newly published, and recently revised instruments in psychology, education, and business. Contains user-oriented information, including practical applications and uses, as well as technical aspects and a critique by a measurement specialist. The companion, *Test Critiques Compendium*, reviews 60 major tests from *Test Critiques* in one volume.

Mental Measurements Yearbook (MMY; Buros Institute of Mental Measurement): Provides reviews of commercially available tests in several areas, including character and personality, achievement, and intelligence. References for most of the tests facilitate further research. The MMY has been published periodically for 60 years. The Buros Institute website (www.unl.edu/buros) includes *Test Reviews Online*, which allows electronic searches of the Buros database.

Tests and Measurements in Child Development: Handbook I and II (Johnson, 1976): Two volumes describe about 900 unpublished tests and instruments for children through age 18.

Sourcebook of Mental Health Measures (Comrey, Backer, & Glaser, 1973): Describes about 1,100 instruments related to mental health, including juvenile delinquency, personality, and alcoholism.

Handbook of Family Measurement Techniques (Touliatos, Perlmutter, Straus, & Holden, 2000): A three-volume set provides overviews and reviews of hundreds of instruments used to measure family variables.

Socioemotional Measures for Pre-School and Kindergarten Children: A Handbook (Walker, 1973): Describes instruments to measure attitudes, personality, self-concept, and social skills of young children.

Handbook for Measurement and Evaluation in Early Childhood Education (Goodwin & Driscoll, 1980): A comprehensive review of affective, cognitive, and psychomotor measures for young children.

Dictionary of Behavioral Assessment Techniques (Hersen & Bellack, 1988): Provides descriptions of approximately 300 instruments that assess psychological and behavioral traits.

In addition to these sources, online resources are very helpful. An excellent one is by the American Psychological Association (www.apa.org/science/faq-findtests.html). The Buros Institute's *Test Reviews Online* (http://buros.un1/edu/buros/jsp) is also excellent. The ERIC database (www.eric.ed.gov) allows online searches by the name of the instrument.

Developing Instruments

Although many instruments are available, there are occasions when researchers have to develop their own measures. The most common situation that requires a locally developed measure is evaluation research for a specific setting. Unless the research will have an important direct impact on programs or individuals, it is unusual for the researcher to systematically establish reliability and validity prior to conducting the study. A more common approach is to develop an instrument that seems reasonable and to gather pilot data on it to revise as needed. While it is probably not necessary to establish sophisticated estimates of reliability and validity, it is still possible for the instrument to be of such inferior quality that the results attained will be uninterpretable. Thus, it is important for a researcher to follow a few basic steps when faced with the development of an instrument:

1. Become acquainted with common approaches to measuring the trait or behavior of interest. Many existing sources summarize approaches for measuring such variables as achievement, attitudes, interests, personality, and self-concept.
2. Write out specific objectives for the instrument, with one objective for each trait or behavior of interest.
3. After reading about the area and conducting discussions with others about what approach would best measure the trait, brainstorm several items for each objective.
4. Ask professionals who are knowledgeable in the assessed area to review the items: Are they clear? Unbiased? Concise? Are the meanings the same for all readers?
5. Find a small sample of individuals who are similar to those who will be used in the actual study and administer the instrument to them. This could be referred to as a *pilot test* of the instrument. Check for clarity, ambiguity in sentences, time for completion, directions, and any problems that may have been experienced.
6. Check for an adequate distribution of scores for each item in the instrument. If all the responses to an item are the same, it will be difficult to know whether the question is inadequate or whether the trait actually lacks variability. As long as the responses result in a spread of scores, the chances are good that the item is an adequate measure of the trait.
7. Revise, delete, and add items where necessary, depending on feedback from the sample subjects in the pilot test.

PROCEDURES

In a quantitative study, the researcher plans the procedures that will be used to collect data and, in the case of experimental research, the nature and administration of the experimental intervention. The researcher decides where the data will be collected (e.g., in a school, city, or laboratory setting), when the data will be collected (time of day and year), how the data will be collected (by whom and in what form), and, if necessary, specifics of the experimental treatment. Any procedures used to control bias (e.g., counterbalancing the order of instruments to control subject fatigue or boredom or being sure observers are unaware of which group is receiving the treatment and which is the control) are planned and implemented as part of the procedures. In reporting the study, the researcher should present the procedures in sufficient detail to permit another researcher to replicate the study.

DESIGN VALIDITY

In the context of research design, the term *validity* (sometimes referred to as *experimental validity*), means the degree to which scientific explanations of phenomena match reality. It refers to the truthfulness of findings and conclusions. Explanations about observed phenomena *approximate* what is reality or truth, and the degree to which explanations are accurate comprises the validity of design.

There are four types of design validity in quantitative research:

- **Statistical conclusion validity** refers to the appropriate use of statistical tests to determine whether purported relationships are a reflection of actual relationships.
- **Internal validity** focuses on the viability of causal links between the independent and dependent variables.
- **Construct validity** is a judgment about the extent to which interventions and measured variables actually represent targeted, theoretical, underlying psychological constructs and elements.
- **External validity** refers to the generalizability of the results and conclusions to other people and locations.

These four types of design validity can also be expressed as questions to be addressed in considering the overall quality of the findings and conclusions:

- Is there a relationship among the variables? (Statistical conclusion validity)
- Is there a causal relationship between the intervention and the dependent variable? (Internal Validity)
- What is the nature of the constructs? (Construct validity)
- What is the generalizability of the results? (External validity)

In designing or reading quantitative research with these four types of design validity in mind, it is necessary to consider who will be assessed (subjects), what they will be assessed by (instruments), how they will be assessed (procedures for data collection), and, for experimental designs, how experimental interventions will be administered. Once statistical conclusion validity has been assured, then it is important to ask Is there anything that occurred or was done that could provide an explanation of the results by means of a rival hypothesis? *Rival* is used in the sense that it is in addition to the stated hypothesis or intent of the research. (A rival hypothesis to the study of whether smoking causes lung cancer, for example, is that diet may contribute to the cause of lung cancer.) This question represents the search for extraneous variability in internal validity.

Campbell and Stanley (1963) refer to such explanations as **plausible rival hypotheses.** The search for plausible rival hypotheses is essential to ensure the quality of the research. Consider, for example, the questions below. Each addresses a possible source of error that could lead to a plausible rival hypothesis that might explain results:

1. Does the researcher have an existing bias about the subjects or about the topic researched?
2. Are the subjects aware that they are being studied?
3. Are the subjects responding honestly?
4. Did both groups receive the intervention as described?
5. Does the sex of the interviewer make a difference?
6. Did very many subjects drop out before the end of the study?
7. Did the time of day the research was done affect the results?

If the researcher believes that the conditions of data collection might affect the results, the study can be designed to ensure that all conditions are as similar as possible. For example, in an observational study of the relationship between teacher behavior and student attention to material, the time of day the observer records data and the subject matter of the lesson (e.g., mornings versus afternoons, math versus history) could make a difference in student attention. One way to control this potential source of error is to make sure that all the observations are done at the same time of day during lessons on the same topic. In this example, the researcher could also control these potential influences by making them independent variables. This could be achieved by assigning observers to each subject of interest and having each topic observed in both the morning and the afternoon. Then the researcher could assess the effect of time of day and subject, rather than simply control for it.

In quantitative studies, control of possible extraneous variables is essential, although educational research rarely exhibits the degree of control evident in studies of physical phenomena or psychology. Thus, the researcher must search constantly for factors (extraneous variables) that might influence the results or conclusions of the study. For quantitative research, the concept of internal validity describes the efficacy with which extraneous variables have been controlled. The concern is with the way the procedures, sampling of subjects, and instruments affect the extent to which extraneous variables are present to complicate the interpretation of the findings. A study high or strong in internal validity successfully controls all or most extraneous variables so that the researcher can be confident that, for instance, X caused changes in Y. Studies low or weak in internal validity are difficult to interpret, since it is impossible to tell whether the results were due to the independent variable or to some extraneous variable that was uncontrolled or unaccounted for. It is important for researchers to be aware of common factors that may be extraneous and to conceptualize and read research with these factors in mind. Since complete control of extraneous variables in educational research is difficult, if not impossible, all relevant threats to internal validity that cannot be prevented should be accounted for in interpreting the results.

Statistical Conclusion Validity

In quantitative research, statistics are used to determine whether a relationship exists between two or more variables. The issue is the extent to which the calculated statistics accurately portray the actual relationship. Doing the statistics is the first step in determining results, interpretations, and conclusions. In other words, statistics guide the findings. While we have not yet discussed typical statistical procedures, it is important to realize that certain factors may invalidate the statistical results. That is, there are reasons that researchers may draw inferences about the relationship between variables that are incorrect. While a complete consideration of these factors, or "threats," as they are called, is beyond the scope of this book, being familiar with these ideas is important to readers.

Shadish, Cook, and Campbell (2002) list nine threats to statistical conclusion validity. The first seven are pertinent to our discussion:

1. ***Low statistical power*** An incorrect conclusion of no relationship due to lack of power, or the ability to detect relationships.
2. ***Violated assumptions of statistical tests*** Violated assumptions may under- or overestimate the size of a relationship.
3. ***"Fishing" and error rate problem*** Repeated tests for statistical significance can inflate statistical significance.
4. ***Unreliability of measures*** Measurement error weakens relationships.
5. ***Restriction of range*** Reduced, small differences among a set of scores weakens relationships.
6. ***Unreliability of treatment implementation*** Unstandardized treatments underestimate the effects of an intervention (also referred to as *treatment fidelity*).
7. ***Extraneous variance in the experimental setting*** Features of an intervention setting may inflate error, making it more difficult to show a relationship.

You may notice that much of the error caused by these factors makes it more difficult to show relationships. This is a critical feature for research that concludes, based on lack of statistical significance, that there really is no relationship. In this case, threats to statistical conclusion, if present, invalidate no-relationship conclusions.

Internal Validity

Internal validity is strongest when the study's design (subjects, instruments, and procedures) effectively controls possible sources of error so that those sources are not reasonably related to the study's results. Several categories or types of threats to internal validity are pertinent to most quantitative studies. Each of these threats is described and illustrated in a following section. These categories are taken from Campbell and Stanley (1963), Cook and Campbell (1979), Shadish, Cook, and Campbell (2002), and McMillan (2004). It is best to keep in mind that the names of these various threats to internal validity should not be interpreted literally. Often, each has a broader meaning than the name may suggest at first. While some of the names are unique to this book, most were originally conceived for experimental research. While many of the threats relate to both experimental and nonexperimental designs, some only make sense in the context of an experiment.

Two conditions must be present to establish whether a threat is plausible: (1) the threat is present for only one level of the independent variable, and (2) the threat is related to the dependent variable. Suppose a researcher is investigating the effect of a special training program for school counselors. If the group receiving the program is more experienced than the comparison group and experience influences the dependent variable, then a clear threat to internal validity will compromise causal inferences.

History In the context of internal validity, **history** refers to extraneous incidents or events affecting the results that occur during the research. This is a threat to any research that is conducted across time, and it becomes more serious as the time between measures increases. If some event occurs during the study that is plausibly related to the dependent variable, it is difficult to know if the independent variable, the event, or a combination of the two produced the result. In this sense, the event is *confounded* with the independent variable; the two cannot be separated.

History can occur *within* the study when subjects are affected by something that happens during the treatment in an experiment or *outside* the research setting. For example, suppose a class is studying the Far East and researchers are trying to determine what effect this unit has on students' multicultural attitudes. During the unit, a major crisis occurs in China. If the students are affected by the crisis, which in turn influences the way they respond to a multicultural attitude questionnaire, this event will constitute a history threat to the internal validity of the study. History threats can also occur within a research setting. For example, a series of unexpected announcements that distract a class receiving one method of instruction adversely will affect the influence of the lesson. Students in this class might score lower than other classes, but the researcher will not know if this result is caused by the distraction or the method of instruction.

Selection There are two types of selection threats to consider: those that occur in experiments and *ex post facto* designs and those that are related to sampling. In experiments, groups of subjects are formed in order to study an independent variable of interest. If there is a systematic difference between the groups, however, the results may be due to these existing differences. The threat of **selection** exists whenever groups of subjects cannot be assigned randomly. While there are several approaches that help control this problem in cases where randomization is undesirable or impossible (e.g., matching, testing subjects more than once, adjusting posttest scores on the basis of initially measured group characteristics, and giving each group every treatment), the researcher should always be concerned with this important threat.

Consider, for example, a teacher who wants to investigate whether the mastery or inductive approach is best for teaching adjectives and adverbs. The teacher secures the cooperation of another class in order to conduct a study. The two teachers flip a coin to decide who will use the discovery approach and who will use the mastery approach. The teachers assess achievement by giving each group a pretest and a posttest to determine growth in knowledge. It happens, however, that the average IQ score of the mastery group is 115 while that of the discovery group 95. Here selection is a major problem, since we would expect the higher-IQ group to achieve more than the lower-IQ group under almost any condition. If uncontrolled and unaccounted for in some way, then such a threat to internal validity could render the study useless. The teacher would falsely conclude that the mastery learning method is more effective, when its apparent success is really due to initial differences in ability.

As discussed previously, selection is also related to the manner in which the researcher chooses a sample. As pointed out, a common problem in research is using volunteers for the sample. The volunteer group may be more motivated or motivated for special reasons; hence, they will respond differently to the treatment or questions than a nonvolunteer group will respond.

Statistical Regression **Statistical regression** (also called *regression artifacts*) refers to the tendency of subjects who score very high or low on a pretest to score closer to the mean (i.e, *regress* to the mean) on the posttest, regardless of the effects of the treatment. All measures have some degree of error, and statistical regression occurs because of changes in error from the pretest to the posttest. Scores on a posttest will be different from the pretest for students on the basis of mathematical probability alone because of this error. For groups of students who score either very high or very low on a pretest, this error works to change the scores on the posttest so that they are closer to the mean of the posttest than they were to the mean of the pretest.

To illustrate this concept, think of Figure 5.5 as representing the same test taken twice by two groups of students in a class in which the average score is 100. The average score for the Superstars on the first test was 150, whereas the score for the Challengers was 40. On the second test, we would expect the average score for the Superstars to be

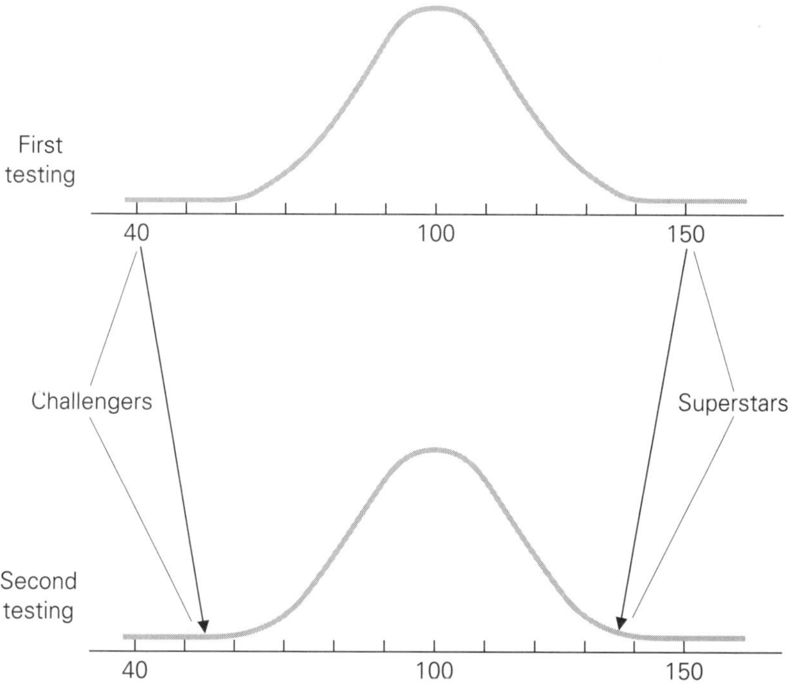

FIGURE 5.5 **Illustration of Statistical Regression**

lower and the Challengers' score to be higher, even if their true ability or knowledge remains the same.

Regression is a problem whenever the researcher purposely chooses groups on the basis of extremely high or low scores. For example, a school district may want to implement a special program to improve the self-concept of children who score low on a self-concept inventory. An assessment of the impact of the program could examine self-concept scores after the program (in a posttest), but the researcher would have to keep in mind that even if there is no program effect whatsoever, the initially low scores (on a pretest) would improve to some degree because of statistical regression. Similarly, it is usually difficult to find positive changes in programs for gifted children. (Because of regression, posttest scores will tend to be slightly lower on average.)

Pretesting Whenever research utilizes a pretest (i.e., some form of measurement that precedes a treatment or experience), it is possible that the test itself will have an impact on the subjects. Just taking a pretest could provide the subject with motivation or practice on the type of questions asked or familiarize the subject with the material tested. This kind of **pretesting** (or *testing*) effect is found in experiments measuring achievement over a short time and in research on attitudes or values when a single group is given a pretest and a posttest. If an attitude questionnaire is used as a pretest, simply reading the questions might stimulate the subject to think about the topic and even change attitudes. A researcher might, for instance, be interested in evaluating the effect of a series of films on changes in students' attitudes toward children with physical disabilities. The researcher would give a pretest, show the films, and then give a posttest to find out whether changes have occurred. Any observed changes, however, might be caused by the pretest. The items in the questionnaire could have been enough to change the attitudes. Pretesting is not a threat for nonexperimental designs.

Instrumentation A threat to internal validity that is related to testing is called **instrumentation.** It refers to the way changes in the instruments or persons used to collect data might affect the results. This threat is particularly serious in observational research, when the observers may become fatigued or bored or change in some other way so as to affect the recording of data. A good example of how instrumentation could affect results occurs when scores from the same standardized test are used to track achievement across several years. If there has been a renorming of the test and a new form, it is problematic to compare results from the old test with those from the new one. The 1995 renorming and other planned changes in the Scholastic Assessment Tests (SAT) is a good illustration of how this can lead to errors in interpretation, since the meaning of the same score, for example, 500, is different in the new form. *Testing* is a change in the subject resulting from taking the test, while *instrumentation* is a recorded change in the results from inadequacies of the testing.

Attrition **Attrition** (also called *mortality*) occurs in a study when subjects systematically drop out or are lost during the investigation. This is a threat to many longitudinal studies that last over several weeks or months. For example, a study of the effect of a program to assist low-achieving ninth-graders conducted between the ninth and the twelfth grades would have apparent success if the lowest-achieving students dropped out of school before twelfth grade and were not even included in the posttest analyses. For most nonexperimental and short-duration research, attrition is not a threat unless the treatment is especially demanding and systematically causes low-performing subjects to drop out. In studies that have differential loss of subjects from different groups because of selection bias or the nature of the treatments, mortality is a serious threat to internal validity. Mortality is essentially the same problem as selection, but it happens after the study is already set up and under way.

Maturation **Maturation** refers to changes in the subjects of a study over time that affect the dependent variable. Subjects develop and change as a part of growing older, and in interpreting research that occurs over an extended time, such changes should be considered. Some changes, such as getting hungry, tired, bored, or discouraged, can occur in a relatively short time and are also considered maturational threats to internal validity. Suppose a researcher is investigating the attitudes of fourth-graders toward reading, mathematics, and science. The researcher has developed an instrument and gives it to all subjects in the same way. It takes the subjects a half hour to finish the reading instrument and another half hour to complete the mathematics questions. How will they respond to the science instrument? They will probably be tired, bored, and inattentive, and maturation would thus be a major problem in using their responses to the science items as an indication of their attitude toward science. Other examples are students who become more knowledgeable because of experience and first-graders who learn to dribble a basketball not because of an effective teacher but because they are maturing physically.

Diffusion of Treatment In an ideal experimental design, an intervention is given to one group, and the control or alternative condition group never comes in contact with the experimental intervention. For instance, if a psychologist is studying cheating behavior and manipulates the incentive to cheat as the independent variable, one group might receive a high incentive for cheating and the other group a low incentive, but neither group would be aware of the treatment the other group was receiving. If, however, a teacher decided to test this notion with a class of students and told half the students they would receive a high incentive and the other half that they would, at the same time, receive a low incentive, then each group would know the conditions of the other. In such circumstances, the treatments would be diffused throughout all subjects. It is possible that both treatments could affect either group, resulting in **diffusion of treatment.** Diffusion also occurs if the effects of the treatment spread to subjects in a control or comparison group.

Experimenter Effects **Experimenter effects** refer to both deliberate and unintentional influences that the researcher has on the subjects. This may be reflected in differential treatment of subjects, such as using a different voice tone, being more reassuring to one group than to others, reinforcing different behaviors, displaying different attitudes, selectively observing different subject responses, and any other demeanor that influences either the subjects' behavior or the evaluation of the behavior by the researcher. Experimenter effects also occur if the characteristics of the investigator or person collecting data, such as clothing, age, sex, educational level, and race, affect subjects' responses. For example, if an experimenter is carrying out a study on the difference in behavior with students of so-called master teachers compared with behavior with students of so-called novice teachers, and if observers are used to record behavior with students of both types of teachers, the observers should not know which teachers have been classified as master or novice. If the observers were aware of which group the students were in (master or novice teacher), this knowledge may influence what the observers notice in the classrooms. In most research that involves the use of researchers as a part of the study, it is best to keep them unaware of the specifics of the research. They need to have only enough information to carry out the research objectively and to collect the information.

Treatment Replications In an experiment, the treatment is supposed to be repeated so that each of the members of one group receives the same treatment separately and independently of the other members of the group. Thus, if the researcher is testing a new method of instruction with a whole class, there is really only one replication of the treatment; that is, the treatment is conducted once. Each class is like one subject, and hence several classes are needed to do the research properly. **Treatment replications** are a threat to internal validity to the extent that the reported number of subjects in the study is not the same as the number of independent replications of the treatment.

ALERT! Be wary of research in which whole classes receive an intervention.

This threat is a particularly troublesome limitation for educational research because it is so difficult to use multiple groups of students. Often a study will compare two treatments: one given to one class, the other to a different class. While this type of design usually results in a technical sample size of two, rather than the number of students in the classes, the threat of treatment replications does not mean the results are completely invalid. Rather, what needs to be recognized is that whatever the results, interpretations and conclusions should be made with great caution. Some experimental treatments are given to students as a group assignment, but the actual treatment condition, such as a particular type of homework assignment, is individualized. In this circumstance, treatment replication is not a threat to internal validity.

Subject Effects In ideal research, the subjects behave and respond naturally and honestly. However, when people become involved in a study they often change their behavior simply because they understand they are subjects, and sometimes these changes affect the results. **Subject effects** refer to subject changes in behavior initiated by the subjects themselves in response to the research situation. If subjects have some idea of the purpose of the study or the motivation for doing well, they may alter their behavior to respond more favorably. Subjects will pick up cues from the setting and instructions, which will motivate them in specific ways. These cues are called **demand characteristics.**

Subjects in most studies will also want to present themselves in the most positive manner. Thus, there may be positive self-presentation, social desirability, or a belief that certain responses are expected, which may affect the results. For instance, most people want to appear intelligent, competent, and emotionally stable, and they may resist treatments that they perceive as manipulating them in negative ways or they may fake responses to appear more positive. Some subjects may increase positive or desirable behavior simply because they know they are receiving special treatment. (This is termed the *Hawthorne effect,* considered by some researchers as a threat to external validity; see the section on ecological external validity.) Control group subjects may try harder because they see themselves in competition with a treatment group or may be motivated because they did *not* get the treatment. (This may be termed the *John Henry effect* or *compensatory rivalry*.) Other subjects, when they realize that they were not selected for what they believe is a preferred treatment, may become demotivated (i.e., *resentful demoralization*). Finally, many individuals will react positively, with increased motivation or participation because they are doing something new and different. (This is termed the *novelty effect.*) As you can see, there are many possible subject effects.

Construct Validity

Research almost always involves making inferences about unobservable mental states (e.g., intelligence, motivation, aggression, and happiness) and experimental interventions. The inference is drawn from what is measured and/or treated pertaining to these mental states. Construct validity refers to inferences that are made from the nature of the measurement and interventions used to the constructs they purportedly represent. Suppose a researcher is studying the effect of curriculum alignment with high-stakes testing on student achievement. The test of student achievement is given to make inferences about what students know and can do, and the specifics of the intervention are used to make inferences about curriculum alignment. Construct validity concerns the efficacy of using the test as a measure of what students know and can do, as well as the representativeness of the intervention as an illustration of curriculum alignment. There are many ways of measuring student achievement and doing curriculum alignment, so if only one test is used and only one model of curriculum alignment is proposed, construct validity will be weak.

Shadish, Cook, and Campbell (2002) list 14 threats to construct validity, some of which were considered earlier as subject effect threats to internal validity. The three threats with the greatest relevance for education research include the following:

1. **Inadequate explication of the constructs** Failure to adequately explain the nature of the construct may lead to inaccurate inferences.
2. **Mono-operation bias** A single example of the intervention or the dependent variables limits inferences (e.g., one method of showing humor in an intervention or using only observation to measure the effect of the humor on attentiveness; humor could be presented by both men and women; observations could use a single format for recording behavior).
3. **Mono-method bias** Use of a single method in implementing the intervention and/or measuring the dependent variable (e.g., humor could be in writing or presented orally; humor could be measured with a paper-and-pencil questionnaire or observations).

Construct validity is closely related to generalizability, since using a weak conceptualization or single method of measurement will limit inferences about the details of the conceptualization and method. Suppose student achievement is limited to how students score on a multiple-choice test. Other ways of measuring achievement might give different results. Thus, what is meant by student achievement is limited to the method of measurement.

External Validity

External validity refers to the generalizability of the results. For quantitative designs there are two general categories of external validity that need to be considered when designing studies or in evaluating research findings: population external validity and ecological external validity.

Population External Validity The subjects used in an investigation have certain characteristics and can be described with respect to such variables as age, race, sex, and ability. Strictly speaking, the results of a study can be generalized only to other people who have the same, or at least similar, characteristics as those used in the experiment. The extent to which the results can be generalized to other people is referred to as **population external validity.**

Consider the prevailing situation in much psychological research. Because of time, money, and other constraints, psychologists often use college students as subjects in research. The results of such research, strictly speaking, are limited in generalizability to other similar college students. In other words, what might be true for certain college students may not be true for sixth-grade students. Similarly, research conducted with elementary students should not be generalized to secondary students, nor males generalized to females, nor Hispanic Americans generalized to African Americans, and so forth. A treatment might be effective with one type of student and be ineffective with another. If subjects are volunteers for research, the findings may be limited to characteristics of the volunteers.

Ecological External Validity **Ecological external validity** refers to the conditions of the research and the extent to which generalizing the results is limited to similar conditions. The conditions of the research include such factors as the nature of the independent and dependent variables, physical surroundings, time of day or year, pretest or posttest sensitization, and effects caused by the presence of an experimenter or treatment. Included in these factors is the well-known **Hawthorne effect:** the tendency for people to act differently simply because they realize they are subjects in research. (It is called the Hawthorne effect because the original study was conducted at the Western Electric Hawthorne Plant in Chicago. Although some research has questioned the validity of the original study, the label *Hawthorne effect* endures.) Much as with threats of subject effects, subjects may become anxious, fake responses in order to look good, or react in many other ways because of their knowledge of aspects of the research.

A variation of external validity is to be careful not to conclude that what may be true for an entire group of subjects is also true for subgroups of subjects. For example, if research with a large high school shows a positive relationship between amount of time spent with homework and achievement for all students, it does not necessarily follow that this same relationship holds for high-ability students or low-ability students or that it is just as true for sophomores as for seniors. This is called generalizing *across* a population and can lead to erroneous interpretations.

It is possible to be so strict with respect to external validity that practically all research is useful only in specific cases. While it is necessary to consider the external validity of studies, we need to be reasonable, not strict, in interpreting the results. It is common, for example, for researchers to cite in the discussion or conclusion section of the article the limitations of generalizing their results.

ETHICAL AND LEGAL CONSIDERATIONS

Since most educational research deals with human beings, it is necessary to understand the ethical and legal responsibilities of conducting research. Often, researchers face situations in which the potential costs of using questionable methods must be balanced by the benefits of conducting the study. Questionable methods come about because of the nature of the research questions and methodology designed to provide valid results. The costs may include injury and psychological difficulties, such as anxiety, shame, loss of self-esteem, and affronts to human dignity, or they may involve legal infringement on human rights. Such costs, if a potential result of the research, must be weighed against the benefits for the research participants, such as increased self-understanding, satisfaction in helping, and knowledge of research methods, as well as more obvious benefits to theory and knowledge of human behavior.

It is ultimately the responsibility of each researcher to weigh these considerations and to make the best professional judgment possible. To do this, it is necessary for the researcher to be fully aware of the ethical and legal principles that should be addressed. We present these principles with a discussion of the implications.

Ethics of Research

Ethics generally are considered to deal with beliefs about what is right or wrong, proper or improper, good or bad. Naturally, there is some degree of disagreement about how to define what is ethically correct in research. But it is a very important issue, one of increasing concern for private citizens, researchers, and legislators. Many professional and governmental groups have studied ethical issues in depth and published guidelines for planning and conducting research in such a way as to protect the rights and welfare of the subjects. Most relevant for educational research are the ethical principles published by the American Educational Research Association. Another useful source is the American Psychological Association.[1] The principles of most concern to educators are discussed here:

1. ***The primary investigator of a study is responsible for the ethical standards to which the study adheres.***
2. ***The investigator should inform the subjects of all aspects of the research*** that might influence willingness to participate and answer all inquiries of subjects on features that may have adverse effects or consequences.

3. ***The investigator should be as open and honest with the subjects as possible.*** This usually involves a full disclosure of the purpose of the research, but there are circumstances in which either withholding information about the research or deceiving the subjects may be justified. Withholding information means that the participants are informed about only part of the purpose of the research. This may be done in studies where full disclosure would seriously affect the validity of the results. For example, in research on students' racial attitudes, it may be sufficient to inform students that the research is investigating attitudes toward others.

   A more volatile issue involves research in which, to put it bluntly, the researcher deliberately misleads the subjects. A good example is the classic study on teacher expectations by Rosenthal and Jacobson (1968). The researchers informed the teachers that certain students had been identified as "bloomers" on a test designed to predict intellectual gain. In fact, the test was a measure of intelligence, and the students were identified at random. In this design, it was necessary to tell the teachers an untruth. Is such deception justified? After all, in this case the students would only benefit from the misinformation, and the results did have very important implications.

   From one perspective, the deception may be justified on the basis of the contribution of the findings. On the other hand, it is an affront to human dignity and self-respect and may encourage mistrust and cynicism toward researchers. It seems that deception should be used only in cases where (1) the significance of the potential results is greater than the detrimental effects of lying; (2) deception is the only valid way to carry out the study; and (3) appropriate debriefing is used, in which the researcher informs the participants of the nature of and reason for the deception following the completion of the study. Deception does not mean that the subjects should not have a choice whether to participate at all in the study.
4. ***Subjects must be protected from physical and mental discomfort, harm, and danger.*** If any of these risks is possible, the researcher must inform the subjects of these risks.
5. ***Many studies require the investigator to secure informed consent from the subjects before they participate in the research.*** **Informed consent** is achieved by providing subjects with an explanation of the research, an opportunity to terminate their participation at any time with no penalty, and full disclosure of any risks associated with the study. Consent is usually obtained by asking subjects (or the parents of minor subjects) to sign a form that indicates understanding of the research and consent to participate. Almost all data gathering in public schools that requires student participation beyond normal testing requires parental as well as school district and principal permission.

   Informed consent implies that the subjects have a choice about whether to participate. Yet there are many circumstances when it seems acceptable that the subjects never know that they have been participants. Sometimes, it is impractical or impossible to locate subjects; sometimes, knowledge of participation may invalidate the results. Some educational research is quite unobtrusive and has no risks for the subjects (e.g., the use of test data of students over the past 10 years in order to chart achievement trends). Still, the researcher infringes on what many believe is the ethical right of participants to make their own decisions about participation. In general, the more the research inconveniences subjects or creates the potential for harm, the more severe the ethical question in using them as subjects without their consent.

   Certainly, people should never be coerced into participating. Coercion is enacted in different degrees. At one extreme, teachers can insist that their students participate, or employers can strongly suggest that their employees cooperate as subjects. Less obvious subtle persuasion is exerted by convincing subjects that they are benefiting science, a program, or an institution. The researcher may indicate freedom of choice to participate or not participate, but the implicit message, "you're letting us down if you don't participate" may also be clear, resulting in partial coercion. In other cases, subjects are simply bribed. Where does freedom of choice end and coercion begin? It is often difficult to know, but it is the responsibility of the researcher to be aware of the power of subtle coercion and to clearly maintain the freedom of the potential participant to decide whether or not to be a subject in the research. Whenever possible, participation should be voluntary and invasion of privacy should be minimized.

6. ***Information obtained about the subjects must be held confidential*** unless otherwise agreed on, in advance, through informed consent. This means that no one has access to individual data or the names of the participants except the researcher(s) and that the subjects know before they participate who will see the data. Confidentiality is ensured by making certain that the data cannot be linked to individual subjects by name. This can be accomplished in several ways, including (1) collecting the data anonymously; (2) using a system to link names to data that can be destroyed; (3) using a third party to link names to data and then giving the results to the researcher without the names; (4) asking subjects to use aliases or numbers; and (5) reporting only group, not individual, results. Boruch and Cecil (1979) provide details of many different procedures for ensuring confidentiality.
7. ***For research conducted through an institution, such as a university or school system, approval for conducting the research should be obtained from the institution before any data are collected.*** Typically, this involves obtaining permission from the institution's **internal review board (IRB),** a committee that prepares guidelines for obtaining permission, conducts reviews of proposals for research, and approves studies. An IRB weighs the potential benefits of the research with possible risks to the participants and may suggest additional procedures to better protect their rights. The IRB process can be very time consuming, so advanced planning is required. It is important for the IRB to make decisions about what must be approved, including research conducted by students. At the very least, students should not go out and collect data without obtaining permission from a professor or administrative head. IRB approval is needed for any research that may be disseminated in a formal manner or in public. This suggests that informal class projects may be exempt from IRB approval, as long as there is assurance that the findings will not be more widely disseminated in the future. All doctoral dissertations require IRB approval, as do many program evaluations.
8. ***The investigator has a responsibility to consider potential misinterpretations and misuses of the research*** and should make every effort to communicate results so that misunderstanding is minimized.
9. ***The investigator has the responsibility of recognizing when potential benefits have been withheld from a control group.*** In such situations, the significance of the potential findings should be greater than the potential harm to some subjects. For example, a new program that purports to enhance achievement of children with learning disabilities may be withheld from some of these children in the belief that an experiment is necessary to document the effectiveness of the program. In the process, the controls who may have benefited are denied participation in the program.
10. **The investigator should provide subjects with the opportunity to receive the results of the study in which they are participating.**

Some research (e.g., studies of the effects of drugs), obviously has potential danger that must be considered carefully by the investigator. While much educational research may not seem to involve any ethical problems, the investigator's view may be biased. It is best to seek the advice and approval of others. Consulting with others provides an impartial perspective and can help the researcher identify procedures for protecting participants from harm.

There is also an interesting, if not frustrating, interaction between being ethical, on the one hand, and designing the research to provide the best, most objective data, on

TABLE 5.5 Keys to Conducting Ethical Research

- Be knowledgeable about ethical principles, professional guidelines, and legal requirements.
- Maximize potential benefits.
- Minimize potential risks.
- Obtain needed permission.
- Minimize potential misinterpretations and misuses of results.
- Obtain informed consent.
- Protect the privacy and confidentiality of the subjects.

the other. It is relatively easy, for example, to observe behavior unobtrusively, such that the subjects might never know they were in an experiment. As previously noted, the Hawthorne effect can reduce the validity of the study. To maximize both internal and external validity, therefore, it seems best for subjects to be unaware that they are being studied. Suppose, for instance, that a researcher planted a confederate in a class in order to record unobtrusively the attending behavior of college students. Does the researcher have an obligation to tell the students that their behavior is being recorded? If the students are aware of being observed, will this awareness change their behavior and invalidate the results? Such situations present ethical dilemmas, and the researcher must weigh the criteria listed above in order to determine the best course of action.

See Table 5.5 for a summary of key points for conducting ethical research.

Legal Constraints

Most of the legal constraints placed on researchers since 1974 have focused on protecting the rights and the welfare of the subjects. These requirements are generally consistent with the ethical principles summarized earlier, and are in a constant state of reinterpretation and change by the courts.

The Family Educational Rights and Privacy Act of 1974, known as the Buckley Amendment, allows individuals to gain access to information pertaining to them, such as test scores, teacher comments, and recommendations. The act also provides that written permission of consent is legally necessary with data that identify students by name. The consent must indicate the information that will be disclosed, the purpose of the disclosure, and to whom it will be disclosed. Exceptions to this requirement are granted for research using school records in which the results are of "legitimate educational interest" and when only group data are reported. It should be noted that data gathered in a study can usually be subpoenaed by the courts, even if confidentiality has been promised to the participants by the researcher.

The National Research Act of 1974 requires review of proposed research by an appropriate group in an institution (school division or university) to protect the rights and welfare of the subjects. While most research involving human subjects must be reviewed by such a group, there are some exceptions, such as research using test data that result from normal testing programs and analyzing existing public data, records, or documents without identifying individuals. These regulations were expanded and modified in 1991 with publication of the *Code of Federal Regulations for the Protection of Human Subjects*. The code was further updated in 2003.

SUMMARY

This chapter introduced the fundamental characteristics of designing quantitative research. It focused particular attention on selecting subjects and instruments and on variables that should be considered in designing and interpreting the research. Key points include the following:

1. Research design refers to the way a study is planned and conducted.
2. The purpose of a good research design is to enhance the credibility of the results by taking into account three sources of variability: systematic, error, and extraneous.
3. Probability sampling is used to be able to generalize to a larger population.
4. Probability sampling is done through simple random sampling, systematic sampling, stratified random sampling, and cluster sampling.
5. Nonprobability sampling includes purposeful, convenience, and quota types. While available and easily obtained, the use of such samples limits generalizability.
6. The size of the sample should be as large as possible without reaching a point at which additional subjects contribute little or no new information.
7. In order to have acceptable reliability and validity for the subjects used in the study, instruments should be chosen carefully. Validity is an estimate of the appropriateness of the use of scores, and reliability is an indication of the consistency of the scores.
8. Researchers should try to locate existing instruments before developing their own.
9. Statistical conclusion validity is concerned with whether there is an actual relationship.
10. Threats to the internal validity of quantitative studies include selection, history, statistical regression, pretesting, instrumentation, subject attrition, maturation, diffusion of treatment, experimenter effects, treatment replications, subject effects, and statistical conclusion.
11. Construct validity considers the match between theoretical constructs and actual interventions and measures.
12. Threats to the external validity of quantitative studies that limit generalizability are classified as population characteristics or ecological conditions.
13. The procedures section of a study should show how the information was collected in detail sufficient to allow other researchers to replicate or extend the study.
14. Researchers should be aware of ethical responsibilities and legal constraints that accompany the gathering and reporting of information.

CHECK YOURSELF

Multiple-choice review items, with answers, are available on the Companion Website for this book:

www.ablongman.com/mcmillanschumacher6e.

APPLICATION PROBLEMS

1. For each case described here, list potential threats to internal and external validity:
   a. Two researchers designed a study to investigate whether physical education performance is affected by being in a class with students of the same sex only or in a class with students of both sexes. A college instructor is found to cooperate with the researchers. Three sections of the same tennis class are offered: an all-male section, an all-female section, and a mixed section. The researchers control the instructor variable by using the same person as the instructor for each section, informing the instructor about the study and emphasizing to the instructor the need to keep instructional activities the same for each section. One section is offered in the morning, one at noon, and one in the afternoon. Students sign up for the course by using the same procedure as for all courses, although there is a footnote about the gender composition in the schedule of courses. A pretest is given to control for existing differences in the groups.

b. In this study, the effect of day care on children's prosocial behavior is examined. A group of volunteer parents agree to participate in the study. (The investigators pay part of the day-care fees.) Children are assigned randomly from the pool of volunteers either to attend a day care of their choice or not to attend. Observers measure the degree of prosocial behavior before and after attending day care for nine months by observing the children on a playground.

c. A superintendent wishes to get some idea of whether or not a bond issue will pass in a forthcoming election. Records listing real estate taxpayers are obtained from the county office. From this list, a random sample of 10 percent of 3,000 persons is called by phone two weeks before election day and asked whether they intend to vote yes or no.

d. The Green County School Board decided that it wanted a status assessment of the ninth-graders' attitudes toward science. A questionnaire was designed and distributed in January to all ninth-grade science teachers. Each teacher was told to give the questionnaire within six weeks, to calculate mean scores for each question, and to return the questionnaires and results to the district office. The instructors were told to take only one class period for the questionnaires in order to minimize interference with the course. Sixty percent of the questionnaires were returned.

NOTE

1. Consider these sources:

American Educational Research Association. (1992). Ethical standards of the American Educational Research Association, *Educational Research, 21*, 23–26.

American Educational Research Association. (2002). Ethical principles of psychologists and code of conduct. *American Psychologist, 47* [Special insert].

American Psychological Association. (1982). *Ethical principles in the conduct of research with human participants*. Washington, DC: APA.

Strike, K. A., Anderson, M. S., Curren, R., van Geel, T., Pritchard, J., & Robertson, E. (2002). *Ethical standards of the American Educational Research Association: Cases and commentary*. Washington, DC: AERA. Available online: www.aera.net/about/policy/ethics.htm

PART

III

QUALITATIVE RESEARCH DESIGNS AND METHODS

Educators frequently ask questions such as these: How do researchers design a qualitative study? How does one address the issues of rigor, validity, subjectivity, and use of the study? When does one employ participant observation and/or in-depth interviews? Should a variety of data collection strategies be employed in a single study? How is systematic data analysis done in qualitative research? Are there guidelines for presenting narrative findings? How does a reader judge the credibility of the findings in a qualitative study?

Qualitative research was classified in Chapter 2 as *interactive research* or *noninteractive research* termed *analytical research*. Qualitative interactive research is addressed in Part III. In Part III, Chapter 6 describes qualitative research design and criteria. Interactive data collection strategies are used primarily in the study of current social happenings, social scenes, and processes. Inductive data analysis uses descriptive data of the meanings people derive from or ascribe to particular events and processes. Qualitative research can suggest grounded propositions, provide explanations to extend understanding of phenomena, or promote opportunities for informed social action. Qualitative research contributes to theory, educational practice, policy-making, and social consciousness.

CHAPTER

6 Designing Qualitative Research

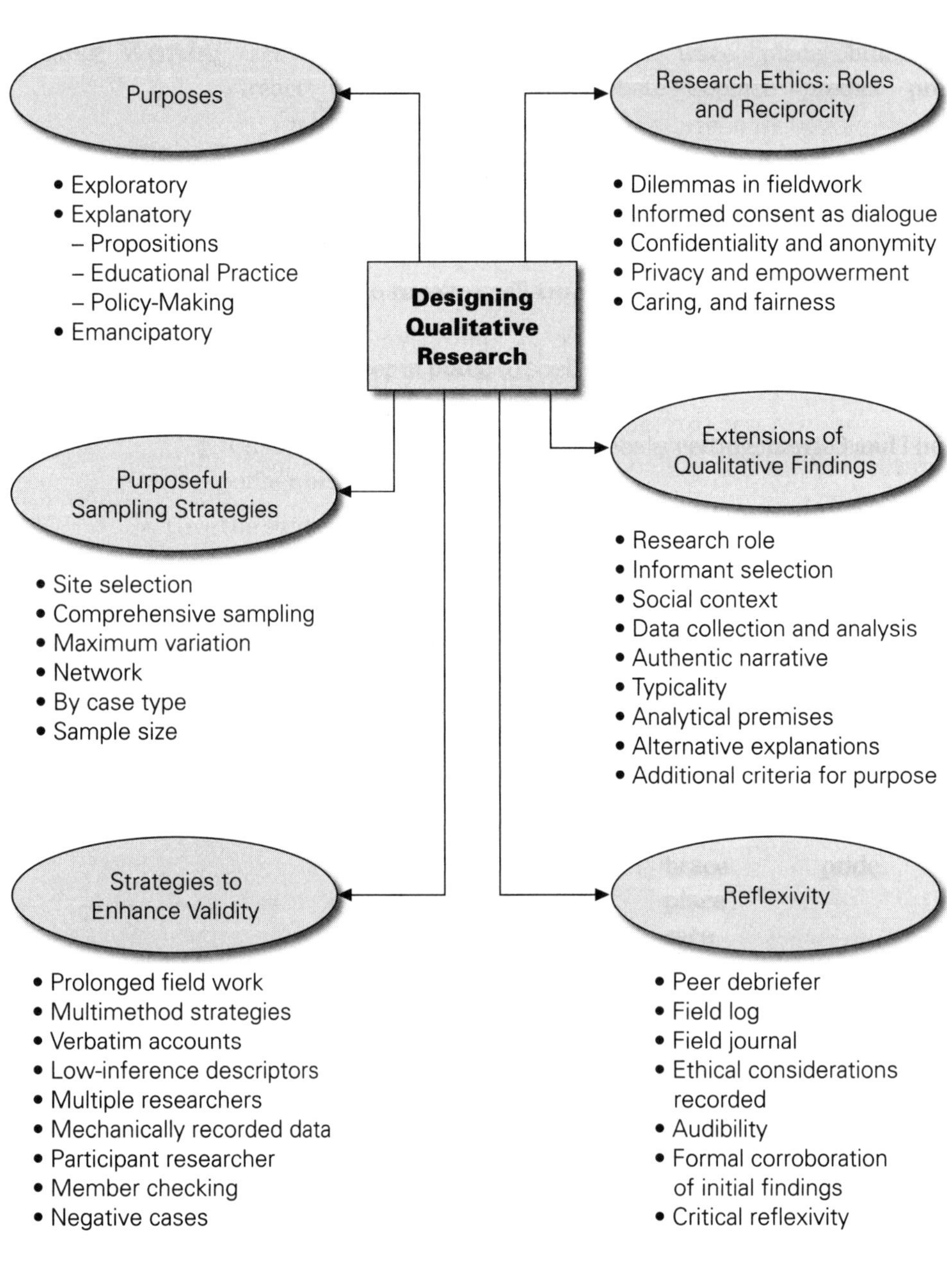

KEY TERMS

- interactive strategies
- field research
- case study design
- emergent design
- purposeful sampling
- site selection
- comprehensive sampling
- maximum variation sampling (quota sampling)
- network sampling (snowball sampling)
- validity of qualitative designs
- reflexivity
- positionality
- audibility
- extension of the findings
- authenticity
- typicality

Qualitative research is inquiry in which researchers collect data in face-to-face situations by interacting with selected persons in their settings (e.g., field research). Qualitative research describes and analyzes people's individual and collective social actions, beliefs, thoughts, and perceptions. The researcher interprets phenomena in terms of the meanings that people assign to them. Qualitative studies are important for theory generation, policy development, improvement of educational practice, illumination of social issues, and action stimulus.

In this chapter, we introduce qualitative design and relate it to the general research question and potential contributions of the study. We explain purposeful sampling strategies, data collection and analysis phases, research ethics, and design standards. A variety of ways to demonstrate evidence-based findings are discussed: strategies to enhance validity, techniques to minimize research bias (reflexivity), and design components to generate extension of results. We point out the differences between traditional and critical approaches to inquiry.

PURPOSES, RESEARCH QUESTIONS, AND CASE STUDY DESIGN

Five of the interactive research approaches (i.e., modes of inquiry) discussed in Chapter 2 were ethnographic, phenomenological, case study, grounded theory, and critical studies. These inquiry modes share assumptions about and goals for research that influence design.

Research Approach and Orientation

Here, we review the research orientation shared among these inquiry modes because it provides a rationale for many design decisions.

Assumptions Qualitative research is based on a constructivist philosophy that assumes that reality is a multilayer, interactive, shared social experience that is interpreted by individuals. Reality is a *social construction;* that is, individuals and groups derive or ascribe meanings to specific events, persons, processes, and objects. People form constructions to make sense of their world and reorganize these constructions as viewpoints, perceptions, and belief systems. In other words, people's perceptions are what they consider real and thus what directs their actions, thoughts, and feelings.

Goal Qualitative research is first concerned with *understanding* social phenomena from participants' perspectives. That understanding is achieved by analyzing the many contexts of the participants and by narrating participants' meanings for these situations and events.

Participants' meanings include their feelings, beliefs, ideas, thoughts, and actions (see Excerpt 6.1). Some qualitative research aims for more than understanding the phenomena and also generates theory or empowerment.

Multimethod Strategies Qualitative researchers study participants' perspectives with **interactive strategies:** participant observation, direct observation, in-depth interviews, artifacts, and supplementary techniques. Research strategies are flexible, using various combinations of techniques to obtain valid data. Most researchers adjust decisions about data collection strategies during the study. The multiple realities are viewed as so complex that one cannot decide a priori on a single methodology.

Research Role Qualitative researchers become immersed in the situations and the phenomena studied. The research role varies from the more traditional neutral stance to an active participatory role, depending on the selected research approach.

Context Sensitivity Other features of qualitative research are rooted in the belief that human actions are strongly influenced by the settings in which they occur. The study is **field research;** that is, the researcher collects data over a prolonged time at a site or from individuals without interfering with the natural events.

Purpose and Research Questions

Historically, qualitative researchers cited two major purposes of a study: *to describe and explore* and *to describe and explain*. Similar terms could be *to examine* or *to document*, *to understand*, and *to discover or generate*.

Exploratory studies add to the literature by building rich descriptions of complex situations and by giving directions for future research. Other qualitative studies are explicitly explanatory. They show relationships between events and meanings as perceived by participants. These studies increase readers' understanding of the phenomena. Other purposes address action, advocacy, or empowerment, which are often the ultimate goals of critical studies (critical, feminist, postmodern, and participatory research). Although researchers can claim empowerment and taking action as part of the study purpose, realistically, they can only note how the inquiry may offer opportunities for informed empowerment (see Table 6.1).

Case Study Design

In a **case study design,** the data analysis focuses on *one phenomenon*, which the researcher selects to understand in depth regardless of the number of sites or participants for the study.[1] The *one* may be, for example, one administrator, one group of students, one program, one process, one policy implementation, or one concept.

An initial plan is necessary to choose sites and participants for beginning data collection. The plan is an **emergent design,** in which each incremental research decision depends

EXCERPT 6.1 Goal of Understanding

More specifically, these narratives can enrich understanding of the culture and daily lives of minority female faculty members. Readers can hear the pain, can see the struggles, and can note the barriers. For example, these voices can help an administrator understand that support and monitoring are critical to minority females in their teaching and scholarship. These voices can help majority faculty members understand. (p. 63)

Source: From Medina, C., & Luna, G. (2000). Narratives from Latina professors in higher education. *Anthropology and Education Quarterly, 31*(1), 47–66.

TABLE 6.1 Research Purpose and Illustrative Research Questions

Research Purpose	Illustrative Research Questions
Descriptive Exploratory	
To examine new or little understood phenomena	What is occurring in this social situation?
To discover themes of participant meanings	What are the categories and themes of participants' meanings?
To develop in detail a concept, model, or hypotheses for future research	How are these patterns linked for propositions/assertions?
Descriptive Explanatory	
To describe and explain the patterns related to the phenomena	What events, beliefs, attitudes, and/or policies impact on this phenomenon?
To identify relationships influencing the phenomena	How do the participants explain the phenomenon?
Emancipatory	
To create opportunities and the will to initiate social action	How do participants describe and explain their problems and take positive action?

Source: Adapted from Marshall & Rossman, 1999, p. 33.

on prior information. The emergent design, in reality, may seem circular, as processes of purposeful sampling, data collection, and partial data analysis are simultaneous and intertwined rather than discrete sequential steps.[2]

Qualitative researchers investigate in-depth small, distinct groups, such as all the faculty in an innovative school, all the students in a selected classroom, or one principal's role for an academic year. These are single-site studies, in which there is a natural sociocultural boundary and face-to-face interaction encompassing the person or group. A study may also focus on individuals who have had a similar experience but may not be interacting with each other, such as families of children who have been physically abused.

Contrasting subunits may also be a focus, such as demographic groups (male/female or black/white) or programmatic groups (dropout/graduates), but the purpose is to understand the *one* phenomenon: the entity or process. Subunits are contrasting groups who are likely to be informative about the research foci.[3] These groups are not viewed as statistically comparative or as mutually exclusive; they often are selected to investigate the extent or diversity of the phenomenon. The researcher examines the first group thoroughly and then selects another group to contrast with or to corroborate findings about the first group.

In the case study design of Excerpt 6.2, the researcher selected one science teacher, Sarah, for a collaborative study. The purpose was to understand Sarah's behaviors and the actions of her students, her colleague teachers, and the school administrators in "terms of what she believed and how she constructed the various contexts in which she taught" (Tobin & LaMaster, 1995, p. 227).

Significance and Justification

To plan a case study design involves selecting the general research question and incorporating components that add to the potential contributions and significance of the study.

EXCERPT 6.2 Case Study Design

The research methodology employed in the study was interpretive and endeavored to make sense of the culture of the [two] classes taught by Sarah in terms of the actions of the participants (Sarah, students, colleague teachers, and school administrators). Accordingly, one rationale of the study was to make sense of Sarah's actions by describing her behaviors, and endeavoring to make sense of them in terms of what she believed and how she constructed the various contexts in which she taught. Our view of collaborative research required that we listen to the voices of Sarah and other participants in the study and also to assign a clear "signature" (Clandinin & Connelly, 1994) to what we learned in terms of interpretation that reflected the perspectives of both authors. (p. 227)

Source: From Tobin, K., & LaMaster, S. (1995). Relationships between metaphors, beliefs, and actions in a context of science curriculum change. *Journal of Research in Science Teaching, 32*(3), 225–242.

Qualitative research can be designed to contribute to theory, practice, policy, and social issues and action. We describe each of these in addition to other justifications.

Contributions to Theory Case study design is appropriate for exploratory- and discovery-oriented research. An *exploratory study*, which examines a topic about which there has been little prior research, is designed to lead to further inquiry. The purpose is to elaborate a concept, develop a model with its related subcomponents, or suggest propositions. Some studies provide an understanding of an abstract concept, such as school-based management, from the participants' social experience. Other studies link participants' perceptions to social science and suggest propositions about humans in general, rather than link the findings to an educational concept. The concepts, models, or hypotheses are *grounded theory* because they are based on observations, rather than deduced from prior theories.

Contributions to Practice Qualitative studies can provide detailed descriptions and analyses of particular practices, processes, or events. Some studies document happenings, and other studies increase participants' own understanding of a practice to improve that practice. A series of qualitative studies over a span of years may contribute to knowledge through the preponderance of evidence accumulated. Specific areas of education for which *quantitative* designs have proven inadequate have begun to accumulate case study evidence. Until quantitative design difficulties can be resolved, knowledge based on a preponderance of evidence cannot easily be ignored.

Contributions to Policy Qualitative research employing a case study design also contributes to policy formulation, implementation, and modification. Some studies focus on the informal processes of policy formulation and implementation in settings with diverse cultural values to explain the outcomes of public policy. These studies frequently identify issues that suggest the need to modify statutes or regulations and to help policy-makers anticipate future issues.

Contributions to Social Issues and Action Critical studies often aim at historical revision and transformation, erosion of ignorance, and empowerment. Some studies focus on the lived experiences of racial and ethnic groups, social classes, and gender roles. Researchers examine qualities such as race, ethnic group, social class, homosexual, and female in a more holistic social context to critique their ideological aspects and the political/economic interests that benefit from a given situation. Studies frequently express the so-called culture of silence experienced by various groups; others describe forms of resistance and accommodation of groups that develop their own values as a force for cohesion and survival within the dominant culture.

Other Justifications *Feasibility issues* related to obtaining valid data can justify a qualitative case study design. Qualitative research is typically done when the nature of the situation or the individuals do not permit use of an instrument. Qualitative strategies, for example, are appropriate with persons who are extremely busy, are expressive nonverbally, or use a second language. When the topic is controversial or confidential or occurred within an institution that has maintained minimal documentation, qualitative inquiry should be chosen. In some situations, an experimental study cannot be done for practical or ethical reasons.

PURPOSEFUL SAMPLING STRATEGIES

Purposeful sampling, in contrast to *probabilistic sampling*, is "selecting information-rich cases for study in-depth" (Patton, 2002, p. 242) when one wants to understand something about those cases without needing or desiring to generalize to all such cases. Purposeful sampling is done to increase the utility of information obtained from small samples. It requires that information be obtained about variations among the subunits before the sample is chosen. The researcher then searches for *information-rich* key informants, groups, places, or events to study. In other words, these samples are chosen because they are likely to be knowledgeable and informative about the phenomena the researcher is investigating.

The power and logic of purposeful sampling is that a few cases studied in depth yield many insights about the topic, whereas the logic of probability sampling depends on selecting a random or statistically representative sample for generalization to a larger population. Probability sampling procedures such as simple random or stratified sampling may be inappropriate when (1) generalizability of the findings is not the purpose; (2) only one or two subunits of a population are relevant to the research problem; (3) the researchers have no access to the whole group from which they wish to sample; or (4) statistical sampling is precluded because of logistical and ethical reasons.

Types of purposeful sampling include site selection, comprehensive sampling, maximum variation sampling, network sampling, and sampling by case type (see Table 6.2).

Site Selection

Site selection, by which a site is selected to locate people involved in a particular event, is preferred when the research focus is on complex microprocesses. A clear definition of the criteria for site selection is essential. The criteria are related to and appropriate for the research problem and purpose. For example, if the initial problem is phrased to describe and analyze teachers' decision making regarding learning activities or students' perspectives regarding classroom management, then the site selected should be one in which these viewpoints or actions are likely present and can be studied.

MISCONCEPTION Self-report surveys of principals' attitudes, behaviors, opinions, and demographic characteristics implied that a principal's job is orderly, routine, and predictable.

EVIDENCE When an ethnography focused on a selected principal's daily professional life, a different image emerged: expedient, rapid problem solving and constant engagement in multitasking with complex human interrelationships to contain any type of conflict immediately.

Comprehensive Sampling

Comprehensive sampling, in which every participant, group, setting, event, or other relevant information is examined, is the preferred sampling strategy. Each subunit is

TABLE 6.2 Purposeful Sampling Strategies

Sample Strategy	Description
Site selection	Select site where specific events are expected to occur.
Comprehensive sampling	Choose entire group by criteria.
Maximum variation sampling	Select to obtain maximum differences of perceptions about a topic among information-rich informants or group.
Network sampling	Each successive person or group is nominated by a prior person as appropriate for a profile or attribute.
Sampling by case type	
Extreme case	Choose extreme cases after knowing the typical or average case—e.g., outstanding successes, crisis events.
Intense case	Select cases that are intense but not extreme illustrations—e.g., below-average students.
Typical case	Know the typical characteristics of a group and sample by cases—e.g., selection of a typical high school principal would eliminate women, persons too young or too old, single males.
Unique case	Choose the unusual or rare case of some dimension or event—e.g., the implementation of a new federal policy mandate.
Reputational case	Obtain the recommendation of knowledgeable experts for the best examples—e.g., principal nominates "competent" teachers or state officials identify "effective" schools.
Critical case	Identify the case that can illustrate some phenomenon dramatically—e.g., the "real test" case or the "ideal" case.
Concept/theory-based	Select by information-rich persons or situations known to experience the concept or to be attempting to implement the concept/theory—e.g., school implementing site-based management, teacher "burnout."
Combination of purposeful sampling strategies	Choose various sampling strategies as needed or desired for purposes, especially in large-scale studies and lengthy process studies.

manageable in size and so diverse that one does not want to lose possible variation. For example, a study of mainstreaming autistic children in one school division would probably require observation of all autistic children. Suppose a study of high school student interns in an external learning program had 35 different sites. Each work setting was so diverse—a hospital speech clinic, a community newspaper, a labor union, two legislative offices, an animal shelter, and others—that comprehensive selection would be necessary. Because groups are rarely sufficiently small and resources are seldom plentiful, researchers use other sampling strategies.

Maximum Variation Sampling

Maximum variation sampling, or **quota sampling,** is a strategy to illuminate different aspects of the research problem. For instance, a researcher may divide a population of elementary school teachers by number of years of service into three categories and select key informants in each category to investigate career development. This is *not* a representative sample because the qualitative researcher is merely using this strategy to describe in detail different meanings of teacher career development for individuals with different years of service. See Excerpt 6.3 for a combination of purposeful sampling strategies.

EXCERPT 6.3 Purposeful Sampling: Nomination and Maximum Variation

The participants in this study were parents of students who graduated from a medium-size Mid-western city school district's program for individuals with cognitive disabilities between 1989 and 1993. The sample included parents whose children attended three of the four high schools in the city and had mild, moderate and severe cognitive disabilities. Using *purposeful sampling,* . . . participants were selected to represent three schools, presence of socio-economic disadvantage, degree of severity of child's disability and the child's current school status. A sample frame . . . was developed with the assistance of special education administrators in the school district. Parents without phone numbers were eliminated from the sampling frame. Twenty-four names . . . were selected, contacted by the researchers, and asked to participate in the study. The number of participants was based on considerations of time and feasibility. Of the 24 families contacted, 19 agreed to participate. (p. 5)

Source: From Hanley-Maxwell, C., Whitney-Thomas, J., & Pogoloff, S. M. (1995). The second shock: A qualitative study of parents' perspectives and needs during their child's transition from school to adult life. *JASH: Journal of the Association for Persons with Severe Handicaps, 20*(1), 3–15.

Network Sampling

Network sampling, also called **snowball sampling,** is a strategy in which each successive participant or group is named by a preceding group or individual. Participant referrals are the basis for choosing a sample. The researcher develops a profile of the attributes or particular trait sought and asks each participant to suggest others who fit the profile or have the attribute. This strategy may be used in situations in which the individuals sought do not form a naturally bounded group but are scattered throughout populations. Network sampling is frequently used for in-depth interview studies, rather than participant observation research.

Sampling by Case Type

Other sampling strategies are used when a study requires an examination of a particular type of case. Remember, *case* refers to an in-depth analysis of a phenomenon and not the number of people sampled. Examples of sampling by case type are extreme-case, intensive-case, typical-case, unique-case, reputational-case, critical-case, and concept/theory-based sampling. Each of these sampling strategies is defined in Table 6.2. A researcher may choose combinations of case types as needed, especially in large-scale studies and lengthy process studies. (See Patton [2002] for additional case-type sampling.)

Purposeful sampling strategies employed in a study are identified from prior information and are reported in the study to enhance data quality. In addition, the persons or groups who actually participated in the study are reported in a manner to protect confidentiality of data. Historical and legal researchers specify the public archives and private collections used and frequently refer to each document or court case in explanatory footnotes. In this manner, researchers using noninteractive techniques to study the past reduce threats to design validity.

Sample Size

Qualitative inquirers view sampling processes as dynamic, ad hoc, and phasic rather than static or a priori parameters of populations. While there are statistical rules for probability sample size, there are only guidelines for purposeful sample size. Thus, purposeful samples can range from 1 to 40 or more. Typically, a qualitative sample seems small compared with the sample needed to generalize to a larger population.

The logic of the sample size is related to the purpose, the research problem, the major data collection strategy, and the availability of information-rich cases. The insights generated from qualitative inquiry depend more on the information richness of the cases and the analytical capabilities of the researcher than on the sample size.

The following are guidelines for determining sample size:

1. ***Purpose of the study*** A case study that is descriptive/exploratory may not need as many persons as a self-contained study that is description/explanatory. Further, a phenomenological study usually has fewer informants than are needed in grounded theory to generate dense concepts.
2. ***Focus of the study*** A process-focused study at one site may have fewer participants than an interview study using network sampling.
3. ***Primary data collection strategy*** Qualitative researchers are guided by circumstances. For instance, a study may have a small sample size, but the researcher may be continually returning to the same situation or the same informants, seeking confirmation. The number of days in the field is usually reported.
4. ***Availability of informants*** Some informants are rare and difficult to locate; others are relatively easy to identify and locate.
5. ***Redundancy of data*** Would adding more individuals or returning to the field yield any new insights?
6. ***Researchers submit the obtained sample size to peer review*** Most qualitative researchers propose a *minimum* sample size and then continue to add to the sample as the study progresses.

ALERT! There are no easy rules for determining sample size. It depends on what you want to know, the purpose of the inquiry, what is at stake, what will be credible, and the available time and resources.

PHASES OF DATA COLLECTION AND ANALYSIS STRATEGIES

The qualitative phases of data collection and analyses are interwoven and occur in overlapping cycles. They are not called *procedures* but *strategies*—that is, techniques that depend on each prior strategy and the resulting data. Figure 6.1 illustrates the five research phases: planning (Phase 1), data collection (Phases 2, 3, 4), and completion (Phase 5). Each phase will be discussed in this section.

Phase 1: Planning Analyzing the problem statement and the initial research questions will suggest the type of setting or interviewees that would logically be informative. In Phase 1, the researcher locates and gains permission to use the site or network of persons.

ALERT! Obtaining permission may take considerable time if you are a complete stranger to the site or the participants, unless someone can vouch for you.

Phase 2: Beginning Data Collection This phase includes the first days in the field, in which the researcher establishes rapport, trust, and reciprocal relations with the individuals and groups to be observed (Wax, 1971). Researchers obtain data primarily to become oriented and to gain a sense of the totality for purposeful sampling. Researchers also adjust their interviewing and recording procedures to the site or persons involved.

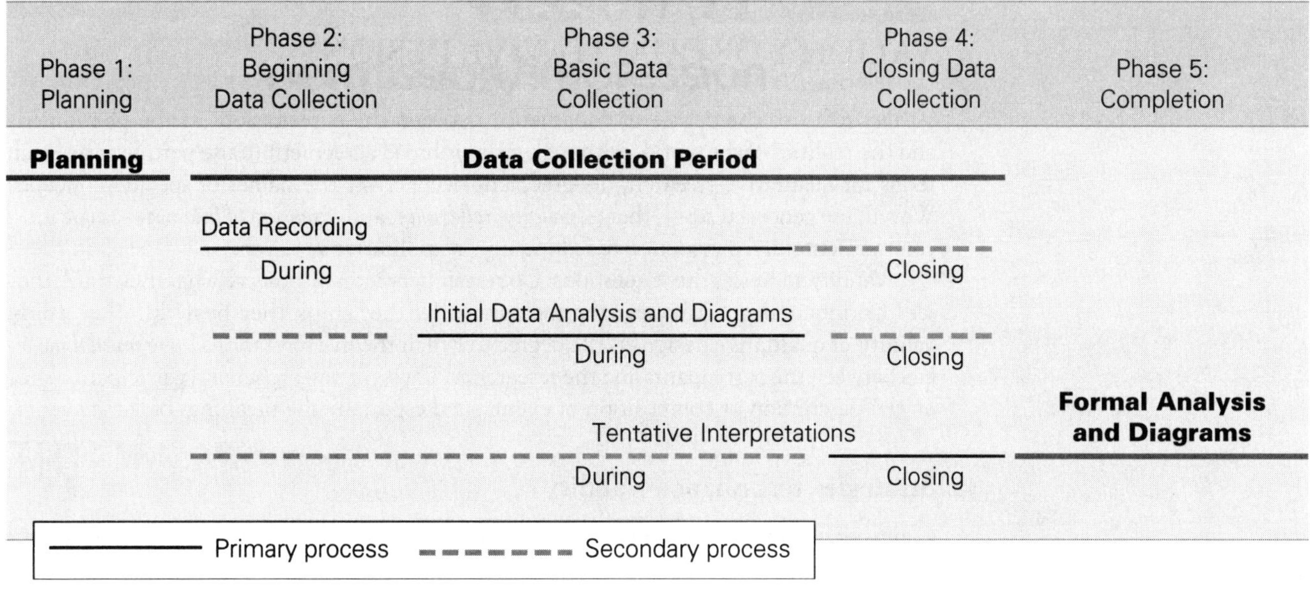

FIGURE 6.1 **Phases of Qualitative Research**

Phase 3: Basic Data Collection The inquirer begins to *hear* and *see* what is occurring, which goes beyond just *listening* and *looking*. Choices of data collection strategies and informants continue to be made. Tentative data analysis begins as the researcher mentally processes ideas and facts while collecting data. Initial descriptions are summarized and identified for later corroboration.

Phase 4: Closing Data Collection The researcher "leaves the field," or conducts the last interview. Ending data collection is related to the research problem and the richness of the collected data. More attention is given to possible interpretations and verifications of the emergent findings with key informants, remaining interviews, and documents. The field may yield more data but *not* yield more insights relevant to the research problem (see Excerpt 6.4).

Phase 5: Completion Completion of active data collecting blends into formal data analysis and construction of meaningful ways to present the data. Integrative diagrams, time charts, frequency lists, process figures, and other graphics can synthesize a sense of the relationship of the parts to the whole. Data analysis and diagrams are essential for interpretations.

EXCERPT 6.4 When to Stop Collecting Data

Eventually, three categories reached theoretical saturation, a point at which, according to Strauss (1987), "additional analysis no longer contributes to discovering anything new about a category" (p. 21). The categories were the roles of religion, poverty, and ethnicity in relationship to second language learning. (p. 130)

Source: From Case, R. (2004). Forging ahead into new social networks and looking back to past social identities: A case study of a foreign-born English as a Second Language teacher in the United States. *Urban Education, 39*(2), 125–148.

VALIDITY OF QUALITATIVE DESIGNS

Validity refers to the degree of congruence between the explanations of the phenomena and the realities of the world. Although there is broad agreement to use pertinent research terms for qualitative research, disagreement occurs over the names of specific concepts. We will use general terms—that is, *validity*, *reflexivity*, and *extension of findings*—as the most common criteria for evidence-based inquiry in qualitative research.

Validity addresses these questions: Do researchers actually observe what they think they see? Do inquirers actually hear the meanings that they think they hear? In other words, **validity of qualitative designs** is the degree to which the interpretations have *mutual meanings* between the participants and the researcher. Thus, the researcher and participants agree on the description or composition of events, and especially the meanings of these events.

Strategies to Enhance Validity

Claims of validity rest on data collection and analysis techniques. Qualitative researchers use a combination of any 10 possible strategies to enhance validity: prolonged field work, multimethod strategies, participant verbatim language, low-inference description, multiple researchers, mechanically recorded data, participant researcher, member checking, participant review, and negative data.

Qualitative researchers typically use as many strategies as possible to ensure design validity. Choosing from strategies involves issues of feasibility and ethics. Strategies are added as appropriate to maintain the least amount of intrusion while increasing the quality of the data (see Table 6.3).

ALERT! *Essential strategies* include prolonged field work, multimethods, verbatim accounts, low-inference descriptions, and negative case searches.

TABLE 6.3 Enhancing Design Validity: Data Collection Strategies to Increase Agreement on the Description by Researcher and Participants

Strategy	Description
Prolonged and persistent field work	Allows interim data analysis and corroboration to ensure match between findings and participant reality
Multimethod stragegies	Allows triangulation in data collection and data analysis
Participant language; verbatim accounts	Obtain literal statements of participants and quotations from documents
Low-inference descriptors	Record precise, almost literal, and detailed descriptions of people and situations
Multiple researchers	Agreement on descriptive data collected by a research team
Mechanically recorded data	Use of tape recorders, photographs, and videotapes
Participant researcher	Use of participant recorded perceptions in diaries or anecdotal records for corroboration
Member checking	Check informally with participants for accuracy during data collection; frequently done in participant observation studies
Participant review	Ask participant to review researcher's synthesis of interviews with person for accuracy of representation; frequently done in interview studies
Negative or discrepant data	Actively search for, record, analyze, and report negative or discrepant data that are an exception to patterns or that modify patterns found in data

Prolonged and Persistent Field Work Participant observation and in-depth interviews are conducted in natural settings to reflect lived experience. The lengthy data collection period provides opportunities for interim data analyses, preliminary comparisons, and corroboration to refine ideas and to ensure the match between evidence-based categories and participant reality.

Multimethod Strategies Most qualitative researchers employ several data collection techniques in a study but usually select one as the central method—either participant observation or in-depth interviews. To some extent, participant observation, open observation, interviewing, and documents are an interwoven web of techniques. How each of these strategies is used varies with the study. Multimethod strategies permits *triangulation* of data across inquiry techniques. Different strategies may yield different insights about the topic of interest and increase the credibility of findings. In its broad sense, *triangulation* also can refer to use of multiple researchers, multiple theories, or perspectives to interpret the data; multiple data sources to corroborate data, and multiple disciplines to broaden one's understanding of the method and the phenomenon of interest (Janesick, 1998). For an example of selecting strategies to enhance design validity, see Excerpt 6.5.

Participant Language and Verbatim Accounts Interviews are phrased in the informant's language, not in abstract social science terms. Researchers are also sensitive to *cultural translators*—that is, informants who translate their words into social class terms. For example, when "tramps" were asked "Where is your home? What is your address?" they interpreted the question as referring to a middle-class residence and said "I have no home." However, an ethnographer found that men labeled as *homeless* by social scientists did, in fact, have "*flops*," which functioned for them as "homes" (Spradley, 1979).

ALERT! Recording verbatim accounts of conversations and transcripts is essential. Direct quotations from the data illustrate participants' meanings and thus ensure validity.

Low-Inference Descriptors Concrete, precise descriptions from field notes and interview elaborations are the hallmarks of qualitative research and the principal method for identifying patterns in the data. *Low inference* means that the descriptions are almost literal and that any important terms are those used and understood by the participants. Low-inference descriptions stand in contrast to the abstract language of a researcher.

EXCERPT 6.5 Enhancing Validity

The study employed an interpretive design (Erickson, 1986) that followed a hermeneutic cycle whereby what was learned was informed by what was already known, reading of the literature, experience in the field, and continuous data framing, analyses, and interpretations. A number of procedures, such as triangulation, were undertaken to ensure that the study had what Guba and Lincoln (1989) referred to as confirmability [validity]. Triangulation, involving the use of numerous data sources, maximized the probability that the emergent assertions were consistent with a variety of data. Because we were in the field for a prolonged time, the tendency of the participants in the study to exhibit contrived behaviors for the benefit of researchers was minimized. Furthermore, researchers were able to see whether given behaviors were typical or atypical. (pp. 227–228)

Source: From Tobin, K., & LaMaster, S. U. (1995). Relationships between metaphors, beliefs, and actions in a context of science curriculum change. *Journal of Research in Science Teaching, 32*(3), 225–242.

EXCERPT 6.6 Mechanically Recorded Data, Participant Researcher, and Member Checking

Data collection . . . occurred over a 10-month period by the first two authors and Millie, Jeffrey's mother. The procedures included semi-structured interviews and an audiojournal. The first two authors conducted five of the six . . . interviews with Millie, Bob, and Chris. Millie conducted the final interview with her husband, Bob. . . . Millie maintained a audiojournal where she recorded her feelings and perceptions of the support process and subsequent changes in Jeffrey's behavior and family functioning. . . . Establishing credibility occurred with member checks, . . . periodically offering Millie the opportunity to respond to the accuracy of the data and . . . coding. (p. 200)

Source: From Fox, L., Vaughn, B., Dunlap, G., & Bucy, M. (1997). Parent-professional partnership in behavioral support: A qualitative analysis of one family's experience. *JASH: Journal of the Association for Persons with Severe Handicaps, 22*(4), 198–207.

Multiple Researchers The use of multiple researchers is one method to enhance validity. The use of more than one researcher is handled in different ways: (1) extensive prior training and discussion during field work to reach agreement on meanings, (2) short-term observations for confirmation at different sites, and (3) more commonly, an arrangement by which each field observer is independently responsible for a research site and periodically meets with the team to share emerging ideas and strategies. Qualitative research based on a large group team approach, however, is infrequently done; most studies involve only two researchers as a team.

Mechanically Recorded Data Tape recorders, photographs, and videotapes provide accurate and relatively complete records. For the data to be usable, situational aspects that affected the data record are noted—for instance, failure of equipment, angles of videotaping, and effects of using technical equipment on the social scene (see Excerpt 6.6).

Participant Researcher Many researchers obtain the aid of an informant to corroborate what has been observed and recorded, interpretations of participant meanings, and explanations of overall processes. Participants may keep diaries or make anecdotal records to share with the researcher.

Member Checking Researchers who establish a field residence frequently confirm observations and participants' meanings with individuals through casual conversations in informal situations. Member checking can also be done within an interview as topics are rephrased and probed to obtain more complete and subtle meanings.

Participant Review Researchers who interview each person in depth or conduct a series of interviews with the same person may ask the person to review a transcript or synthesis of the data obtained from him or her. The participant is asked to modify any information from the interview data for accuracy. Then, the data obtained from each interviewee are analyzed for a comprehensive integration of findings.

Negative and/or Discrepant Data Researchers actively search for, record, analyze, and report negative cases or discrepant data. A *negative case* is a situation, a social scene, or a participant's view that contradicts the emerging pattern of meanings. *Discrepant data* present a variant to the emerging pattern. For example, a school ethnographer may find that faculty interact freely among themselves in six situations. No negative situations are found. Discrepant data, however, may suggest that faculty interactions are free in five situations and only semi-free in the sixth situation, depending on who is present.

REFLEXIVITY IN QUALITATIVE RESEARCH

Reflexivity is a broad concept that includes rigorous examination of one's personal and theoretical commitments to see how they serve as resources for selecting a qualitative approach, framing the research problem, generating particular data, relating to participants, and developing specific interpretations (Altheide & Johnson, 1998; Fine; 1998, Mason, 1996; Marcus, 1998; Schwandt, 2001; MacBeth, 2001). Further, all data are processed through and reconstructed in the researcher's mind as the report is written.

In other words, **reflexivity** is rigorous self-scrutiny by the researcher throughout the entire process. The researcher's very act of posing difficult questions to himself or herself assumes that he or she cannot be neutral, objective, or detached. Reflexivity is an important procedure for establishing credibility. Qualitative researchers thus do not deny human subjectivity, but rather take it into account through various strategies.

Interpersonal Subjectivity and Reflexivity

Qualitative research depends to a great extent on the interpersonal skills of the inquirer, such as building trust, keeping good relations, being nonjudgmental, and respecting the norms of the situation. Researchers use all their personal experiences and abilities of engagement, balancing the analytical and creative through empathetic understanding and profound respect for participants' perspectives. Interpersonal emotions in field work are essential in data collection activities because of the face-to-face interaction. Feelings serve several useful functions throughout the research process (Kleinman & Copp, 1993).

The progress of the study often depends primarily on the relationship the researcher builds with the participants. The interactive process is relatively personal; no two investigators observe, interview, or relate to others in exactly the same way. These issues are handled primarily within the actual study to enhance reflexivity.

Data obtained from informants are valid even though they may represent particular views or have been influenced by the researcher's presence. Such data are problematic only if they are claimed to be representative beyond the context. Potential researcher bias can be minimized if the researcher spends enough time in the field and employs multiple data collection strategies to corroborate the findings. Providing sufficient details about the design, including reflexivity strategies, is necessary.

What exactly is *reflexivity*? Pillow (2003) suggests these four validated strategies of reflexivity:

1. Reflexivity as recognition of self—personal self-awareness
2. Reflexivity as recognition of the other—capturing the essence of the informant, or "let them speak for themselves"
3. Reflexivity as truth gathering—the researcher's insistence on getting it right or being accurate
4. Reflexivity as transcendence—the aim that the researcher, through transcending her own subjectivity and cultural context, can be released from the weight of (mis)representation for accuracy in reporting

Reflexivity also involves discomfort, as researchers seek to minimize predispositions through self-questioning. Patton (2002) suggests this questioning focus on several screens that the researcher uses for self, audience, and participants (see Figure 6.2).

Some critical studies may require the use of additional strategies. Critical researchers are wary that their empirical work will be viewed as an ideological discourse and fearful of duplication of social, racial, ethnic, and gender biases in their studies. For example, one difficult question relates to *voice:* Were all the voices allowed to emerge, especially those of the socially silenced, whose perspectives are often counter to the situation?

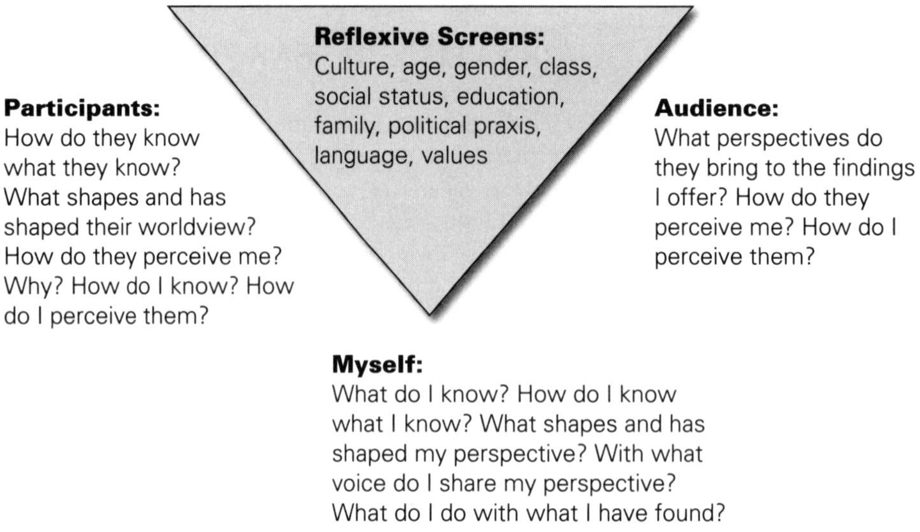

Reflexive Screens:
Culture, age, gender, class, social status, education, family, political praxis, language, values

Participants:
How do they know what they know? What shapes and has shaped their worldview? How do they perceive me? Why? How do I know? How do I perceive them?

Audience:
What perspectives do they bring to the findings I offer? How do they perceive me? How do I perceive them?

Myself:
What do I know? How do I know what I know? What shapes and has shaped my perspective? With what voice do I share my perspective? What do I do with what I have found?

FIGURE 6.2 **Reflexive Questions**

Adapted from M. Q. Patton. (2002). *Qualitative research and evaluation methods,* 3rd ed. Thousand Oaks, CA: Sage (p. 66).

Another reflex strategy is **positionality,** which assumes that only texts in which researchers display their own positions (standpoints) and contextual grounds for reasoning can be considered good research (Lincoln, 1995; Lather, 1991; J. K. Smith, 1993). Critical researchers often write in the introduction their individual social, cultural, historical, racial, and sexual location in the study (see Excerpt 6.7). However, positionality statements can be only a gesture.

In participatory research, the inquirer writes into the data his or her own actions. The complicated dual role of researcher and participant requires scrutiny of both the role and the resulting data. This is not an easy task nor should it be taken lightly.

Strategies to Enhance Reflexivity

Qualitative researchers combine any of seven possible strategies to monitor and evaluate the impact of their subjectivity (see Table 6.4). The most important strategies are keeping a field log and a field (reflex) journal and documenting for audibility. Other strategies are added as needed to obtain valid data.

Peer Debriefer A *peer debriefer* is a disinterested colleague who discusses the researcher's preliminary analysis and next strategies. Such a discussion makes more

EXCERPT 6.7 The Researcher's Stance

My status as a White, European American, male college professor would play an important role as a researcher in Mr. Wilson's class. . . . I hoped to break down the hegemonic relationships that form when a White, European American male college professor enters the classroom of a Black, African American male teacher. I began keeping a reflexive journal before I started the study in which I recorded my reactions to readings I had completed on the experience of Muslims and Africans in United States. This was the first step. (p. 131)

Source: From Case, R. (2004). Forging ahead into new social networks and looking back to past social identities: A case study of a foreign-born English as a Second Language teacher in the United States. *Urban Education, 39*(2), 125–148.

TABLE 6.4 Strategies to Enhance Reflexivity: Strategies to Monitor and Evaluate Researcher Subjectivity and Perspective

Strategy	Description
Peer debriefer	Select a colleague who facilitates the logical analysis of data and interpretation; frequently done when the topic is emotionally charged or the researcher experiences conflicting values in data collection
Field log	Maintain a log of dates, time, places, persons, and activities to obtain access to informants and for each datum set collected
Field (reflex) journal	Record the decisions made during the emerging design and the rationale; include judgments of data validity
Ethical considerations recorded	Record the ethical dilemmas, decisions, and actions in field journal, and self-reflections
Audibility	Record data management techniques, codes, categories, and decision-rules as a "decision trail"
Formal corroboration of initial findings	Conduct formal confirmation activities such as a survey, focus groups, or interviews
Critical reflexivity	Self-critique by asking difficult questions; positionality

explicit the tacit knowledge that the inquirer has acquired. The peer debriefer also poses searching questions to help the researcher understand his or her own posture and its role in the inquiry. In addition, this dialogue may reduce the stress that normally accompanies field work.

Field Log A *field log* documents the persistent field work and provides a chronological record by date and time spent in the field, including getting access to sites and participants. The field log also contains, for each entry, the places and person involved.

Reflex Journal A *reflex journal* is a continuous record of the decisions made during the emergent design and rationale. This allows for justification, based on the available information at the time, of the modifications of the research problem and strategies. The reflex journal also contains assessments of the trustworthiness of each data set. A reflex journal traces the researcher's ideas and personal reactions throughout the field work.

Ethical Considerations Recorded Researchers make strategy choices in the field, some of which are based primarily on ethical considerations. A record of ethical concerns helps to justify choices in data collection and analysis.

Audibility **Audibility** is the practice of maintaining a record of data management techniques and decision rules that document the chain of evidence or decision trail. That record includes the codes, categories, and themes used in description and interpretation as well as drafts and preliminary diagrams. Thus, the chain of evidence will be available for inspection and confirmation by outside reviewers.

Audibility criteria can be met with or without an outside reviewer—that is, an *auditor* who submits a reviewer's appraisal. An alternative is to place a list of files, codes, categories, and decision rules in an appendix for readers' perusal.

ALERT! An auditor must be knowledgeable about *both* the methodology and the topic.

Formal Corroboration of Initial Findings Surveys, focus groups, and in-depth interviews with those not selected originally may be used for formal confirmation, especially when the findings depend on a few informants. As a corroboration activity, the data must be completely analyzed first. Confirmation activities ensure that the patterns found have not been unduly contaminated by the researcher.

EXTENSION OF QUALITATIVE FINDINGS

Qualitative researchers provide for the logical **extension of findings,** which enables others to understand similar situations and apply the findings in subsequent research or practical situations. Knowledge is produced by the preponderance of evidence found in separate case studies over time.

Authenticity is the faithful reconstruction of participants' perceptions. In other words, readers can relate to or connect with informants and situations. Some studies, such as grounded theory, cite the theoretical frameworks for other researchers. Other studies are more contextual for practical implications. A study that is idiosyncratic and has a minimum of design description has limited usefulness for future inquiry.

Design Components to Generate Extension of Findings

Ten design components can affect logical extensions; those actually employed should be described. The components are research role, informant selection, social context, data collection strategies, data analysis strategies, authentic narrative, typicality, analytical premises, alternative explanations, and other criteria associated with a particular research purpose (see Table 6.5).

Research Role The importance of the inquirer's social relationship with the participants neccessitates a description of his or her role and status within the group or site. The preferred research role is that of a person who is unknown at the site—in other words, an *outsider*. Researchers often cite personal or professional experiences that enable them to empathize with the participants—that is, they recognize more readily the observed processes and subtle participant meanings than those who lack such experiences. Participatory research requires planning the dual role of participant and researcher, which usually limits extension of the findings.

Informant Selection The rationale and decision-making process for choosing the participants is described. Future studies will require researchers to contact individuals similar to those used in the prior study. If a particular person is not cooperative or not available, researchers will search for other informants until a pattern emerges. Increasing the number of sites or persons does not aid in extension of findings; the criterion is information-rich individuals or social scenes (see Excerpt 6.8).

Social Context The social context influences data content and is described physically, socially, interpersonally, and functionally. Physical descriptions of the people, the time, and the place of the events or the interviews all assist in data analysis. The purpose of group meetings, such as inservice training or official business, requires other researchers to find similar social contexts for further study.

TABLE 6.5 Design Components to Generate Extension of Findings

Strategy	Adequate Description in the Study
Research role	The social relationship of the researcher with the participants
Informant selection	Criteria, rationale, and decision process used in purposeful sampling
Social context	The physical, social, interpersonal, and functional social scenes of data collection
Data collection strategies	The multimethods employed, including participant observation, interview, documents, and others
Data analysis strategies	Data analysis process described
Authentic narrative	Thick description presented as an analytical narrative
Typicality	Distinct characteristics of groups and/or sites presented
Analytical premises	The initial theoretical or political framework that informs the study
Alternative explanations	Retrospective delineation of all plausible or rival explanations for interpretations
Other criteria by research approach (after study completed)	
Ethnography	Comprehensive explanation of complexity of group life
Phenomenology	Understand the essence of lived experience; generates more research questions
Case study	Understand the practice; facilitates informed decision making
Grounded theory	Concepts or propositions relate to social science; generates verification research with more structured designs
Critical traditions	Informs or empowers participants about their situation and opportunities; generates further research; action stimulus

EXCERPT 6.8 Informant Selection

Participants: Richness of professional background and willingness to participate in a series of personal in-depth interviews were the primary considerations in identifying participants for the study. . . . A male superintendent, who had supervised two women principals at different times and in different districts, suggested their names to the first author. A family friend of the first author suggested a third choice. . . . This study included 3 participants, all African American women who had been principals in urban school settings. (p. 149)

Source: From Bloom, C., & Erlandson, D. (2003). African American women principals in urban schools: Realities, (re)constructions, and resolutions. *Educational Administration Quarterly, 39*(3), 339–369.

Data Collection Strategies Using the study for future inquiry will be impossible without precise descriptions of data collection techniques: the varieties of observational and interviewing methods and data recording techniques used. How different strategies were employed is noted, as well. For example, if the primary interest was observing a group process, then individual interviews and documents would be corroborative data collection strategies.

Data Analysis Strategies Simply asserting that data analysis was done carefully or citing that a certain software program was used is insufficient. The researcher must provide retrospective accounts of how data were synthesized and identify the general analytical strategies used. Frequently, the categories used in data analysis and their decision rules are listed in an appendix.

Authentic Narrative Most qualitative studies contain thick description in the narrative, interspersed with brief quotations representing participants' language. A good narrative is one that may be read and lived vicariously by others. A narrative is authentic when readers connect to the story by recognizing particulars, by visioning the scenes, and by reconstructing them from remembered associations with similar events (Connelly & Clandinin, 1990). It is the particular, not the abstract, that triggers emotions and moves people. Stories stand between the abstract and the particular by mediating the basic demands of research along with the personal aspects.

Typicality Another design component is the extent of **typicality** of the phenomenon (Wolcott, 1973)—that is, the degree to which it may be compared or contrasted along relevant dimensions with other phenomena. Qualitative researchers' virtual obsession with describing the distinct characteristics of groups studied is, in fact, an appreciation of the importance of this information for extension of findings. The attributes of groups and sites can include socioeconomic status, educational attainment, age range, racial or ethnic composition, time period, and contextual features of the location. Unique historical experiences of groups and cultures may limit extension, but few groups' experiences are totally ethnocentric (see Excerpt 6.9). Once typicality has been established, a basis for extension will be evident and can be used to provide insights across time frames and situations.

Analytical Premises The choice of conceptual framework made by one researcher for a given study will necessitate other researchers to begin from similar analytical premises (see Excerpt 6.10). Because one major outcome of qualitative research is the generation and

EXCERPT 6.9 Typicality of Site and Persons Related to the Research Problem

To explore the authenticity dilemma confronting Asian ethnics, . . . ninety-five third, fourth, and fifth generation Chinese and Japanese ethnics living in northern and southern California [have been interviewed.] . . . All the participants are well-educated and from urban areas; many are white collar professionals. . . . Those who are not included are housewives, small business owners, students and a few artists. The youngest participants were in their early 20s while the oldest were into their 70s. . . .

The fact that this study was conducted in California is of special significance. . . . California has remained the state with the largest concentration of Asian-Americans. . . . Whether their numbers and long history have promoted greater social acceptance or the reverse—greater hostility—is not at all clear [even though] . . . they are well integrated into its social fabric. . . . In addition, the general climate towards immigrants, both legal and illegal, is decidedly less hospitable today. (pp. 106–107)

Source: From Tuan, M. (1999). Neither real Americans nor real Asians? Multigeneration Asian ethnics navigating the terrain of authenticity. *Qualitative Sociology, 22*(2), 105–125.

EXCERPT 6.10 Analytical Premises and Prior Research

Not surprisingly, then, the girls whose families were *not* like the television families thought the television families were more unrealistic. Following McRobbie's (1991) culturalist approach, the girls were interpreting and assessing media based on their own lived experiences. Greenberg and Reeves (1996) also find that children's personal experiences affect their perceptions of reality on television. Children in general do not have multiple reference points regarding family life, so the girls in this study saw any family as deviating from those they know as unrealistic. This data also empirically supports Greenberg and Reeves's prediction that television content is perceived as more like real life if the child's attitudes and behaviors, or in this case, family dynamics, are consistent with the television content. (pp. 398–399)

Source: From Fingerson, L. (1999). Active viewing: Girls' interpretations of family television programs. *Journal of Contemporary Ethnography, 28*(4), 389–418.

refinement of concepts, inquirers contrast their findings to those of prior research. When discrepancies are presented, researchers cite the attributes of the group, time period, and settings. This alerts other researchers when they use these same findings. Much qualitative research, however, is nontheoretical.

Alternative Explanations During data analysis, qualitative researchers search for negative evidence and discrepant data to challenge or modify emerging patterns. Negative and discrepant data are useful for identifying alternative explanations. Observers and interviewers actively search for informants and social scenes that appear to vary from or disagree with prior data. A major pattern becomes an explanation only when alternative patterns do not offer reasonable explanations related to the research problem. Major and alternative explanations are discussed in the study because both might generate further research.

Other Criteria by Research Approach (After Study Completed) In addition to providing adequate descriptions of the general components mentioned, specific qualitative approaches may emphasize additional criteria. For example, phenomenology, grounded theory, and critical studies have slightly different effects on research communities, readers, and participants. An *ethnography* provides a comprehensive understanding of the complexity of group life, which leads to further case studies. A *phenomenological study* increases the understanding of lived experiences by readers and others. A *case study* promotes better understanding of a practice or issue and facilitates informed decision making. A *grounded theory study*, however, usually leads to more structured designs to test a concept or to verify a proposition. Some forms of critical traditions not only inform through historical revisionism but also empower and stimulate action. Thus, the researcher frequently has a meeting with the major informants or all participants, reviews the findings, and initiates a dialogue. The researchers also may provide additional resource information to foster personal and group empowerment.

When qualitative researchers appropriately address the issues of design validity, reflexivity, and extension of findings, as noted previously, their work is regarded as credible by other qualitative investigators. Many design issues are handled by planning and conducting studies based on the appropriate criteria for evidence-based research.

RESEARCH ETHICS: ROLES AND RECIPROCITY

Qualitative research is more likely to be personally intrusive than quantitative research. Thus, ethical guidelines include policies regarding informed consent, deception, confidentiality, anonymity, privacy, and caring. Field workers, however, must adopt these principles in complex situations.

Ethical Dilemmas in Fieldwork

A credible research design involves not only selecting informants and effective research strategies but also adhering to research ethics. Qualitative researchers need to plan how they will handle the ethical dilemmas in interactive data collection. Some qualitative researchers, for example, have collected data after gaining the confidence of persons potentially involved in illegal activities. Other researchers have investigated controversial and politically sensitive topics. When researchers study, say, drugs on campus, lesbian and gay youth, and violence in schools or families, profound ethical dilemmas arise.

Researchers may also be drawn unexpectedly into morally problematic situations. Some typical questions that a qualitative inquirer may face are Do I observe this abuse, or do I turn away from it? Do I record this confession, and if I do record it, do I put it in a public report? If I see abuse or neglect, do I report it to the officials? Am I really seeing abuse or projecting my own values into the situation? If I promised confidentiality when I entered the field, am I breaking my bargain if I interfere? These questions suggest that it is difficult to separate research ethics from professional ethics and personal morality.

Most qualitative researchers devise roles that elicit cooperation, trust, openness, and acceptance. Sometimes, researchers assume helping roles, dress in a certain manner, or allow themselves to be manipulated. When people adjust their priorities and routines to help a researcher or even tolerate his or her presence, they are giving of themselves. A researcher is indebted to these persons and should devise ways to reciprocate, within the constraints of research and personal ethics. Some researchers prefer to collaborate with their informants and share authorship. Reciprocity can be the giving of time, feedback, attention, appropriate token gifts, or specialized services. Some inquirers, upon completion of the report, become advocates for a particular group in the larger community, including policy-making groups.

Research Ethics in Fieldwork

Most qualitative researchers use discussion and negotiation to resolve ethical dilemmas in fieldwork. Negotiations revolve around obtaining consensus on situational priorities.

Informed Consent as a Dialogue In gaining permission, most researchers give participants assurances of confidentiality and anonymity and describe the intended use of the data. Institutional review boards (IRBs) require a protocol for informed consent to be signed by each participant. As Malone (2003) demonstrates, the typical protocol is usually not accurate for most qualitative research because one cannot anticipate what will be intrusive for each participant.[4]

Many researchers (L. M. Smith, 1990) view informed consent as a dialogue with each new participant. However, in some situations, such a dialogue is impossible—for instance, in a sudden and unexpected trauma that brings persons to the scene during the observation or the observation of public behavior in a crowd. Usually, the time required for participation and the noninterfering, nonjudgmental research role is explained. Informants select interview times and places. Because researchers need to establish trusting relationships, they plan how to handle the dialogue. Most participants can detect and reject insincerity and manipulation.

Confidentiality and Anonymity The settings and participants should not be identifiable in print. Thus, locations and features of settings are typically disguised to appear similar to several possible places, and researchers routinely code names of people and places (see Excerpt 6.11). Officials and participants should review a report before it is finally released. Researchers have a dual responsibility: to protect the individuals' confidences from other persons in the setting and to protect the informants from the general reading public.

However, the law does *not* protect researchers if the government compels them to disclose matters of confidence. The report, the field notes, and the researcher can all be subpoenaed. For example, one researcher was asked to be an expert witness in a school desegregation case. The researcher initiated the "ethical principle of dialogue" (L. M. Smith, 1990, p. 271) in presenting the dilemma to several school officials for mutual problem solving. Finally, a top official said the lawyer would not call the researcher as a witness because it violated the confidentiality commitments. Spradley (1979) suggests that one should consider an alternative project if protecting informants is not possible.

Privacy and Empowerment Deception violates informed consent and privacy. Although some well-known ethnographers have posed as hobos, vagrants, and even army recruits (Punch, 1994), they claim that no harm to informants resulted from their research. However, even informed persons who cooperate may feel a sense of betrayal upon reading the research findings in print.

Field workers negotiate with participants so that they understand the power that they have in the research process. This power and the mutual problem solving that results from it may be an exchange for the privacy lost by participating in a study (Lincoln, 1990).

Feminist researchers may focus on communitarian ethics, rather than the normal research ethics (Denzin, 1997). The mission of social science is to enable community life to transform itself. From this perspective, qualitative research is "authentically sufficient when it fulfills three conditions: represents multiple voices, enhances moral discernment, and promotes social transformation" (Christians, 2000, p. 145). These inquirers focus more on general morality rather than on professional ethics per se.

Caring and Fairness Although physical harm to informants seldom occurs in qualitative research, some persons may experience humiliation and loss of trust. Justifying the possible harm to one individual because it may help others is unacceptable. A sense of caring and fairness must be part of the researcher's thinking, actions, and personal morality.

Many inquirers argue for *committed relativism* or *reasonableness* in particular situations. Open discussions and negotiation usually promote fairness to the participants and to the research inquiry.

EXCERPT 6.11 Anonymity of School and Persons

Most of the data . . . were collected . . . in several urban communities in San Diego . . . and in one urban high school. . . . We refer to this school by the pseudonym, Auxilio High School. The names of all the participants are also pseudonyms. (p. 235)

Source: From Stanton-Salazar, R. D., & Spina, S. U. (2003). Informal mentors and role models in the lives of urban Mexican-origin adolescents. *Anthropology and Education Quarterly, 34*(3), 231–254.

STANDARDS OF ADEQUACY

Qualitative designs are judged by several criteria. Following are the questions readers typically ask about a qualitative design before accepting the study as evidence-based inquiry:

1. Is the one phenomenon investigated clearly articulated and delimited?
2. Are the qualitative approach (i.e., ethnographic, grounded theory, critical) and the purpose of the study stated?
3. Are the research questions focused and phrased to discover and describe the how's and why's of the phenomenon?
4. Which purposeful sampling technique(s) were selected to obtain information-rich informants or sites? Are the informants described and is the type of site obtained identified? If potentially useful groups were not selected, is a rationale presented?
5. Did the sample size seem logical, given the research purpose, time, and resources?
6. Is the design presented in sufficient detail to enhance validity? That is, does it specify essential strategies such as prolonged field work, collection of verbatim accounts with descriptive data, and negative case search? If the design was modified during data collection, is justification presented for the change?
7. Which multimethod data collection strategies were employed to ensure agreement between the researcher and informants? Did the researcher have knowledge and experience with the primary strategy used? How were different data collection strategies employed?
8. If multiple researchers or participant researchers collected data, how were issues of data quality handled?
9. Which strategies did the researcher employ to enhance reflexivity? Did these seem appropriate to the study?
10. Which design components were included to encourage the usefulness and the logical extensions of the findings? Could others have been incorporated into the study? If so, which ones?
11. Does the researcher specify how informed consent, confidentiality, and anonymity were handled? Was any form of reciprocity employed? If any design decisions were made due to ethical considerations, is the justification reasonable?

SUMMARY

The following statements summarize the major aspects of qualitative research design:

1. Qualitative researchers study participants' perspectives—feelings, thoughts, beliefs, ideals—and actions in natural situations.
2. Qualitative researchers use interactive strategies to collect data for exploratory, explanatory, and emancipatory studies.
3. Qualitative researchers employ emergent designs.
4. A case study design focuses on one phenomenon to understand in depth, regardless of the number of persons or sites in the study.
5. Case studies are significant for theory, practice, policy, and social action stimulus.
6. Purposeful sampling is selecting small samples of information-rich cases to study in depth without desiring to generalize to all such cases.
7. Types of purposeful sampling include site selection, comprehensive sampling, maximum variation sampling, network sampling, and sampling by case type.
8. Sample size depends on the purpose of the study, the data collection strategies, and the availability of information-rich cases.
9. Data collection and analysis are interactive and occur in overlapping cycles.
10. The use of research strategies rather than procedures allows for flexibility to study and corroborate each new idea as it occurs in data collection.

11. The five phases of qualitative research are planning, beginning data collection, basic data collection, closing data collection, and formal data analysis and diagrams.
12. The validity of a qualitative design is the degree to which the interpretations and concepts have mutual meanings between the participants and researcher.
13. Qualitative researchers enhance validity by making explicit all aspects of their designs.
14. Data collection strategies to increase validity are a combination of the following strategies: prolonged field work, multimethod, verbatim accounts, low-inference descriptors, multiple researchers, mechanically recorded data, participant researcher, member checking, participant review, and negative case reporting.
15. Qualitative researchers employ interpersonal subjectivity to collect data and reflex strategies or evidence-based inquiry.
16. Qualitative studies aim at extension of findings, rather than generalization of results. Generalizability is usually not the intent of the study.
17. Design components that enhance the extension of findings are specification of the researcher role, informant selection, the social context, data collection and analysis strategies, authentic narrative, typicality, analytical premises, and alternative explanations.
18. Field researchers employ dialogue and reciprocity while following ethical and legal principles with participants.

CHECK YOURSELF

Multiple-choice review items, with answers, are available on the Companion Website for this book:

www.ablongman.com/mcmillanschumacher6e.

APPLICATION PROBLEMS

1. The director of an inner-city preschool program wants to obtain parent perspectives of the program. She is especially interested in this year's innovation in one class: a parent education program. Materials are sent home twice a week for a parent or guardian to work with the child, and records of teacher/parent contacts are made. There are twelve children in the preschool class. Four children live with a single parent, six live with both parents, and two children live with one parent and their grandparents.
   a. What type of sampling is appropriate and why? (probability or purposeful)
   b. How should the sampling be done?
   c. Which qualitative strategies would be appropriate?
2. A researcher is interested in how principals make decisions about retention of elementary schoolchildren. How would you design this study?
3. A researcher wants to understand the concept of site-based school management. He has located a school district that has spent one year in planning and writing guidelines for site-based management at six selected schools. The researcher is primarily interested in how a site-based management team operates and whether this affects the role of the principal and the school's relationship to the district central management. A site-based management team consists of six members from the community and three teachers plus the principal as an ad hoc member. A central office facilitator frequently attends the monthly meetings after conducting six orientation sessions. How would you design the study?
   a. Which type of sampling is appropriate and why? (probability or purposeful)
   b. How should the sampling be done?
   c. Which qualitative methods would be appropriate?
4. For Problem 1 above, which research strategies could increase design validity, enhance reflexivity, and encourage extension of findings?
5. For Problem 3 above, which research strategies could enhance design validity, enhance reflexivity, and foster extension of findings?

NOTES

1. *Case study design* does not refer to a *case study*—that is, a study that may employ both qualitative and quantitative researcher techniques without comparison groups and not an in-depth study.
2. See Bogdan and Biklen (2003), Giesne and Pushkin (1992), Marshall and Rossman (1999), Strauss and Corbin (1999), Stake (1995), Le Compte and Preissle (1993), and Lincoln and Guba (1985).
3. Bogan and Biklen (2003) call an examination of subunits a *multicase study*. A multicase study is *not* a multisite study, which uses a modified analytical induction approach, frequently with multiple researchers.
4. Malone (2003) rewrote an informed consent letter to represent what actually occurred in interviews from her study and concluded that no one would have signed the revised version.

PART

IV

EMERGING METHODS OF RESEARCH

The methodologies of educational research are constantly evolving and changing. As we have already noted, qualitative designs became much more popular over the last 25 years, and experimental designs are making a comeback in popularity. In the past decade, three additional trends have emerged, and this part provides an introduction to each. The first and perhaps most significant trend is the use of mixed-method designs, which are studies that combine quantitative and qualitative features. The second trend, which is just under way among all researchers, is the use of secondary data analysis. (Some researchers have used secondary data analysis for many years.) This kind of study, which depends on being able to obtain electronic databases, uses data that have already been collected and analyzes them in new and different ways. Finally, conducting action research is becoming standard practice in some schools of education and local school districts, as teachers and administrators focus on researching local problems and questions.

Chapter 7 summarizes the essential characteristics of each of these emerging methods and provides examples from the literature. We hope this introduction will generate interest and further reading.

CHAPTER

7 Mixed-Method Designs, Secondary Data Analysis, and Action Research

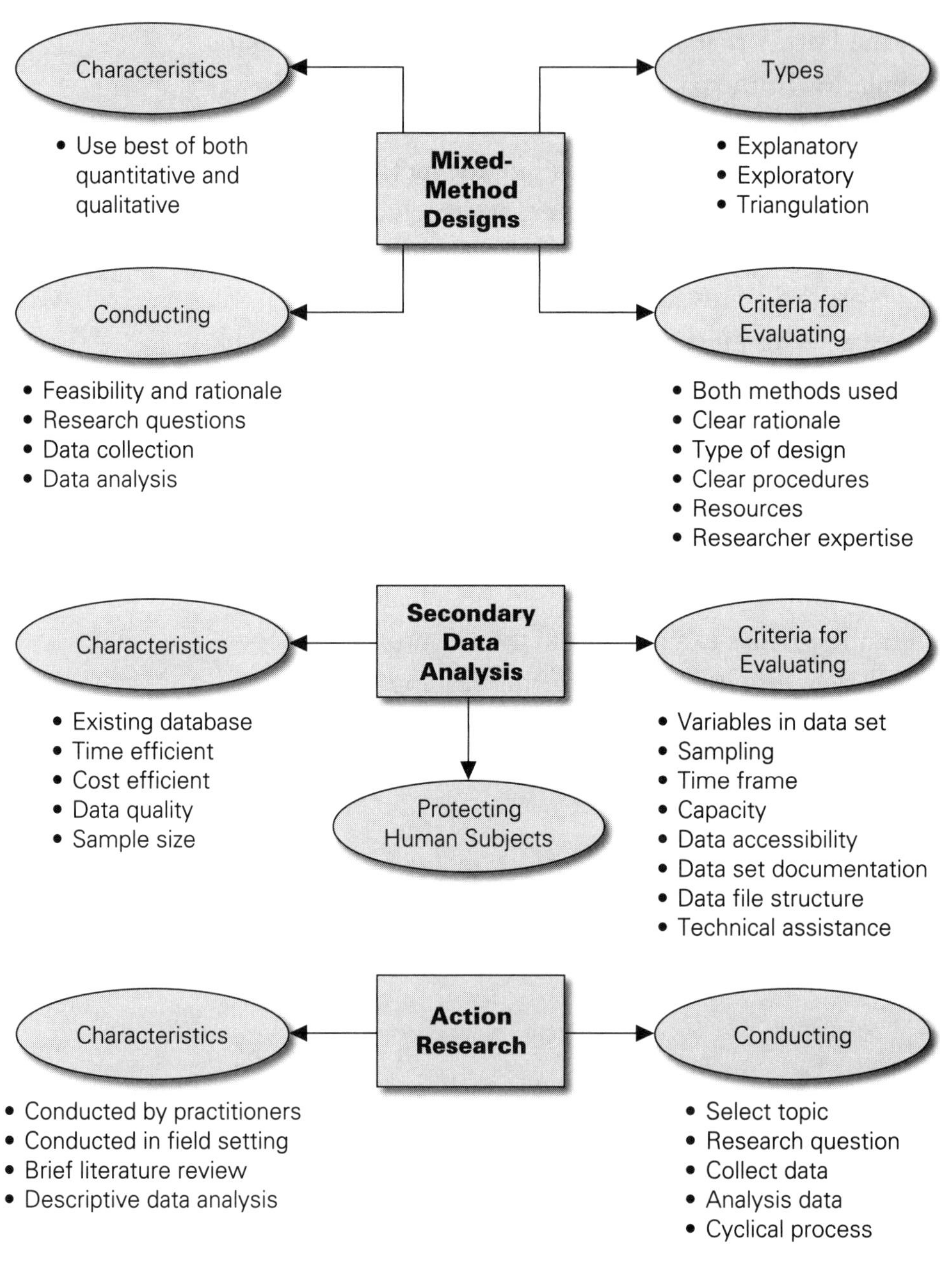

KEY TERMS

mixed-method designs
explanatory design
exploratory design
triangulation design
secondary data
secondary data analysis
action research

This chapter introduces three approaches to educational research that have become increasingly common in the last 10 years: mixed-method designs, secondary data analysis, and action research. These designs are helpful for integrating qualitative and quantitative methods, for using existing databases, and for helping practitioners conduct research in school settings.

MIXED-METHOD DESIGNS

by Angela L. Snyder

The development and use of **mixed-method designs** (also called *mixed-mode*) have increased in recent years as researchers have realized that often the best approach to answering research questions is to use both quantitative and qualitative methods in the same study. For example, consider investigating whether there is a relationship between high-stakes testing and dropout rate when successful achievement is needed for graduation. On the surface, this question lends itself nicely to a nonexperimental, quantitative study, in which characteristics of students, including their scores on graduation tests, can be entered into a regression model to determine if performance on the tests predicts dropping out once other variables have been controlled. On a deeper level, it would also be helpful to understand *why* students did not perform better on the tests and how having graduation tests affects students' motivation. These issues could be studied most effectively using interviews with students, teachers, and parents. By combining quantitative data with qualitative data, a more complete understanding of the relationship between high-stakes testing and dropping out can be developed.

There are both advantages and disadvantages to using a mixed-method design. On the positive side, using both approaches allows the researcher to incorporate the strengths of each method. This provides for a more comprehensive picture of what is being studied, emphasizing quantitative outcomes as well as the process that influenced the outcomes. In addition, the nature of the data collected is not confined to one type of method, which encourages producing a more complete set of research questions as well as conclusions. It is also helpful to supplement a primarily quantitative or qualitative study with some data from the other method.

There are also some negatives to using mixed-method designs. First, combining qualitative and quantitative methods in a single study requires that the researcher have competence in each type. While it is relatively easy to gain an introductory understanding of both methodologies, greater depth of knowledge is needed to avoid less than credible findings. Second, a mixed-method study requires extensive data collection and more resources than many studies using only a quantitative or qualitative approach. This suggests that it may not always be feasible to conduct a mixed-method study. Finally, with the popularity of mixed methods, researchers may use one of the approaches superficially. For example, a researcher conducting a survey of school administrators about school climate could use both closed-ended (quantitative) and open-ended questions (presumably qualitative). Such a study would not be an example of a mixed-method design, however, since the "qualitative" part would not include characteristics of an actual qualitative investigation. Similarly, if a researcher used random sampling to identify a group of counselors and then conducted in-depth interviews, it would be misleading to call this a mixed-method study. There is a small trend toward using the term *mixed method* rather liberally to include any study that has some degree of each method in the research. We believe that it is best to use this term only for studies that include extensive aspects of both methodologies. It should not simply be a case of having more than one type of data collection or one type of data analysis.

A mixed-method study can be quickly identified by the title, methodology section, or research questions. Often, the title of the article will use the words *mixed method* or *quantitative and qualitative*. The title could also use the terms *mixed model, mixed approaches, combined,* and *integrated*. In the methodology section, there will be a clear indication of collecting both quantitative and qualitative data, usually in different sections or parts. Often, the research questions or purpose will include reference to using mixed methods or having both quantitative and qualitative purposes. Excerpt 7.1 shows how the methodology section of an article indicates the use of mixed methods.

Types of Mixed-Method Designs

Mixed-method designs can differ to a great extent, depending on the purpose of the research design as well as the sequence in which quantitative and qualitative methods are used and the emphasis given to each method. We will begin to examine these designs by discussing a notation system that helps clarify the nature of the study.

Notation System

Creswell (2002) describes the following notation system to represent different mixed-method designs:

- Uppercase letters (e.g., *QUAL* or *QUANT*) indicate a priority given to the method identified.
- Lowercase letters (e.g., *qual* or *quant*) show a lower priority given to the method.
- An arrow (⟶) indicates the sequence of the collection of data.
- A + indicates the simultaneous collection of both quantitative and qualitative data.

Explanatory Design In an **explanatory design,** quantitative and qualitative data are gathered sequentially, often in two phases, with the primary emphasis on quantitative methods. Initially, quantitative data are collected and analyzed. This is followed by qualitative data collection and analysis.

QUANT ⟶ qual

The qualitative data are needed to explain quantitative results or to further elaborate on quantitative findings.

An explanatory design is generally used when quantitative data collection is clearly warranted but further analysis—specifically, using qualitative methods—is necessary to

EXCERPT 7.1 Mixed-Method Study Identified by Methodology

Types of issues discussed and the impact of the support community on beginning teachers were examined using three data sources: messages generated by participants, follow-up phone interviews, and an online survey.

Source: From Helsel DeWert, M., Babinski, L., & Jones, B. (2003). Safe passages: providing online support to beginning teachers. *Journal of Teacher Education, 54*(4), 311–321.

elucidate the quantitative findings. For example, in a study comparing alternatively and traditionally prepared teachers, Miller, McKenna, and McKenna (1998) used three separate phases to answer their primary research question regarding differences in teaching practices between teachers who were traditionally certified and those who were alternatively certified (i.e., individuals who became teachers after having careers in other fields). The first two phases of the study were quantitative and utilized random sampling techniques and a 15-item rating scale to determine differences in teaching ability between the two groups. The last phase of the study used qualitative, in-person interviews to "gain insight into . . . teachers' perceptions of their teaching abilities" (p. 169). While this study focused primarily on quantitative data, the qualitative interviews provided a richer understanding of the teachers' perceptions of their own abilities and how their training and certification program provided them with preparation for their teaching careers.

Another example of a mixed-method explanatory study was conducted by McMillan (2000). In this study, a large sample of teachers (850) was surveyed to determine the extent to which they used different factors in classroom assessment and grading. This provided a general overview of the teachers' practices. In the second phase, teachers were selected who represented high or low scores on the factors. Qualitative interviews were conducted with these teachers to determine why certain factors were emphasized. Thus, the qualitative phase was used to augment the statistical data to provide explanations for the practices.

Exploratory Design A second type of mixed-method research is the **exploratory design,** in which qualitative data collection and analysis is followed by a quantitative phase. Generally, the purpose of an exploratory design is either to use the qualitative data exploring a particular phenomenon to develop a quantitative instrument to measure that phenomenon or to use the quantitative portion of the study to explore relationships found in the qualitative data. If the main purpose is to test out an instrument, there may be a greater emphasis on the quantitative part of the study:

$$\text{Qual} \longrightarrow \text{QUANT}$$

If the quantitative portion of the study is used to confirm, determine, or expand on qualitative findings, then the qualitative part of the study will be emphasized:

$$\text{QUAL} \longrightarrow \text{quant}$$

Using quantitative data to explore relationships found in qualitative studies allows the researcher to gather in-depth information from participants. This can be achieved by listening during interviews or focus groups and determining if any of the themes appear to be related and then following up with a quantitative measure to further explore those relationships, basically quantifying the connection established during the qualitative phase.

In developing a quantitative instrument from qualitative data, the researcher can use the language and emphasis of the participants in the wording of the items for the survey or scale. Doing so increases the validity of the scores from the newly developed instrument. For example, in a study by Rue, Dingley, and Bush (2002), the researchers utilized qualitative interviews and language from many different participants with chronic health conditions to develop a quantitative instrument to measure the inner strength of women. This study relied heavily on participant language and experiences with chronic conditions in order to develop items for a survey that could then quantitatively measure inner strength—a new concept in the field and one that had not previously been studied quantitatively.

Like explanatory designs, exploratory designs have both advantages and disadvantages. One advantage is that the quantitative portion of an exploratory study actually relies on the qualitative analysis to drive its direction, providing a greater understanding of the purpose of the quantitative data collection and analysis. However, like explanatory designs, exploratory designs require extensive data collection and analysis for both the qualitative and quantitative phases of the study. Moreover, it is sometimes difficult to indicate specifically how the qualitative findings were used to determine or influence the quantitative part of the study.

Triangulation Design The third type of mixed-method study is a **triangulation design,** in which the researcher simultaneously gathers both quantitative and qualitative data, merges them using both quantitative and qualitative data analysis methods, and then interprets the results together to provide a better understanding of a phenomenon of interest. Approximately equal emphasis is given to each method, even though one can follow the other:

QUAL + QUANT or QUANT + QUAL

Or both can be conducted at the same time:

QUANT
+
QUAL

The interpretation of results is the key to this method, as it provides a convergence of evidence in which the results of both methods either support or contradict each other. When the results of different methods converge and support one another, researchers have *triangulated* the findings. In this case, the use of different methods results in very strong results. Often, the strengths of one method offset the weaknesses of the other, which allows for a much stronger overall design and thus more credible conclusions. Quantitative results enhance generalizability while qualitative results help explain context. For example, a recent study examined the relationship between working and family involvement in a child's education (Weiss et al., 2003). The researchers used concurrent quantitative and qualitative data collection and analysis to fully explore the relationship. They used data from an ongoing longitudinal study and also conducted interviews with working mothers and their children in order to determine the impact of working on family involvement in education. The researchers explain their methods in Excerpt 7.2.

While giving equal priority to both methods is great for validity, triangulation requires that researchers be able to conduct both qualitative and quantitative methods. It is also a challenge to merge the qualitative and quantitative data so that there is a single study, not two studies.

Table 7.1 summarizes the three major types of mixed-method designs.

EXCERPT 7.2 Triangulation Mixed-Method Design

For this study we employed a mixed-method approach, using both quantitative and qualitative analyses. The added value of mixed-method analysis has been well documented in the literature, allowing, for example, better data triangulation and expansion of findings. We conducted the quantitative analyses in two phases: (a) We estimated the associations between demographic characteristics of mothers and their work/school statuses and their levels of school involvement; and (b) we estimated the association between mothers' work/school statuses and their levels of school involvement. Qualitative techniques supporting description and interpretation included reviewing ethnographic field notes, writing analytic memos, and systematically coding interviews. . . . Presented separately in the results below, these quantitative and qualitative analyses occurred in part on "parallel tracks." However, we also employed a "cross-over tracks" approach—an iterative mixed-method process, such that emergent findings from one method helped to shape subsequent analyses.

Source: From Weiss, H. B., Mayer, E., Kreider, H., Vaughan, M., Dearing, E., Hencke, R., & Pinto, K. (2003). Making it work: Low-income working mothers' involvement in their children's education. *American Educational Research Journal, 40*(4), 879–901.

TABLE 7.1 Types and Purposes of Mixed-Method Designs

Type	Design	Purpose(s)
Explanatory	Quantitative method followed by qualitative method	Qualitative data are used to elucidate, elaborate on, or explain quantitative findings (e.g., outliers or different groups). Qualitative data are used to develop a quantitative instrument or survey.
Exploratory	Qualitative method followed by quantitative method	Using qualitative data to establish groups to be compared. Using quantitative data to explore relationships found in qualitative data.
Triangulation	Quantitative and qualitative methods are concurrent	To provide a more comprehensive and complete picture of data by converging data analysis methods and offsetting strengths and weaknesses of each method.

Conducting Mixed-Method Research

Creswell (2002) identifies seven sequential steps in conducting mixed-method studies:

1. ***Determine the feasibility of doing a mixed-method study.*** Feasibility is a function of the adequacy of training of study personnel and resources to collect and analyze the data. Sufficient time is needed to complete the data collection and analysis, and researchers must have expertise in both quantitative and qualitative methods.

2. ***Determine the rationale.*** It is important to identify the reasons for conducting a mixed-method study and to determine whether these reasons provide sufficient justification. Researchers must be explicit about why a mixed-method study is preferable to one that is entirely either quantitative or qualitative.

3. ***Identify a data collection strategy and design.*** It is also important to identify the extent to which each of the two methods will be used, whether priority will be given to one method, and in what sequence the two methods will be used. This information will be used to identify the design as exploratory, explanatory, or triangulation. It is helpful at this point to construct a diagram to show data collection methods in the sequence used with assigned emphasis. Often, different *phases* are used to identify different stages of the design.

4. ***Determine research questions.*** While it is important to formulate a general purpose prior to establishing a design, at this point, specific research questions can be formulated. Both quantitative and qualitative questions should be developed (although in an explanatory study, it may not be possible to establish qualitative questions until the quantitative questions have been addressed). Quantitative research questions should state expected relationships, while qualitative questions should be nondirectional.

5. ***Collect the data.*** The sequence for collecting data is determined by the design (i.e., exploratory, explanatory, or triangulation). This stage of conducting the study will be lengthy, and appropriate principles for credible data collection for both the quantitative and qualitative phases should be followed.

6. ***Analyze the data.*** The data are analyzed depending on the nature of the design. Data analyses for exploratory and explanatory designs are done separately. With a triangulation design, the quantitative and qualitative data are analyzed concurrently in an integrated fashion.

7. ***Write the report.*** Like many aspects of planning and conducting mixed-method studies, the preparation of the report also depends on the nature of the design. The report can be constructed to reflect each phase by providing separate sections for each phase and then reflecting the synthesis of the results of each phase in drawing conclusions. Triangulation designs integrate the qualitative and quantitative findings for each research question.

The key to carrying out a credible mixed-method study is to ensure that both quantitative and qualitative methods are well executed and then to make reasonable interpretations. Given a clear rationale and appropriate resources, the quality of the conclusions rests on how well each method was conducted. The criteria for evaluating a mixed-method study include those identified earlier for both quantitative and qualitative results. The following questions should be considered (Creswell, 2002):

- Is it clear that both quantitative and qualitative methods were used?
- Is it identified as a *mixed-method study?*
- Is there a clear rationale that states a convincing case for doing a mixed-method study?
- Is the type of mixed-method design indicated?
- Is a priority stated for using different methods, and is an explanation made for the sequence of data collection used?
- Considering the available resources and the expertise of the researcher, is the study feasible?
- Are there both quantitative and qualitative research questions?
- Have data collection and analysis procedures been clearly described?
- Is the written structure consistent with the nature of the design?

SECONDARY DATA ANALYSIS

by Kirsten Barrett

Defining Secondary Data

Secondary data, simply put, are data that have already been collected. They are different from primary data in that the data user had no involvement in the data collection effort. When a researcher analyzes data that have been collected by some other organization, group, or individual at some prior time, the work is called **secondary data analysis**[1] (Kiecolt & Natham, 1985). Examples include a local school administrator analyzing decennial census data to better understand the socioeconomic status of parents in the community, a principal examining trends in high-stakes testing from a state database, and a parent analyzing achievement test scores across a number of schools to inform decisions about family relocation.

Reasons for Using Secondary Data

A researcher may choose to use secondary data for a number of reasons. Four of the most significant are the benefits of time efficiency, cost effectiveness, data quality, and increased sample size.

Using secondary data can save considerable time. The researcher does not need to spend time designing the research study and collecting primary data. When using secondary data, this work has already been done. Time savings can be a significant benefit when a person or an organization needs to make program or policy decisions within a short period of time. Also, students completing coursework, master's theses, or doctoral dissertations can often expedite their efforts by using secondary data.

Using secondary data also can be cost effective. Cost savings are realized because the researcher does not need to fund the primary data collection. Costs related to photocopying, postage, telecommunication charges, personnel time, and data entry are minimized, as well. Also, many secondary data sets are freely available in electronic format from reputable organizations such as the Inter-University Consortium for Social and Political Research, the National Center for Education Statistics, the U.S. Census Bureau, and the National Center for Health Statistics. Further, state-level department of education websites often contain accessible, downloadable data pertaining to, among other things, achievement and accountability test scores, graduation rates, and disciplinary actions. Table 7.2 contains a listing of the key sources of secondary data and the Internet address for each.

A third benefit is data quality. Depending on the data set being used, the findings that result from secondary analyses may well have a high degree of validity and reliability. Reputable data collection organizations have the fiscal and human resources necessary to develop and extensively test surveys prior to implementing them. These organizations also have the resources necessary to field surveys using sampling methods and sample sizes that allow for reliable and valid population estimates.

ALERT! The term *secondary* does not mean less important or significant in this context.

Finally, secondary data sets usually provide very large samples. With increased sample size comes greater flexibility in examining identified subgroups (especially small segments of the population), improved reliability, and generally credible results. However, large samples can also result in producing statistically significant findings that have little practical significance.

Considerations for Using Secondary Data

A number of factors should be considered when deciding if secondary data and secondary data analyses are appropriate to answer a research question or to test a research hypothesis:

1. ***Does the data set contain variables that will allow the research question to be answered or the research hypothesis to be tested?*** If the answer is *no* or *probably not*, then the data set is not appropriate. If the data set does contain the variables of

TABLE 7.2 Key Sources of Secondary Data

Source	Internet Address
Inter-University Consortium for Social and Political Research (ICPSR)	www.icpsr.com
National Center for Education Statistics	http://nces.ed.gov
U.S. Census Bureau	www.census.gov
National Center for Health Statistics	www.cdc.gov/nchs
State-level departments of education	*Examples:* *Virginia:* www.pen.k12.va.us/VDOE/Publications *Texas:* www.tea.state.tx.us/research *Maine:* www.state.me.us/education/data/homepage.htm

interest, the researcher needs to determine how the data were collected. That is, how were the questions worded, and what response categories were made available to the respondents? In other words, the potential data user needs to determine how the variables of interest were operationally defined. Information about variables can usually be found in the technical documentation and code book that accompanies the data set. If these documents do not exist or exist only in part, the researcher should be wary about using the data set.

2. ***Were data collected from the population of interest?*** A survey may yield a data set containing the variables of interest, but the data may not have been collected from a sample that is representative of the population the researcher is interested in. For example, if a researcher is interested in children in a specific age bracket, the data set should contain data collected from children in the age bracket of interest. Similarly, if the researcher intends to generalize his or her findings to a specific geographic area, the data should have been collected from individuals living in the geographic area of interest.

3. ***When were the data collected?*** The researcher should consider the time period in which the data were collected. If the research has implications for current practice, the data used for the analyses should be relatively current. If the research is historical in nature or examines change over time, then the data set may be older or may contain data collected over a number of years. Also, the researcher should consider the timing of data collection relative to major social or political events. For example, data from a survey about attitudes toward women in sport conducted prior to the passage of Title IX should not be used to make inferences about current attitudes toward women in sport.

4. ***Is there adequate computing capacity to work with the secondary data set?*** This consideration relates both to computer software and computer storage capacity and processor speed. Many secondary data sets from reputable data repositories are derived from surveys that involved complex, multistage sampling designs. Some researchers may not have access to the statistical software necessary to analyze such data, or they may not have the expertise needed to use the software appropriately. Secondary data sets can range in size from less than one megabyte to many gigabytes. The larger the dataset, the greater the amount of free disk space needed. Also, as the size of the data set increases, so should the speed of the computer processor.

5. ***Are the data easily accessible?*** Some secondary data sets can be downloaded via the Internet, while others need to be ordered. If a data set needs to be ordered, it is important to determine how it will be provided to the end user. Will it be sent via electronic mail as an attachment or provided on a CD, DVD, or diskette? Also, in what format will the data file be provided? Does the end user have the skills to manipulate the data file? Data provided as hard copy (i.e., printed pages) can be useful but will require scanning or manual data entry. A final consideration with regard to accessibility is the extent to which the variables of interest are available. In some cases, certain variables may be removed from the data file due to issues of confidentiality. For example, if data are available for a number of cities within a specific state, city identifiers may be removed so that researchers cannot identify individuals by combining their demographic characteristics with their geographic information. Removal of the city identifier can be problematic if the research question is focused on an issue in specific city.

6. ***Is documentation about the dataset available?*** It is important for the researcher to have technical documentation that describes what data were collected through what method(s) and in what time interval(s). The technical documentation should provide the end user with the variable names, their locations in the data file, the associated survey question and response categories, and, ideally, the number of respondents for each response category. Figure 7.1 is an example of an entry from the technical documentation from the *Health Behavior in School-Aged Children Survey, 1997–1998* (WHO, 2002). The different elements in the entry can be explained as follows:

a. Q1 is the column heading in the data set for the variable denoting sex of the child.
b. "Are you a boy or a girl?" is the question that was asked of each respondent.

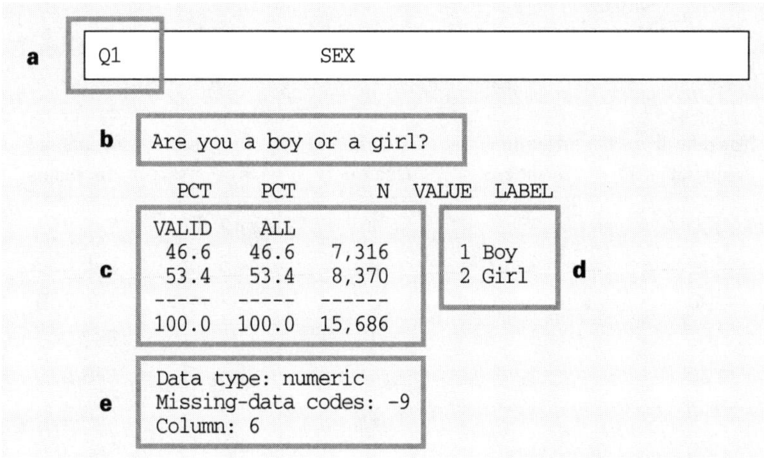

FIGURE 7.1 **Example of Technical Documentation**

c. These are the counts and percentages of respondents in the "Boy" and "Girl" categories. There were 7,316 boys and 8,370 girls for a total of 15,686 cases. The sample was 46.6 percent male and 53.4 percent female.

d. In the dataset, in the column identified as Q1, a value of 1 will indicate that the respondent was a boy and a value of 2 will indicate that the respondent was a girl.

e. The data are numeric in nature, rather than string. If a respondent did not answer this question, he or she would have a value of –9 in the Q1 field in the dataset. Finally, the variable is located in column 6 of the dataset.

Imagine receiving a dataset with a column labeled Q1 with respondent values of 1, 2, or –9. Without the technical documentation just described, the end user would not know what question Q1 corresponded to or what the values 1, 2, and –9 denoted.

7. ***What is the structure of the data file?*** This is an important and more technical consideration. Some secondary data sets contain data at different levels—say, an individual, a family, and/or a household. Figure 7.2 is an example of a data set that contains data at a number of different levels. In this example, although there are 10 records, only 5 unique households are represented (i.e., 100, 200, 300, 400, and 500). Household 100, comprised of three people (Person Numbers 1, 2, and 3), contains two families. This could be a husband and wife (Record IDs 1 and 2) and a nonrelated renter (Record ID 3). Contained within the dataset are two variables: age and household income. Age is a person-level variable, whereas Household Income is a household-level variable. As can be seen in the example, all people with a Household Number of 100 have the same household income. This distinction is important. Suppose that the researcher wants to report average household income by household. It would be incorrect to simply add all 10 household income values and divide by 10. If this were done, the average household income would appear to be $41,585. To determine the average household income by household, the researcher should add the household incomes of all the households and divide by 5, since there are 5 households in the file. The result would be an average household income of $40,970.

What is important with data file structures is to recognize that care needs to be taken to ensure that analysis is done at the appropriate level (household, family, and/or person) and that the interpretations are accurate based on the file structure and the variables used.

8. ***Is technical assistance available relative to the data set and its use?*** When working with secondary data, researchers may come across unanticipated problems, such as frequency counts that do not match those identified in the technical documentation, difficulty applying sample weights, or a lack of knowledge about how best to account for

FIGURE 7.2 Example of Data Set with Household, Family, and Person Records

Record ID	Household Number	Family Number	Person Number	Age	Household Income
1	100	1	1	42	$45,650
2	100	1	2	45	$45,650
3	100	2	3	32	$45,650
4	200	1	1	21	$32,000
5	300	1	1	35	$48,200
6	300	1	2	32	$48,200
7	400	1	1	54	$43,250
8	500	1	1	36	$35,750
9	500	2	2	42	$35,750
10	500	2	3	46	$35,750

a complex sample design. When such a situation arises, support from the individual or organization providing the data is needed. If support is not available, the researcher should find someone who has used the data set previously and seek his or her help.

Protecting Human Subjects

Secondary data that are publicly available, whether free or at cost, are usually coded so that the identification of any single individual is not possible. Thus, research involving the collection or study of existing data, documents, or records in which subjects cannot be identified—directly or through identifiers linked to them—is usually exempt from needing the subjects' informed consent. Regardless, most organizations and universities still require their researchers to submit their study protocols to the institutional review board (IRB), which allows a third party to review the proposed study and confirm that the criteria for exemption have indeed been met. As a general rule of thumb, users of secondary data should be familiar with the policies of their individual organizations with regard to human subjects' protection and IRB review requirements.

Not all secondary data sets are devoid of identifying information about participants. It is therefore important to look beyond the obvious identifiers, such as name, Social Security number, and address information. Sometimes, through a combination of variables in the data set, an individual can be identified. For example, consider a small data set of 200 individuals living in a small community. In the data set is information about individuals' jobs, types of cars, and numbers of people in households, as well as information about age, race, and marital status. This information, in combination, could be enough to allow for the identification of an individual person. Although no one variable would serve to identify an individual, combining variables could allow for identification. Reputable federal statistical agencies and data repositories address this issue by ensuring that there is an adequate number of respondents for key variables in the data set prior to its release.

Myths about Secondary Data

1. ***Secondary data require manipulation before they can be useful.*** One has to go no further than the U.S. Census Bureau website to realize that this statement is indeed a myth. Many data tables are available and ready for direct application to social issues without any data manipulation at all. Figure 7.3 is an example of a data table that is readily

PCT63. SEX BY COLLEGE OR GRADUATE SCHOOL ENROLLMENT BY AGE FOR THE POPULATION 15 YEARS AND OVER [23] - Universe: Population 15 years and over
Data Set: Census 2000 Summary File 4 (SF 4) - Sample Data

NOTE: Data based on a sample. For information on confidentiality protection, sampling error, nonsampling error, and definitions see http://factfinder.census.gov/home/en/datanotes/expsf4.htm.

	United States
Total:	221,148,671
Male:	107,027,405
Enrolled in college or graduate school:	7,919,628
15 to 17 years	32,945
18 to 24 years	4,241,329
25 to 34 years	1,957,404
35 years and over	1,687,950
Not enrolled in college or graduate school	99,107,777
15 to 17 years	6,085,188
18 to 24 years	9,590,257
25 to 34 years	17,945,333
35 years and over	65,486,999
Female:	114,121,266
Enrolled in college or graduate school:	9,563,615
15 to 17 years	41,644
18 to 24 years	4,961,751
25 to 34 years	2,202,202
35 years and over	2,358,018
Not enrolled in college or graduate school	104,557,651
15 to 17 years	5,709,745
18 to 24 years	8,274,173
25 to 34 years	17,472,418
35 years and over	73,101,315

U.S. Census Bureau
Census 2000

FIGURE 7.3 **Data Table from the U.S. Census Bureau**

available that contains information about college and graduate school enrollment for individuals 15 years of age or older in the United States. Another agency, the National Center for Education Statistics, allows the user to build custom tables by selecting variables of interest for specified years and/or geographic areas. Figure 7.4 shows a custom table detailing the number of guidance counselors at various grade levels in Chesterfield, Virginia. As can be seen in this figure, the data can be downloaded in a variety of formats, including Excel. Furthermore, the data can be formatted for printing. The user can also reorder or resort the columns based on his or her needs.

2. ***Secondary data files are analysis ready.*** It would be convenient if secondary data files could be downloaded and opened with a statistical software package ready for statistical analyses. The process is not that simple, however. Often, expertise is required to manipulate data files of various formats, including .txt, .dat, and .xls. To do so requires an understanding of data file structure, knowledge of variable location, and skill at working with multiple computer files simultaneously. In addition, once a data file is in a statistical software package, a number of manipulations may be required, such as assigning variable names and value labels, recoding variables and collapsing response categories, and converting variables from string to numeric formats or vice versa.

3. ***Research using secondary data is less rigorous than other types of research.*** Although the researcher who uses secondary data is saving time and money by foregoing primary data collection, he or she still must have a sound theoretical basis for the research and the research questions must be clearly stated. Furthermore, the researcher needs to have a firm understanding of the research methodology that resulted in the data set being used. That includes an understanding of the target population, the sampling methods, the data collection methods, and the data management techniques. The operational definitions of the variables also need to be understood as well as the structure and characteristics of the data file. The researcher may spend months or longer identifying an appropriate

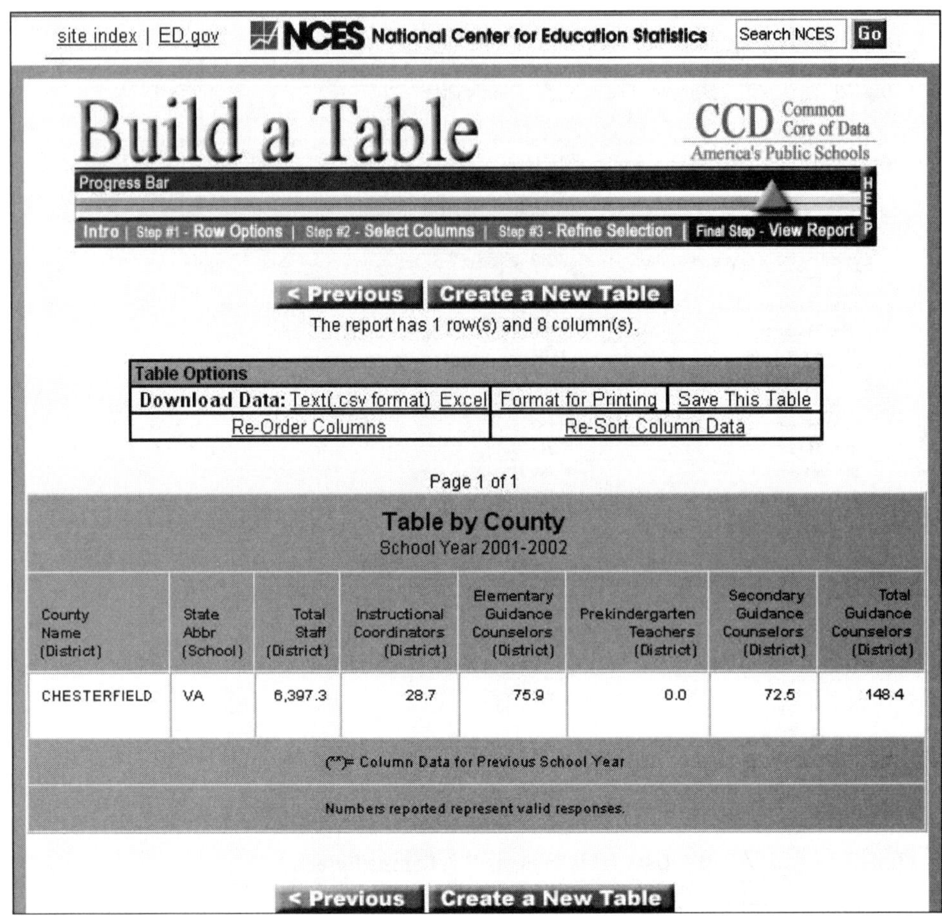

County Name (District)	State Abbr (School)	Total Staff (District)	Instructional Coordinators (District)	Elementary Guidance Counselors (District)	Prekindergarten Teachers (District)	Secondary Guidance Counselors (District)	Total Guidance Counselors (District)
CHESTERFIELD	VA	6,397.3	28.7	75.9	0.0	72.5	148.4

FIGURE 7.4 **Custom Table from the National Center for Education Statistics**

data set and deciding on the analysis plan once the data file has been selected and its characteristics are known.

Combining Secondary Data with Primary Data Collection

Using a combination of primary and secondary data can often strengthen research findings. Not only can analyzing existing data inform primary data collection efforts, but it can also lead to discovering new research questions, to refining existing research questions, and to informing primary data collection efforts. For example, if a researcher is analyzing secondary data and finds that a high percentage of the respondents refused to answer a particular question, he or she may use this information in developing new survey instruments.

Secondary data also can provide a context for interpreting the findings that result from primary data collection efforts. Consider the issue of school consolidation. When school leaders are making decisions about consolidating students and closing schools, they often solicit feedback from key stakeholders, including parents and teachers. School leaders could survey parents and teachers in order to learn about their attitudes about school consolidation, and the survey data could be augmented with data about student enrollment over time based on analysis of school administrative records. In this example, the survey data would be the primary data and the school administrative data would be the secondary data.

Secondary data can be used to help researchers identify where members of the target population are most likely to be located. An example would be a survey of households in which there are children under the age of 18. Decennial census data could be used to identify at very small levels of geography areas with the highest proportion of households with children under 18. Once this was determined, the sampling methods could be targeted so that these areas would be maximally surveyed and other areas would be surveyed to a lesser extent.

After data have been collected, there is a chance that the sample will be distributed in ways that are inconsistent with what is known about the target population. For example, in a hypothetical survey of a local community, 50 percent of the respondents have less than a high school education, 30 percent are married, and 20 percent have at least one child under the age of 18. However, through secondary analysis of decennial census data, you determine that the true percentages in the community in each of these categories are 35 percent, 50 percent, and 15 percent, respectively. The discrepancy identified through the secondary data analysis suggests that the researcher should apply statistical weighting procedures so that the sample will better represent the target population. This is one method of enhancing external validity.

Research Articles and Secondary Data

For the most part, journal articles written by researchers who have used secondary data follow the same form as journal articles written by researchers conducting primary data collection. However, when describing the sampling and data collection methods, researchers using secondary data write about what was done by the individual or group who initially collected the data. Researchers who conduct primary data collection write about what they did to collect the data used in the study yielding the findings being reported.

The following should be included in the research methods section of a journal article written by a researcher using secondary data:

- The name of the data set and its source should be clearly identified.
- If more than one data set is used and they are linked, the names of all data sets should be provided and their sources identified.
- The time period in which the data were collected should be identified. If the data were pooled over a number of years, this should be identified, as well.
- The sampling methods and the characteristics of the sample should be described.
- If the researcher is interested in a subset of cases in a data set, any procedures used to limit the data set to select cases should be identified in sequence.
- The key variables used in the analysis should be identified and, in some cases, the specific survey questions identified.

Excerpts 7.3 and 7.4 show examples from parts of secondary analysis research studies. In Excerpt 7.3, the researchers identify the source of data and how the sampling was done.

EXCERPT 7.3 Survey Identification and Sample Description in Secondary Analysis

The data for this study were drawn from the 1994 NAEP Trial State Data collection. Data from the 1998 NAEP had not been released when the study was completed and other recent data sets did not contain state-level data with student and teacher questionnaires on reading. In this assessment, a multistage sampling design was used to include the following: (a) selection of schools, both public and private and (b) selection of students within the identified schools. Sampling weights were computed to account for disproportionate representation of African American and Hispanic students from urban schools and lower sampling weights from very small schools. In the present analyses, the weighting was applied to the Maryland sample of 577 students used in HLM analyses, which allowed generalizations to the full population of Grade 4 students in Maryland.

Source: From Guthrie, J. T., Schafer, W. D., & Chun-Wei, H. (2001). Benefits of opportunity to read and balanced instruction on the NAEP. *Journal of Educational Research, 94*(3), 145–163.

EXCERPT 7.4 Description of Key Variables in Secondary Analysis

Two measures were used to determine demonstrated academic ability in grammar school, namely Grades and Repeat Grade. Respondents were asked what grades they received overall in the 8th grade. The measure Grades was coded such that 1 = Mostly B's or Better and 0 = Mostly C's or Worse. Respondents were also asked if they ever repeated a grade. Repeat Grade was coded such that those who reported that they repeated at least one grade in elementary school = 1, while others = 0.

Source: From Caputo, R. K. (2003). Early education experiences and school-to-work program participation. *Journal of Sociology and Social Welfare, 30*(4), 141–157.

Excerpt 7.4 shows how key variables were described and how they were coded for analytic purposes.

ACTION RESEARCH

Defining Action Research

With the current emphasis on data-driven decision making, educational professionals are increasingly asked to provide evidence that documents best practice. There is also an emphasis on *critical reflection* about practice that provides a systematic approach to gathering and analyzing information. It is the intersection, then, between systematic inquiry (i.e., research) and its use by practitioners that characterizes *action research*. **Action research** is the process of using research principles to provide information that educational professionals use to improve aspects of day-to-day practice. The research questions are rooted in practice, perhaps by K–12 teachers working in classrooms, administrators identifying and implementing guidelines, counselors practicing in schools and colleges, or faculty teaching at colleges and universities. It is simply a systematic approach to help professionals change practice, usually using a collaborative model that includes several individuals.

In K–12 education, the terms *teacher/researcher, teacher research, research practitioner,* and *teacher-as-researcher* are all used to focus on the action research of a single teacher. Action research is also completed in teams using a collaborative model and with entire schools (i.e., school-based action research). In other fields and at other levels of education, the broader term *applied* may be used to describe what is essentially action research. For example, teachers in a high school mathematics department may work together (or collaborate) to determine if a specific method of presenting a concept is effective, or the same question could be posed and answered by a single teacher.

Action research is not limited to a specific methodology (although in most cases, there is at least some use of qualitative methods), and typically quantitative data are used descriptively (with little or no emphasis on inferential statistics). The goal is to introduce a more systematic process than what is typically employed, be it qualitative, quantitative, or mixed method. One important difference is that the intent of action research is only to address specific actions in a single context, while applied research seeks to have implications for the field more generally. However, that does not mean that action research does not have implications for the overall field. Because practitioners are involved throughout the study, action research promotes change in classrooms and schools, greater collaboration among those with a vested interest in the results, an integration of research with practice, and a willingness to test new ideas.

Table 7.3 summarizes the differences between action research and traditional research. The reader should keep in mind, however, that there can be significant variability in the extent to which characteristics of traditional research are used in action research.

TABLE 7.3 Characteristics of Action Research versus Traditional Research

Characteristic	Action Research	Traditional Research
Who identifies the research question(s) and conducts the research	Practitioners: teachers, principles, counselors	Trained researchers: university professors, scholars, graduate students
Where the research is conducted	Schools, universities, day cares, and other institutions where practice is implemented	Settings in which appropriate control can be implemented, from laboratories to field settings
Goal	Knowledge that is relevant to the local setting	Knowledge that can be generalized to the field
Literature review	Brief, with a focus on secondary sources	Extensive, with an emphasis on primary sources
Instrumentation	Use of instruments that are convenient and easy to administer and score	Measures are selected based on technical adequacy
Sampling	Convenient sampling of students or employees in the targeted setting	Tends to be random or representative
Data analysis	Descriptive	Descriptive and inferential
Dissemination	To the specific individual, classroom, or organization	To other professionals in different settings

Source: Adapted from Gall, Gall, & Borg (2003).

Conducting and Using Action Research

Action research is conducted in four phases: (1) selecting a focus, topic, or issue to study; (2) collecting data; (3) analyzing data; and (4) taking action based on the results. Each will be considered in more detail with some examples in a following section.

ALERT! Action researchers must be careful not to let their biases or wishes influence their results or actions.

Selecting a Focus, Topic, or Issue to Study The first step in any research endeavor is to determine the research question, goal, or purpose. A good topic is one that is important and relevant and that provides results that will immediately impact professional practice. Sometimes, an informal needs assessment is used to identify a topic; sometimes, a review of literature is used. Usually, the experiences of the researcher are used to identify topics. Research is often suggested because there is a problem in implementing practice, or something that is not going well.

Eventually, researchable questions need to be formulated to determine methods of data collection. Here are some examples of such questions:

- What is the effect of assigning greater responsibility to students in completing the yearbook on their attitudes toward writing?
- How effective is peer tutoring in the advanced placement (AP) history course?
- What teaching methods most motivate students to write detailed research proposals?
- Is there a difference in school climate after the introduction of more strict hall monitoring?

Collecting Data The second phase of conducting action research is to collect data that will answer the research questions. Decisions need to be made about what type or types of data need to be collected and the sample from which data will be collected. Both quantitative and qualitative methods should be considered; using a variety of data collection tools usually strengthens the study by providing triangulation. Often, initial data gathering will lead to collecting additional data. For example, a teacher might begin to study the effectiveness of cooperative learning groups by first doing some informal observation while the groups are deliberating. From these data, a more structured observation could be developed, along with specific questions that students could be asked.

Typically, action researchers will use one of three approaches to data collection: experiencing, enquiring, and examining (Mills, 2003). *Experiencing* takes the form of observation, with a focus on understanding the variables, participants, and relevant phenomena. *Enquiring* occurs when the researcher needs to gather data that have not yet been obtained. This could involve interviews, questionnaires, and tests. *Examining* occurs when the researcher uses data that have already been conducted. Whatever the approach, one challenge is to decide what data really need to be collected. The researcher does not want to be swamped with so much data that it will be difficult to analyze and summarize them.

As in any research project, attention must be given to issues of credibility, transferability, dependability, validity, and reliability. While highly technical conceptualizations

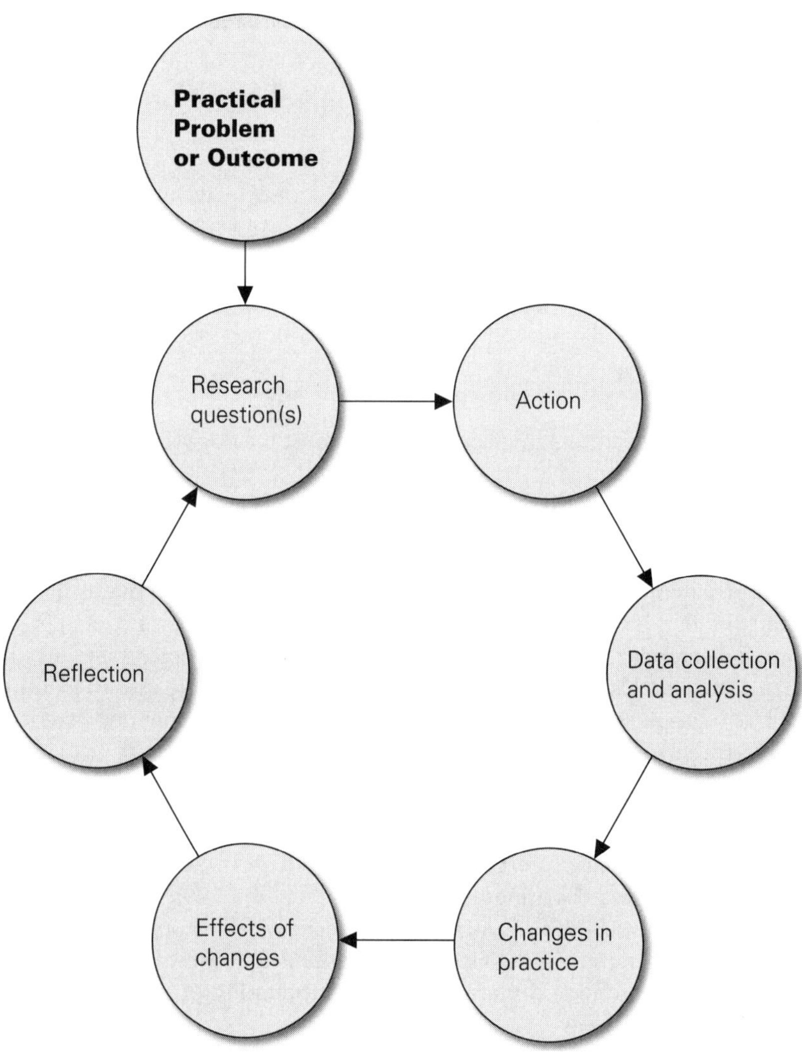

FIGURE 7.5 **Cyclical Nature of Action Research**

EXCERPT 7.5 Cyclical Process in Action Research

This study was conducted in three phases over a two-year period, and involved students and staff from three faculties of the Queensland University of Technology. A total of 1,654 students and 30 staff participated in the project. An action research process based on cycles of action and reflection . . . was used to develop peer assessment procedures that were responsive to student and staff needs and concerned. This process was participatory, collaborative and reflexive.

Source: From Ballantyne, R., Hughes, K., & Mylonas, A. (2002). Developing procedures for implementing peer assessment in large classes using an action research process. *Assessment and Evaluation in Higher Education, 27*(5), 427–441.

will not be used (e.g., statistical calculations such as correlations and multiple raters), the *ideas* or notions of validity, reliability, and related principles must be addressed. This is often best accomplished by simply having others review the procedures and results to determine whether any factors could invalidate the findings or provide competing explanations. The *ideas* are more important than complex definitions, typologies of error, and statistical indices.

Analyzing Data Next, the data need to be examined and interpreted. It is important that the data are clear and well organized. For qualitative analyses, action researchers will look for redundancy in what is being communicated *after* they have gained a complete understanding of what has been observed and recorded. Usually, some kind of categorization is utilized to organize the information. Quantitative data are summarized using simple descriptive statistics (e.g., frequencies, mean, mode, range) and graphs. It is helpful to ask others to review at least a portion of the data analyses, as well as the interpretations and conclusions, to help ensure that the analyses, interpretations, and conclusions make sense.

Action researchers often use the results from their initial data collection and analysis to change practice, which is evaluated, and then to suggest new research questions, which are followed by new data collection and analysis procedures. This is essentially a cyclical process, as illustrated in Figure 7.5. This process is essential to the action research project in Excerpt 7.5, in which college professors investigate the effect of using peer assessment in large classes.

Evaluating Action Research

The quality of action research is judged by criteria related to its primary purpose—that is, to change practice and resolve the identified problem that prompted the study. It is in the usefulness of the action taken that credibility is assessed. This judgment is made by addressing the following questions:

- Is the research problem one that addresses the effectiveness of professional practice?
- Is the research question stated in a way that can be addressed empirically?
- Were sufficient data collected?
- Could anything about the sampling, instrumentation, or procedures distort the findings?
- Were there multiple methods of data collection and analyses?
- Does the suggested action follow logically from the findings?
- Will the findings result in a change of practice?
- Has implementation of suggested changes improved the targeted participant outcomes?

Clearly, the evaluation rests as much, if not more on use of the results as on the technical adequacy of the research. This is in contrast to most other kinds of studies, in which details related to subject selection, instrument validity, and internal validity are stressed as the criteria for determining credibility. Consider Excerpt 7.6, in which four high school teachers

EXCERPT 7.6 Action Research Outcomes

A majority of students indicated that the alternative grading system did affect their academic preparation and performance in class (in a positive way), and that they had a more positive attitude toward the class. . . . We believe that the increased focus on personal learning, growth, and improvement that evolved from de-emphasizing grades made it less likely for students to fail and more likely for students to accept responsibility for their learning and to provide the evidence that they had learned. . . . By far the most rewarding part of working on an action research team was the opportunity to learn and grow with a small group of teacher colleagues. . . . By working with these colleagues consistently throughout the year, we were able to explore new ideas and takes risks in the classroom. . . . We will continue to conduct action research. (pp. 101–102)

Source: From Mills, G. E. (2003). *Action research: A guide for the teacher researcher,* 2nd ed. Upper Saddle River, NJ: Merrill Prentice Hall.

implement changes in the grading system to determine the effects on student effort, responsibility, and attitudes. Surveys, observations, and student interviews were used to collect data. Also consider the importance of collaboration among these teachers. Action research is usually most effective when teams of professionals work together on the same problem, issue, or practice.

SUMMARY

This chapter presented an introduction to mixed-method designs, secondary data analysis, and action research. Following is a summary of the key points in each area:

Mixed-Method Designs

1. Quantitative and qualitative methods and analyses are combined in a single study.
2. Mixed-method studies incorporate the strengths of different approaches to research.
3. Mixed-method studies require researcher competence in both quantitative and qualitative methods.
4. There are explanatory, exploratory, and triangulation mixed-method designs.
5. In explanatory designs, quantitative methods are used first, followed by qualitative methods that explain the quantitative findings.
6. Exploratory designs use qualitative findings to determine the best quantitative method.
7. Triangulation designs use quantitative and qualitative methods concurrently.

Secondary Data Analysis

8. Secondary data analysis studies use previously gathered data from existing sources.
9. Secondary data analysis may be efficient, cost effective, and provide a large sample.
10. Many existing databases can be used in secondary analyses.
11. It is important to review the structure of the data file, data set documentation, and accessibility, as well as whether technical assistance is available.
12. Secondary analysis can be used with primary data collection to strengthen and extend findings.

Action Research

13. Action research is conducted by practitioners with the goal of changing actions in classrooms, schools, universities, and other settings.
14. Action research emphasizes the use of the data.
15. Action research is a systematic inquiry that may utilize both quantitative and qualitative methods.
16. Research is conducted in the settings in which changes in action are anticipated.
17. Data analyses are primarily narrative and descriptive, with the use of graphs when appropriate.
18. Highly sophisticated statistics and research principles are typically not employed, even though concepts such

as validity and reliability must be considered to some extent to ensure producing credible results.

19. Action research often has a cyclical nature. Beginning with research questions, action leads to research, which leads to changes in practice, effects on targeted individuals, reflection, and then research questions.
20. Action research is evaluated primarily on the extent to which the investigation provided credible data that were used to successfully change practice.

CHECK YOURSELF

Multiple-choice review items, with answers, are available on the Companion Website for this book:

www.ablongman.com/mcmillanschumacher6e.

APPLICATION PROBLEMS

1. For each of the following descriptions, indicate the type of design being used: mixed method, secondary data analysis, or action research.
   a. A researcher is interested in examining the correlation between high-stakes testing and grades. The test scores and grades are from 2000–2003.
   b. A doctoral student is interested in studying the effects of small-group counseling on students' self-esteem. Thirty students participate as subjects. The Coopersmith Self-Esteem Inventory is given as a pretest and a posttest, and interviews are used to follow up with students every month.
   c. Service learning is becoming very popular in both public schools and colleges and universities. However, relatively little is known about the perceptions of the beneficiaries of the services. A study is prepared to examine these perceptions using focus group interviews and a questionnaire to ask participants about the characteristics of effective volunteers.
   d. A principal is interested in knowing whether a new procedure for aligning classroom assessments with graduation requirements will result in more students graduating.
   e. To compare student achievement in the United States with that of students in other countries, a professor bought and used a CD containing three years of relevant data.
2. Give an original example of each of the three types of mixed-method designs.
3. A researcher has conducted a series of interviews about job stress and burnout with teachers of students with disabilities. Following the interviews, additional data could be collected to provide even more description of teachers' job stress and burnout as well as its effects on students. What procedures could be used to extend the study to be an exploratory design? What procedures could be used to extend the study to be a triangulation design?
4. For each of the following characteristics, indicate whether it is typical of action research or traditional research.
   a. Tends to use mostly secondary sources
   b. Is done in classrooms by teachers
   c. Uses inferential statistics or qualitative software
   d. Measures are selected to provide generalizability
   e. Involves limited dissemination
   f. Researcher bias is a particular concern
   g. Findings are relevant for the field in general
5. In your own field of work and study, suggest an action research study that uses a mixed-method design.
6. Suppose a teacher decides to study the impact of technology on the attention behavior of her fifth-grade students. She makes observations of students for three weeks before the technology is introduced and then continues her observations for the next three weeks while students use the technology. The results suggest that students pay

increased attention when they use technology, so the teacher decides to use it for the rest of the semester.

a. What should the teacher do to ensure credible results?
b. How can teacher bias be controlled?
c. Is this an example of cyclical research? Why or why not?
d. Using Table 7.3 (p. 175), explain how this could become an applied, more traditional study.

NOTE

1. Kiecolt, K. J. & Natham, L. E. (1985). *Secondary Analysis of Survey Data*. Beverly Hills, CA: Sage Publications.

APPENDIX

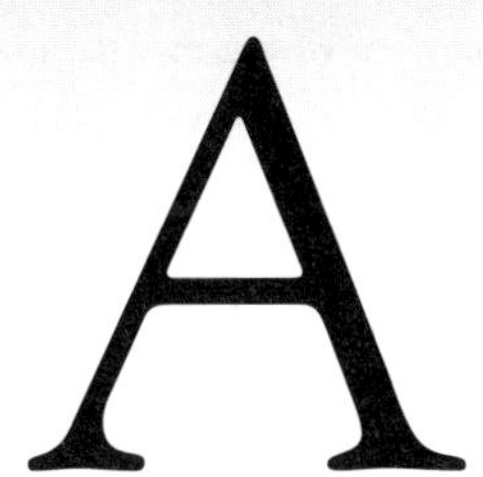

Glossary

action research Studies undertaken by practitioners in schools that address an actual problem or issue in the school or classroom

analytical research An analysis of documents to investigate historical concepts and events

applied research Research that is conducted in a field of common practice and is concerned with the application and development of research-based knowledge

attrition A threat to internal validity in which loss of subjects affects the results

audibility A record of data management techniques and decision rules that documents the "chain of evidence" or "decision trail."

authenticity The faithful reconstruction of participants' multiple perceptions

basic research Research that tests or refines theory; not designed to be applied immediately to practice

case A particular situation selected by the researcher in which some phenomena will be described by participants' meanings of events and processes

case study Qualitative research that examines a bounded system (i.e., a case) over time in detail, employing multiple sources of data found in the setting

case study design A research design in which the researcher selects one phenomenon to understand in depth, regardless of the number of settings, social scenes, or participants in a study

categorical variable A variable used to divide subjects, objects, or entities into two or more groups

cluster sampling A form of probability sampling in which subjects are first grouped according to naturally occurring traits

comparative *See* comparative research

comprehensive sampling The type of sampling in qualitative research in which every participant, group, setting, event, or other information is examined

concept analysis A study that clarifies the meaning of a concept by describing its generic meaning, different meanings, and appropriate use; also called *philosophical research*

construct A complex abstraction that is not directly observable, such as anxiety, intelligence, and self-concept; a meaningful combination of concepts

construct validity A type of external validity that refers to the extent to which a study represents the underlying construct

continuous variable A variable in which the property or attribute of an object, subject, or entity is measured numerically and can assume an infinite number of values within a range; also called a *measured variable*

convenience sampling A nonprobability method of selecting subjects who are accessible or available

correlation A measure of relationship that uses a correlation coefficient

correlation coefficient A calculation that represents the size and direction of the degree of relationship between two variables

correlational research Research in which information on at least two variables is collected for each subject in order to investigate the relationship between the variables

credibility The extent to which the results of a study approximate reality and are thus judged to be trustworthy and reasonable

criterion variable In a prediction study, the variable that is predicted

critical studies Qualitative research in which the researcher is committed to exposing social manipulation and changing oppressive social structures and in which he or she may have emancipatory goals

data The results obtained by research from which interpretations and conclusions are drawn

demand characteristics A possible source of bias when any aspect of a study reveals its purpose and may influence subjects to respond differently because they know that purpose

dependent variable The measured variable that is the consequence of or depends on antecedent variables

descriptive Refers to research that describes an existing or past phenomenon in quantitative terms

diffusion of treatment A threat to internal validity in which the subjects are influenced by other conditions of the independent variable

ecological external validity The extent to which the results of research can be generalized to other conditions and situations

electronic resources Literature that is stored in a computer database

emergent design A research plan in which each step depends on the results of the field data obtained in the previous step

empirical Refers to what is guided by evidence, data, and sources

ERIC (Educational Resources Information Center) A comprehensive database and index of education literature

ERIC digest Short reports that synthesize the available education literature on a topic

evaluation research Research that is designed to assess the worth of a specific practice in terms of the values operating at the site

exhaustive search A literature search about a narrowly focused problem that spans 10 or more years and uses the most relevant reference services

experimental variable The variable in an experimental or quasi-experimental design that is manipulated or changed by the researcher to see the effect on (i.e., relationship to) the dependent variable

experimenter effects A threat to internal validity in which the researcher's differential treatment of the subjects affects results, also called *experimenter contamination*

explanation A theory or analytical generalization that states cause-and-effect relationships in simple statements

explanatory design A mixed-method design in which a quantitative phase is followed by a qualitative phase

exploratory design A mixed-method design in which a qualitative phase is followed by a quantitative phase

evidence-based inquiry A search for knowledge that uses systematically gathered empirical data and that reports them in such a way that the reasoning can be examined

***ex post facto* design** *See ex post facto* research

extension of the findings Using the results of a qualitative study to enable others to understand similar situations and to apply them in conducting subsequent research

external validity The extent to which the results of a study can be generalized to other subjects, conditions, and situations

field research Research that views the setting as a natural situation in which the researcher collects data over a prolonged time

foreshadowed problems Anticipated research problems that will be reformulated during data collection

generalization The extent to which the results of one study can be used as knowledge about other populations and situations

grounded theory Qualitative procedures that are used to develop detailed concepts or conditional propositions for substantive theory

Hawthorne effect The tendency of people to act differently upon realizing that they are subjects in a study

historical analysis The application of analytical methodology to the study of the past, as in biographies and studies of movements, institutions, and concepts

history A threat to internal validity in which incidents or events that occurred during the research affect results

inadequate explication of the constructs A threat to the construct validity of a study in which insufficient explanation is provided of the nature of the construct being measured or manipulated

independent variable A variable that is antecedent to or that precedes the dependent variable; in experimental design, also called the *experimental* or *manipulated variable*

informed consent Obtaining permission from individuals to participate in research before the research begins

instrument reliability An indication of the consistency of measurement

instrument validity An indication of the extent to which inferences made on the basis of scores are appropriate

instrumentation A threat to internal validity in which changes in instruments and unreliability affect the results

interactive strategies The use of participant observation, direct observation, in-depth interviewing, artifacts, and supplementary techniques to study participants' perspectives

internal criticism The use of analytical procedures to determine the credibility of the statements in a source; the accuracy and trustworthiness of the facts

literature review A summary and analysis of related literature that is conducted to provide insights about a study

manipulated variable The independent variable in an experiment, as determined by the researcher

maximum variation sampling (quota sampling) In qualitative research, a strategy that is used to sample the anticipated different meanings of the research phenomenon or concept

maturation A threat to internal validity in quantitative research in which maturational changes in the subjects (e.g., growing older or becoming tired or hungry) affect the results

MAXMINCON An acronym for maximizing systematic variance, minimizing error variance, and control extraneous variance

meta-analysis A research procedure that uses statistical techniques to synthesize the results of prior independently conducted studies

mixed-method Refers to a study that combines qualitative and quantitative techniques and/or data analysis within different phases of the research process

mono-method bias A threat to construct validity due to the use of a single exemplar or measure

mono-operation bias A threat to construct validity due to the use of a single method in implementing an intervention or measuring the dependent variable

multistage cluster sampling The use of several stages of clustering in selecting a sample

narrative descriptions Detailed narrations of people, incidents, and processes

network sampling (snowball sampling) A qualitative strategy in which each successive participant or group is named by a preceding group or individual

nonexperimental Research that requires no direct manipulation of variables, such as descriptive and correlational research

nonprobability sampling A sampling procedure in which the probability of selecting elements from the population is not known

nonproportional sampling Stratified sampling in which the number of subjects selected from each stratum is not based on the percentage of the population represented by that stratum

objectivity Refers to data collection and analysis procedures from which only one meaning or interpretation can be made

operational definition A definition of a variable that is produced by specifying the activities or operations necessary to measure, categorize, or manipulate it

participants Individuals from whom data are collected; also called *subjects* in quantitative studies

phenomenological study Research that describes the meanings or essence of a lived experience

plausible rival hypotheses Possible explanations (i.e., other than the effect of the independent variable) for cause-and-effect relationships

population A group of individuals or events from which a sample is drawn

population external validity The extent to which the results of a research study can be generalized to other people

positionality A researcher's display of position or standpoint by describing his or her own social, cultural, historical, racial, and sexual location in the study

predictor variable The antecedent variable in a prediction study

preliminary search A search limited by use of one or two reference services, the number of years to be reviewed, or the number of sources desired; usually conducted to select a research problem

pretesting A threat to internal validity in which taking a pretest can affect the results

primary literature The original research studies or writings by researchers and theorists

probability sampling A type of sampling in which subjects are drawn from a population in known probabilities

proportional sampling A type of stratified sampling in which the number of subjects selected from each stratum is based on the percentage of subjects in the population in that stratum

purposeful sampling A type of sampling that allows choosing small groups or individuals who are likely to be knowledgeable and informative about the phenomenon of interest; selecting cases without needing or desiring to generalize to all such cases

qualitative Refers to an in-depth study using face-to-face techniques to collect data from people in their natural settings

qualitative field records Data that are recorded as participant observation field notes, in-depth interview records, or researcher notes of historical documents

quasi-experimental designs Research designs in which there is no random assignment of subjects; rather, cause-and-effect relationships are examined by manipulating the independent variable

quota sampling A nonprobability method of sampling in which subjects are selected in proportion to the characteristics they represent in the general population

random assignment A procedure used to assign subjects to different groups so that every subject has an equal chance of being assigned to each group

random sampling A procedure for selecting subjects from a population in such a way that every member of the population has an equal chance of being selected

refereed Refers to a review procedure for journal articles by experts in the field

reflexivity Refers to the researcher's rigorous self-scrutiny throughout the entire qualitative research process

related literature Literature that is relevant to the research problem or related to the design in some essential way

replication A study that duplicates the findings of a prior study using different settings or techniques

report literature Documents other than journals that are in the ERIC Document Microfiche Collection and indexed by *Resources in Education;* that is, presentations, final reports of projects, or evaluation studies

research A systematic process of collecting and logically analyzing data for a specific purpose

research design The plan that describes the conditions and procedures for collecting and analyzing data

research hypothesis A tentative statement of the expected relationship between two or more variables

research methods The procedures used to collect and analyze data

research problem A formal statement of the question or hypothesis that will be investigated through empirical research

sample The group of subjects from which data are collected; often representative of a specific population

secondary data Data that were collected previously and are available in a database for further use

secondary data analysis Statistical analysis that is conducted using secondary data

secondary literature A synthesis of existing research literature; can be theoretical, empirical, or both

selection A threat to internal validity in which differences between groups of subjects affect the results

significance of the problem The rationale for a research problem or the importance of a study as it relates to developing educational theory, knowledge, and/or practice

simple random sampling *See* random sampling

single-subject designs Research done with individual subjects in order to study the changes in behavior that are associated with the intervention or removal of a treatment

site selection The specification of site criteria implied in the foreshadowed problems; used to obtain a suitable and feasible research site

sources of variability Systematic, error, and extraneous influences related to research design

statistical conclusion validity The extent to which statistics provide accurate information about the relationship being studied

statistical regression The tendency for extreme scores to move closer to the mean score on a second testing

stratified random sampling A form of random sampling in which a population is first divided into subgroups (i.e., strata) and then subjects are selected from each subgroup

subject effects Changes in subject behavior that results from being in a study

subjects The person or persons from whom data are collected in a study

survey The use of a questionnaire or interview to assess the current opinions, beliefs, and attitudes of members of a known population

synthesized abstractions Summative generalizations and explanations of the major research findings of a study; format varies with the selected qualitative tradition

systematic sampling A form of sampling in which subjects are selected from a continuous list by choosing every *n*th subject

theory A prediction and explanation of natural phenomena

thesaurus A publication that lists and cross-references the key terms used in an index for a reference service (database), such as ERIC or *Psychological Abstracts*.

treatment replications A threat to internal validity that occurs when the number of treatment replications does not equal the number of subjects

triangulation Qualitative cross-validation among multiple data sources, data collection strategies, time periods, and theoretical schemes

triangulation design A type of mixed-method design in which quantitative and qualitative methods are used simultaneously

typicality The degree to which a phenomenon may be compared or contrasted with other phenomena along relevant dimensions

validity of qualitative designs The degree to which the interpretations have mutual meanings between the participants and the researcher

variability *See* measures of variability

variable An event, category, behavior, or attribute that expresses a construct and has different values, depending on how it is used in a study

verification Confirming or modifying the results of a research study in subsequent research

APPENDIX B

Calculations for Selected Descriptive and Inferential Statistics

In this appendix, we will present a step-by-step guide for performing calculations for several simple statistical procedures.* Our intent is not to derive formulas but to show how the statistics are calculated. We believe that being able to apply these formulas assists greatly in understanding the meaning of the statistics.

MEASURES OF CENTRAL TENDENCY

Measures of *central tendency* are descriptive statistics that measure the central location or value of sets of scores. They are used widely to summarize and simplify large quantities of data.

The Mean

The *mean* is the arithmetical average of a set of scores. It is obtained by adding all the scores in a distribution and dividing the sum by the number of scores. The formula for calculating the mean is

$$\bar{X} = \frac{\Sigma X}{n}$$

where

$\bar{X}$ is the mean score
ΣX is the sum of the X_s (i.e., $X_1 + X_2 + X_3 \ldots X_n$)
n is the total number of scores

Example: Calculation of Mean If we have obtained the sample of eight scores—17, 14, 14, 13, 10, 8, 7, 7—the mean of this set of scores is calculated as

$$\Sigma X = 17 + 14 + 14 + \ldots + 7 = 90$$
$$n = 8$$

Therefore,

$$\bar{X} = \frac{90}{8} = 11.25$$

*Statistical tables are located at the end of the appendix.

The Median

The *median* is the score in a distribution below which half the scores fall. In other words, half the scores are above the median and half are below the median. The median is at the 50th percentile.

To calculate the median, the scores are rank ordered from highest to lowest; then one simply counts, from one end, one half of the scores. In distributions with an odd number of scores, the median is the middle score, as illustrated here:

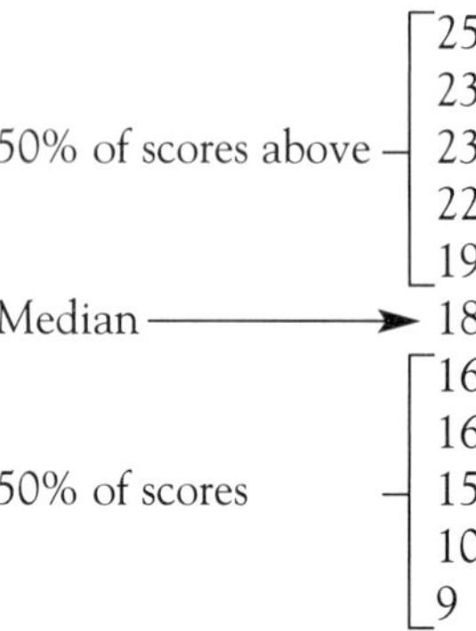

If the distribution has an even number of scores, the median is the average of the two middle scores. In this case, the median is a new score or point in the distribution, as shown here:

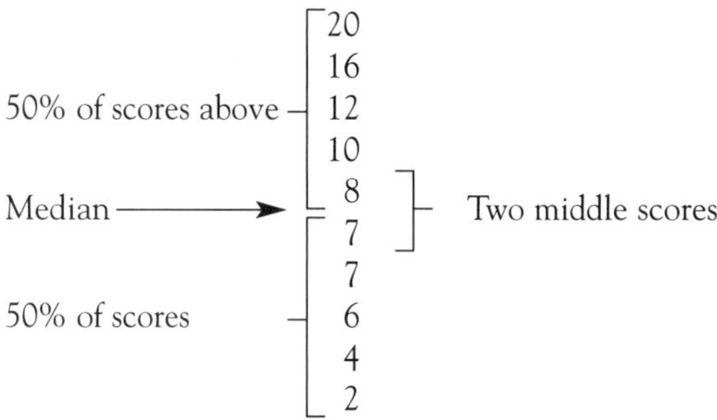

Thus, the median in this example is

$$7 + \frac{8}{2} = \frac{15}{2} + 7.5$$

The median is relatively easy to find in studies with a small number of subjects. As the number of scores increases, the calculation is done either by a formula or by placing the scores into intervals of scores and using the intervals to make the calculations. Computers are able to apply these more complicated calculations easily, quickly, and reliably.

The Mode The *mode* is simply the most frequently occurring score in a distribution, and it is found by counting the number of times each score was received. The mode in this distribution, for example, is 22:

23 22 22 22 20 18 18 17 16

MEASURES OF VARIABILITY

Measures of variability are used to show the differences among the scores in a distribution. We use the term *variability* or *dispersion* because the statistics provide an indication of how different, or dispersed, the scores are from one another. We will discuss three measures of variability: range, variance, and standard deviation.

The Range

The *range* is the simplest but also least useful measure of variability. It is defined as the distance between the smallest and the largest scores and is calculated by simply subtracting the bottom, or lowest, score from the top, or highest, score:

$$\text{Range} = X_H - X_L$$

where

X_H = the highest score
X_L = the lowest score

For the following scores, then, the range is 26 – 6 = 20:

6 8 10 11 15 20 26

The range is a crude measure of variability and is unstable. Because the range can be biased, it is rarely used as the only measure of variability.

Variance

The *variance* (s^2 or σ^2) is a measure of dispersion that indicates the degree to which scores cluster around the mean. The variance provides the researcher with one number to indicate, in a sense, the average dispersion of scores from the mean. Computationally, the variance is the sum of the squared deviation scores about the mean divided by the total number of scores:

$$s^2 = \frac{\Sigma(X - \bar{X})^2}{N}$$

where

s^2 is the variance
$\Sigma(X - X)^2$ is the sum of the squared deviation scores
$(X - \bar{X})$ is the deviation score
N is the total number of scores

For any distribution of scores, the variance can be determined by following these five steps:

1. Calculate the mean: $(\Sigma X/N)$.
2. Calculate the deviation scores: $(X - \bar{X})$.

3. Square each deviation score: $(X - \bar{X})^2$.
4. Sum all the deviation scores: $\Sigma(X - \bar{X})^2$
5. Divide the sum by N: $\Sigma(X - \bar{X})^2/N$.

These steps are illustrated with actual numbers as follows:

(1) Raw Scores	(2) $(X - \bar{X})$	(3) $(X - \bar{X})^2$	(4)	(5)
20	7	49		
15	2	4		
15	2	4		
14	1	1		
14	1	1	$\Sigma(X - \bar{X})^2 = 120$	$\frac{\Sigma(X - \bar{X})^2}{N} = 12$
14	1	1		
12	–1	1		
10	–3	9		
8	–5	25		
8	–5	25		
$\Sigma X = 130$				
$N = 10$				
$\bar{X} = 13$				

Substituting directly in the formula:

$$s^2 = \frac{120}{10} = 12$$

Here is another formula that can be used to calculate the variance that is computationally more simple:

$$s^2 = \frac{\Sigma\bar{X}^2 - N\bar{X}^2}{N}$$

Because the variance is expressed as the square of the raw scores, not the original units, it is not usually reported in research. To return to units that are consistent with the raw score distribution, we need to take the square root of the variance. Taking the square root of the variance yields the standard deviation.

Standard Deviation

The *standard deviation* (s, σ, or *SD*) is the square root of the variance. It is a measure of dispersion that uses deviation scores expressed in standard units about the mean; hence the name *standard deviation*. The standard deviation is equal to the square root of the sum of the squared deviation scores about the mean divided by the total number of scores. The formula is

$$s = \sqrt{\frac{\Sigma(X - \bar{X})^2}{N}}$$

where

s	is the standard deviation
$\sqrt{}$	is the square root
$\Sigma(X - \bar{X})^2$	is the sum of the squared deviation scores
$(X - \bar{X})$	is the deviation score
N	is the total number of scores

To calculate the standard deviation, simply add one step to the formula for variance: take the square root. In our example for variance, for instance, the standard deviation would be

$$s = \sqrt{\frac{\Sigma(X - \bar{X})^2}{N}} = \sqrt{\frac{120}{10}} = \sqrt{12} = 3.46$$

The standard deviation is commonly reported in research and, with the mean, is the most important statistic in research. It tells the number of scores (i.e., the percentage of scores) that are within given units of the standard deviation around the mean. This property of standard deviation is explained in the section called "Normal Distribution," which follows.

STANDARD SCORES

Standard scores are numbers that are transformed from raw scores to provide consistent information about the location of a score within a total distribution. They are numbers that are related to the normal distribution.

Normal Distribution

The *normal distribution* is a set of scores that, when plotted in a frequency distribution, result in a symmetrical, bell-shaped curve with precise mathematical properties. The mathematical properties provide the basis for making standardized interpretations. These properties include possessing a mode, mean, and median that are the same; having a mean that divides the curve into two identical halves; and having measures of standard deviation that fall at predictable places on the normal curve, with the same percentage of scores between the mean and points equidistant from the mean.

This third characteristic is very important. We know, for example, that at $+1s$, we will always be at about the 84th percentile in the distribution. (The percentile score is the percentage of scores at or below the designated score.) This is because the median is at the 50th percentile, and $+1s$ contains an additional 34 percent of the scores (50 + 34 = 84). Similarly, the percentage of scores between $+1s$ and $+2s$ is about 14 percent, which means that $+2s$ is at the 98th percentile. These characteristics are illustrated in Figure B.1, the graph of the standard normal distribution.

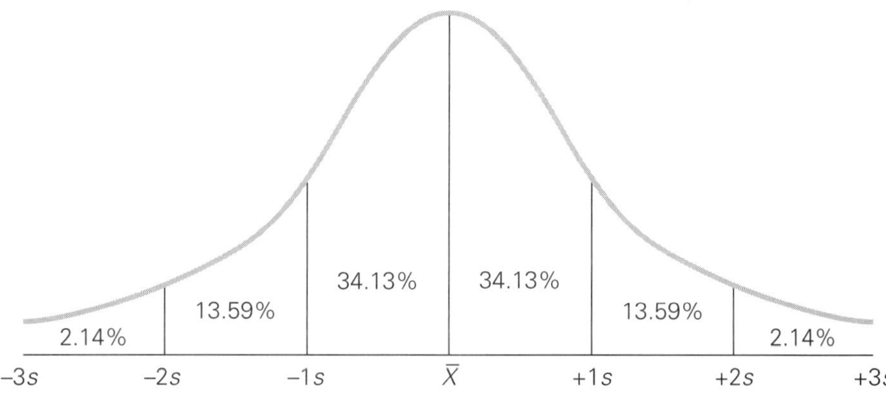

FIGURE B.1 **Graph of the Standard Normal Distribution or Normal Curve**

The pleasing aspect of this property is that for any raw score distribution with unique units, such as 1 or 2 as s, the interpretation is always the same. If one distribution has a mean of 10, therefore, and a standard deviation of 3, and a second distribution has a mean of 50 and a standard deviation of 7, a score of 4 in the first case is at about the same percentile (the second) as a score of 36 in the second case.

z-Scores

The most basic standard score is called a *z*-score, and it is expressed as a deviation from the mean in standard deviation units. A *z*-score of 1 is thus at one standard deviation, –1 is at minus one standard deviation, +2 at two standard deviations, and so forth.

After the mean and standard deviation are calculated for a set of scores, it is easy to convert each raw score to a *z*-score, which then indicates exactly where each score lies in the normal distribution.

The formula for calculating a *z*-score is

$$z = \frac{X - \bar{X}}{s}$$

where

z is the *z*-score value
X is any particular score
$\bar{X}$ is the arithmetic mean of a distribution of scores
s is the standard deviation of that same distribution

Taking the scores used to illustrate variance and standard deviation, the *z*-scores would be found as follows:

$$\text{For the raw score of 20: } z = \frac{20 - 13}{3.46} = 2.02$$

$$\text{For the raw score of 14: } z = \frac{14 - 13}{3.46} = 0.29$$

$$\text{For the raw score of 10: } z = \frac{10 - 13}{3.46} = -0.87$$

Once the *z*-score has been calculated, it is easy to refer to conversion tables to find the percentile rank corresponding to each *z*-score.

T-Scores

One limitation of using *z*-scores is the necessity for being careful with the negative sign and with the decimal point. To avoid these problems, other standard scores are used by converting the *z*-scores algebraically to different units. The general formula for converting *z*-scores is

$$A = \bar{X}_A + s_A(z)$$

where

A is the new standard score equivalent to z
$\bar{X}_A$ is the mean for the new standard-score scale
s_A is the standard deviation for the new standard-score scale
z is the *z*-score for any observation

For *T*-scores, $\bar{X}_A = 50$ and $s_A = 10$. The equation for converting *z*-scores to *T*-scores is thus

$$T = 50 + 10(z)$$

For example, the *T*-scores for our earlier illustration would be as follows:

For the raw score of 20: $T = 50 + 10(2.02) = 70.2$
For the raw score of 14: $T = 50 + 10(0.29) = 52.9$
For the raw score of 10: $T = 50 + 10(-0.87) = 41.3$

Other Standard Scores

Other common standard scores include the following:

1. Normal Curve Equivalent (NCE) has a mean of 50 and *s* of 21.06. Thus, NCE = 50 + 21.06 (*z*-score).
2. IQ score has a mean of 100 and *s* of 15 or 16. Thus, IQ = 100 + 15 (*z*-score).
3. College Entrance Examination Boards (CEEB, such as SAT) use a mean of 500 and an *s* of 100. Thus, CEEB = 500 + 100 (*z*-score).
4. ACT (American College Testing Program) uses a mean of 20 and an *s* of 5. Thus, ACT = 20 + 5 (*z*-score).
5. Stanine. The stanine is also commonly reported. Stanines are standardized on a mean of 5 and *s* of 2, but unlike other standard scores, the numbers refer to intervals rather than to specific points on the normal distribution. Stanine 5 is located in the center of the distribution and includes the middle 20 percent of scores; stanines 4 and 6 include 17 percent of the scores; 3 and 7, 12 percent; 2 and 8, 7 percent; and 1 and 9, 4 percent.

MEASURES OF RELATIONSHIP

Measures of relationship are used to indicate the degree to which two sets of scores are related, or covary. We intuitively seek relationships by such statements as "If high scores on variable X tend to be associated with high scores on variable Y, then the variables are related" and "If high scores on variable X tend to be associated with low scores on variable Y, then the variables are related." The relationship can be either positive or negative and either strong or weak.

We use correlation coefficients as a statistical summary of the nature of the relationship between two variables. They provide us with an estimate of the quantitative degree of relationship. The numbers are almost always between –1.00 and +1.00. We will show how to calculate two common correlation coefficients: the Pearson product-moment and the Spearman rho correlations.

Pearson Product-Moment (Pearson *r*)

The *Pearson product-moment correlation coefficient* is the most widely used measure of relationship. The Pearson *r* is calculated to show the linear relationship between two variables. To compute the Pearson *r*, two measures on each subject are needed. Suppose, for example, we have a group of 10 subjects, and for each subject we have measures of self-concept and achievement. We can then calculate the Pearson *r* between self-concept and achievement for these 10 subjects using the following formula:

$$\text{Pearson } r = \frac{N\Sigma XY - (\Sigma X)(\Sigma Y)}{\sqrt{N\Sigma X^2 - (\Sigma X)^2} \cdot \sqrt{N\Sigma Y^2 - (\Sigma Y)^2}}$$

where

ΣXY is the sum of the XY cross-products
ΣX is the sum of the X scores
ΣY is the sum of the Y scores
ΣX^2 is the sum of the squared X scores
ΣY^2 is the sum of the squared Y scores
N is the number of pairs of scores

This formula may appear complex but is actually quite easy to calculate. The scores can be listed in a table, as follows. To use it, one simply finds the values for each summation in the formula, substitutes where appropriate, and performs the math indicated.

Subject	Self-Concept Score *X*	X^2	Achievement Score *Y*	Y^2	$X \cdot Y$
1	25	625	85	7,225	2,125
2	20	400	90	8,100	1,800
3	21	441	80	6,400	1,680
4	18	324	70	4,900	1,260
5	15	225	75	5,625	1,125
6	17	289	80	6,400	1,360
7	14	196	75	5,625	1,050
8	15	225	70	4,900	1,050
9	12	144	75	5,625	900
10	13	169	60	3,600	780
	$\Sigma X = 170$	$\Sigma X^2 = 3{,}038$	$\Sigma Y = 760$	$\Sigma Y^2 = 58{,}400$	$\Sigma X \bullet Y = 13{,}130$
	$(\Sigma X)^2 = 28{,}900$		$(\Sigma Y)^2 = 577{,}600$		

To conduct the Pearson r, follow these steps:

1. Pair each set of scores; one set becomes X, the other Y.
2. Calculate ΣX and ΣY.
3. Calculate X^2 and Y^2.
4. Calculate ΣX^2 and ΣY^2.
5. Calculate $(\Sigma X)^2$ and $(\Sigma Y)^2$.
6. Calculate $X \times Y$.
7. Calculate $\Sigma X \times Y$.
8. Substitute the calculated values into the formula.

$$\text{Pearson } r = \frac{10(131{,}300) - (170)(760)}{\sqrt{10(30{,}380) - 28{,}900} \bullet \sqrt{10(58{,}400) - 577{,}600}}$$

$$= \frac{131{,}300 - 129{,}200}{\sqrt{30{,}380 - 28{,}900} \bullet \sqrt{584{,}000 - 577{,}600}}$$

$$= \frac{2{,}100}{\sqrt{1{,}480} \bullet \sqrt{6{,}400}}$$

$$= \frac{2{,}100}{(38.47) \bullet (80)}$$

$$= \frac{2{,}100}{3{,}078}$$

$$= .68$$

The value of 0.68 shows a moderate positive relationship between self-concept and achievement for this set of scores. The level of significance of correlation coefficients are indicated in Table B.2 at the end of this appendix.

Spearman Rank (r ranks or Spearman rho)

The *Spearman rho* is used when ranks are available on each of two variables for all subjects. Ranks are simply listings of scores from highest to lowest. The Spearman rho correlation shows the degree to which subjects maintain the same relative position on two measures. In other words, the Spearman rho indicates how much agreement there is between the ranks of each variable.

The calculation of the Spearman ranks is more simple than calculating the Pearson r. The necessary steps are as follow:

1. Rank the Xs and Ys.
2. Pair the ranked Xs and Ys.
3. Calculate the difference in ranks for each pair.
4. Square each difference.
5. Sum the squared differences.
6. Substitute calculated values into formula.

The formula is:

$$\text{Spearman rho} = 1 - \frac{6\Sigma D^2}{n(n^2 - 1)}$$

For the data used in calculating the Pearson r, the Spearman rho would be found as follows:

Subject	Self-Concept Rank *X*	Achievement Rank *Y*	Difference *D*	D^2
1	1	2	−1	1
2	3	1	2	4
3	2	3.5	−1.5	2.25
4	4	5.5	−1.5	2.25
5	6.5	8	−1.5	2.25
6	5	3.5	1.5	2.25
7	8	8	0	0
8	6.5	5.5	1	1
9	10	8	2	4
10	9	10	−1	1
				$\Sigma D^2 = 20$

Note: When ties in the ranking occur, all scores that are tied receive the average of the ranks involved.

$$\begin{aligned} r \text{ ranks} &= 1 - \frac{6(20)}{10(100 - 1)} \\ &= 1 - \frac{120}{990} \\ &= 1 - 0.12 \\ &= .88 \end{aligned}$$

In most data sets with more than 50 subjects, the Pearson r and Spearman rank will give almost identical correlations. In the example used here, the Spearman is higher because of the low n and the manner in which the ties in rankings resulted in low difference scores.

CHI-SQUARE

Chi-square (χ^2) is a statistical procedure that is used as an infererential statistic with nominal data, such as frequency counts, and ordinal data, such as percentages and proportions. In the simplest case, the data are organized into two categories, such as *yes* and *no*, *high* and *low*, *for* and *against*. If, for example, a researcher is interested in the opinions of college professors about tenure and asks the question Should tenure be abolished? then all responses could be categorized as either *yes* or *no*. The total frequency in each category (observed frequencies) is then compared to the expected frequency, which in most cases is chance. This means that with two categories, half the responses should be *yes* and half *no*. Assume the following results:

Should tenure be abolished?

	Yes	**No**
Observed	40	60
Expected	50	50

These values are then used in the following formula to calculate the chi-square statistic:

$$\chi^2 = \Sigma \frac{(f_o - f_e)^2}{f_e}$$

where

χ^2 is the chi-square statistic
Σ is the sum of
f_o is the observed frequency
f_e is the expected frequency

Inserting the values from the table, the result is

$$\chi^2 = \frac{(40 - 50)^2}{50} + \frac{(60 - 50)^2}{50}$$

$$= \frac{100}{50} + \frac{100}{50}$$

$$= 2 + 2$$

$$= 4.0$$

The obtained value, in this case 4, is then used with the degrees of freedom in the problem ($df = k - 1$, where k equals the number of categories; in our example, $df = 2 - 1$, or 1) to find the value of the chi-square in the critical values of chi-square table (Table B.3 at the end of this appendix) to determine the level of significance of the results. By referring to the table and locating 4.00 within the table with 1 *df*, the result is significant at just less than a p value of .05. Consequently, it would be appropriate to say that there is a significant difference in the number of professors responding *yes* as compared to the number responding *no*.

Suppose the researcher wanted to go a step further with this problem and learn whether administrators and professors differ in their responses to the question about abolishing tenure. The researcher would then have what is called a contingency table, which is a cross-tabulation of the frequencies for the combinations of categories of the two variables. A hypothetical contingency table is shown below for administrators and professors.

Should tenure be abolished?

	Professors	Administrators	Raw Totals
Yes	40(p = 0.40)	40(p = 0.80)	80(p_e = 0.53)
No	60(p = 0.60)	10(p = 0.20)	70(p_e = 0.47)
	n = 100	n = 50	n = 150

Notice in the table that the proportion of responses in each response category (*yes* and *no*) is shown for both professors and administrators, and the total proportions are shown in the last column. These proportions are used in the following equation:

$$\chi^2 = \frac{\Sigma n(P - P_e)^2}{P_e}$$

where

χ^2 is the chi-square statistic
Σ is the sum of all cells in the problem (in our example, there are four cells)
n is the number of total observations in each column
P is the proportion of observed frequencies in each cell
P_e is the expected proportion for each row

For our example, therefore, the result would be

$$\chi^2 = 100\,\frac{(.4 - .53)^2}{.53} + 100\,\frac{(0.60 - .47)^2}{.47}$$

$$= 50\,\frac{(.80 - .53)^2}{.53} + 100\,\frac{(.20 - .47)}{.47}$$

$$= 100\,\frac{.017}{.53} + 100\,\frac{.017}{.47} + 50\,\frac{.07}{.53} + 50\,\frac{.07}{.47}$$

$$= 3.19 + 3.61 + 6.60 + 7.45$$

$$= 20.85$$

In contingency tables, the degrees of freedom are equal to $(r - 1)(c - 1)$, where r is the number of rows and c is the number of columns. In our example, the $df = (2 - 1)(2 - 1) = 1$. By locating 22.08 with 1 degree of freedom in the critical values of chi-square table (Table B.3), we note that the result is highly significant, $p < .001$. This result indicates that there is a significant association or relationship between the two variables (*professors* and *administrators*, and *yes* and *no*).

t-TEST

The *t*-test is used to indicate the probability that the means of two groups are different. We will present two common forms of the *t*-test: one used with independent samples and the other with dependent samples.

Independent Samples *t*-test

The *independent samples t-test*, or *t*-test for independent groups, is used to determine whether the mean values of a variable on one group of subjects is different from a mean value on the same variable with a different group of subjects. It is important to meet three statistical assumptions: (1) that the frequency distributions of scores for both the populations of each group are normal, (2) that the variances in each population are equal, and (3) that the observation of scores in one group is independent from the other group. If the sample size is greater than 30, violating the assumption of normality is not serious, and as long as the sample sizes are equal, violation of the assumption of homogeneity of variance is not a problem. It is crucial, however, that the observations for each group are independent.

The formula for calculating the *t*-test statistic is

$$t = \frac{\bar{X}_1 - \bar{X}_2}{s_{\bar{X}_1 - \bar{X}_2}}$$

where

t is the *t*-test statistic
$\bar{X}_1$ is the mean of one group
$\bar{X}_2$ is the mean of the second group
$s_{\bar{X}_1 - \bar{X}_2}$ is the standard error of the difference in means

The standard error of the difference in means is estimated from the variances of each distribution. This part of the formula is calculated by pooling the variances of each distribution to result in s. This is done using the following formula:

$$s = \sqrt{\frac{\Sigma x_1^2 + \Sigma x_2^2}{df_1 + df_2}}$$

Then,

$$s_{\bar{X}_1 - \bar{X}_2} = s\sqrt{\frac{1}{n_1} + \frac{1}{n_2}}$$

As an example, consider the data we present below:

Group x_1	Group x_2
$\bar{X}_1 = 18$	$\bar{X}_2 = 25$
$n_1 = 20$	$n_2 = 20$
$\Sigma X_1^2 = 348$	$\Sigma X_2^2 = 425$

From this point, we can calculate the *t*-test statistic using the following steps:

1. Calculate s:

$$s = \sqrt{\frac{348 + 425}{19 + 19}}$$
$$= \sqrt{20.34}$$
$$= 4.51$$

2. Calculate $s_{\bar{X}_1 - \bar{X}_2}$:

$$s_{\bar{X}_1 - \bar{X}_2} = 4.51\sqrt{\frac{1}{20} + \frac{1}{20}}$$

$$= 4.51\sqrt{\frac{1}{10}}$$

$$= 4.51(0.32)$$

$$= 1.44$$

3. Substitute into *t*-test formula:

$$t = \frac{18 - 25}{1.44}$$

$$= \frac{7}{1.44}$$

$$= 4.86$$

Once the *t*-test statistic is calculated, it is found in the critical values for *t*-table (Table 11.1) with corresponding degrees of freedom (which for the independent samples *t*-test is $n_1 + n_2 - 2$, or in our example, $20 + 20 - 2 = 38$) to determine the significance level of the results. In this example, the *t*-test statistic of 4.86, with 38 *df*, is significant at $p < 0.001$.

Here is another example of a computation with the *t*-test, beginning with raw data:

Group 1		Group 2	
x^1	x_1^2	x_2	x_2^2
7	49	7	49
8	64	7	49
8	64	8	64
6	36	6	36
5	25	6	36
5	25	4	16
6	36	4	16
6	36	3	9
9	81	5	25
8	64	5	25
$\Sigma x_1 = 68$	$\Sigma x_1^2 = 480$	$\Sigma x_2 = 55$	$\Sigma x_2^2 = 325$
$n = 10$	$n = 10$	$\bar{X}_2 = 5.5$	
$\bar{X}_1 = 6.8$			

Following the three steps outlined earlier:

$$s = \sqrt{\frac{480 + 325}{9 + 9}} = \sqrt{44.72} = 6.69$$

$$s_{\bar{X}_1 - \bar{X}_2} = 6.69\sqrt{\frac{1}{10} + \frac{1}{10}} = 6.69\sqrt{\frac{1}{5}} = (6.69)(0.45) = 2.99$$

$$t = \frac{6.8 - 5.5}{2.99} = \frac{1.3}{2.99} = 0.43$$

In this case, the *t*-test statistic of 0.43, with 18 *df*, is not statistically significant. Even though the means for the groups are different, therefore, there is a good possibility that they can be different by chance alone.

Dependent Samples *t*-Test

When two groups that have been matched are being compared, as in a pretest-posttest design, the *t*-test formula must take into account the interrelationship between the groups: that is, the groups are not independent but rather related. The formula for this type of *t*-test is easier to calculate than for the independent samples *t*-test:

$$t = \frac{\bar{D}}{\sqrt{\dfrac{\Sigma D^2 - \dfrac{(\Sigma D)^2}{N}}{N(N-1)}}}$$

where

D is the mean difference for all pairs of scores
ΣD^2 is the sum of the squares of the differences
$(\Sigma D)^2$ is the square of the sum of the differences
N is the number of pairs of scores
$N - 1$ is the degrees of freedom (one less than the number of pairs of scores).

Consider the following example and steps:

	Posttest Scores	**Pretest Scores**		
Subjects	x_1	x_2	$\bar{D}$	D_2
1	22	15	7	49
2	21	16	5	25
3	20	17	7	49
4	23	16	7	49
5	19	14	5	25
6	21	15	6	36
7	18	12	6	36
8	22	18	4	16
			$\Sigma D = 47$	$\Sigma D^2 = 285$

To perform the first step, calculate $\bar{D}$:

$$\bar{D} = \frac{\Sigma D}{N} = \frac{47}{8} = 5.9$$

To perform step 2:

$$(\Sigma D)^2 = 47^2 = 2{,}209$$

Finally, substitute into the formula:

$$t = \frac{5.9}{\sqrt{\dfrac{285 - \dfrac{2{,}209}{8}}{8(8-1)}}}$$

$$= \frac{5.9}{\sqrt{\frac{285 - 276}{56}}}$$

$$= \frac{5.9}{\sqrt{\frac{9}{56}}}$$

$$= \frac{5.9}{0.40}$$

$$= 14.75$$

The calculated *t*-test statistic (14.75) is located in the critical values of the *t*-table, with the degrees of freedom ($N - 1$, or in this example, $8 - 1 = 7$). The result from the table is that the group means are clearly different from each other and statistically significant at $p < .001$.

TABLE B.1 Random Numbers

03 47 43 73 86	36 96 47 36 61	46 98 64 71 62	33 26 16 80 45	60 11 14 10 95
97 74 24 67 62	42 81 14 57 20	42 53 32 37 32	27 07 36 07 51	24 51 79 89 73
16 76 62 27 66	56 50 26 71 07	32 90 79 78 53	13 55 38 58 59	88 97 54 14 10
12 56 85 99 26	96 96 68 27 31	05 03 72 93 15	57 12 10 14 21	88 26 49 81 76
55 59 56 35 64	38 54 82 46 22	31 62 43 09 90	06 18 44 32 53	23 83 01 30 30
16 22 77 94 39	49 54 43 54 82	17 37 93 23 78	87 35 20 96 43	84 26 34 91 64
84 42 17 53 31	57 24 55 06 88	77 04 74 47 67	21 76 33 50 25	83 92 12 06 76
63 01 63 78 59	16 95 55 67 19	98 10 50 71 75	12 86 73 58 07	44 39 52 38 79
33 21 12 45 29	78 64 56 07 82	52 42 07 44 38	15 51 00 13 42	99 66 02 79 54
57 60 86 32 44	09 47 27 96 54	49 17 46 09 62	90 52 84 77 27	08 02 73 43 28
18 18 07 92 46	44 17 16 58 09	79 83 86 19 62	06 76 50 03 10	55 23 64 05 05
26 62 38 97 75	84 16 07 44 99	83 11 46 32 24	20 14 85 88 45	10 93 72 88 71
23 42 40 64 74	82 97 77 77 81	07 45 32 14 08	32 98 94 07 72	93 85 79 10 75
52 36 28 19 95	50 92 26 11 97	00 56 76 31 38	80 22 02 53 53	86 60 42 04 53
37 85 84 35 12	83 39 50 08 30	42 34 07 96 88	54 42 06 87 98	35 85 29 48 39
70 29 17 12 13	40 33 20 38 26	13 89 51 03 74	17 76 37 13 04	07 74 21 19 30
56 62 18 37 35	96 83 50 87 75	97 12 25 93 47	70 33 24 03 54	97 77 46 44 80
99 59 57 22 77	88 42 95 45 72	16 64 36 16 00	04 43 18 66 79	94 77 24 21 90
16 08 15 04 72	33 27 14 34 09	45 59 34 68 49	12 72 07 34 45	99 27 72 95 14
31 16 93 32 43	50 27 89 87 19	20 15 37 00 49	52 85 66 60 44	38 68 88 11 80
68 34 30 13 70	55 74 30 77 40	44 22 78 84 26	04 33 46 09 52	68 07 97 06 57
74 57 25 65 76	59 29 97 68 60	71 91 38 67 54	13 58 18 24 76	15 54 55 95 52
27 42 37 86 53	48 55 90 65 72	96 57 69 36 10	96 46 92 42 45	97 60 49 04 91
00 39 68 29 61	66 37 32 20 30	77 84 57 03 29	10 45 65 04 26	11 04 96 67 24
29 94 98 94 24	68 49 69 10 82	53 75 91 93 30	34 25 20 57 27	40 48 73 51 92
16 90 82 66 59	83 62 64 11 12	67 19 00 71 74	60 47 21 29 68	02 02 37 03 31
11 27 94 75 06	06 09 19 74 66	02 94 37 34 02	76 70 90 30 86	38 45 94 30 38
35 24 10 16 20	33 32 51 26 38	79 78 45 04 91	16 92 53 56 16	02 75 50 95 98
38 23 16 86 38	42 38 97 01 50	87 75 66 81 41	40 01 74 91 62	48 51 84 08 32
31 96 25 91 47	96 44 33 49 13	34 86 82 53 92	00 52 43 48 85	27 55 26 89 62
66 67 40 67 14	64 05 71 95 86	11 05 65 09 68	76 83 20 37 90	57 16 00 11 66
14 90 84 45 11	75 73 88 05 90	52 27 41 14 86	22 98 12 22 08	07 52 74 95 80
68 05 51 18 00	33 96 02 75 19	07 60 62 93 55	59 33 82 43 90	49 37 38 44 59
20 46 78 73 90	97 51 40 14 02	04 02 33 31 08	39 54 16 49 36	47 95 93 13 30
64 19 58 97 79	15 06 15 93 20	01 90 10 75 06	40 78 78 89 62	02 67 74 17 33
05 26 93 70 60	22 35 85 15 13	92 03 51 59 77	59 56 78 06 83	52 91 05 70 74
07 97 10 88 23	09 98 42 99 64	61 71 62 99 15	06 51 29 16 93	58 05 77 09 51
68 71 86 85 85	54 87 66 47 54	73 32 08 11 12	44 95 92 63 16	29 56 24 29 48
26 99 61 65 53	58 37 78 80 70	43 10 50 67 42	32 17 55 85 74	94 44 67 16 94
14 65 52 68 75	87 59 36 22 41	26 78 63 06 55	13 08 27 01 50	15 29 39 39 43
17 53 77 58 71	71 41 61 50 72	12 41 94 96 26	44 95 27 36 99	02 96 74 30 83
90 26 59 21 19	23 52 23 33 12	96 93 02 18 39	07 02 18 36 07	25 99 32 70 23
41 23 52 55 99	31 04 49 69 96	10 47 48 45 88	13 41 43 89 20	97 17 14 49 17
60 20 50 81 69	31 99 73 68 68	35 81 33 03 76	24 30 12 48 60	18 99 10 72 34
91 25 38 05 90	94 58 28 41 36	45 37 59 03 09	90 35 57 29 12	82 62 54 65 60
34 50 57 74 37	98 80 33 00 91	09 77 93 19 82	74 94 80 04 04	45 07 31 66 49
85 22 04 39 43	73 81 53 94 79	33 62 46 86 28	08 31 54 46 31	53 94 13 38 47
09 79 13 77 48	73 82 97 22 21	05 03 27 24 83	72 89 44 05 60	35 80 39 94 88
88 75 80 18 14	22 95 75 42 49	39 32 82 22 49	02 48 07 70 37	16 04 61 67 87
90 96 23 70 00	39 00 03 06 90	55 85 78 38 36	94 37 30 69 32	90 89 00 76 33

Source: Taken from Table XXXII of Fisher and Yates': *Statistical Tables for Biological, Agricultural and Medical Research* (6th Edition 1974) published by Longman Group UK Ltd. London (previously published by Oliver and Boyd Ltd, Edinburgh) and is reprinted by permission of the authors and publishers.

TABLE B.2 Critical Values for the Pearson Correlation Coefficient

	Level of Significance for a One-Tail Test				
	.05	.025	.01	.005	.0005
	Level of Significance for a Two-Tail Test				
df	.10	.05	.02	.01	.001
1	.9877	.9969	.9995	.9999	1.0000
2	.9000	.9500	.9800	.9900	.9990
3	.8054	.8783	.9343	.9587	.9912
4	.7293	.8114	.8822	.9172	.9741
5	.6694	.7545	.8329	.8745	.9507
6	.6215	.7067	.7887	.8343	.9249
7	.5822	.6664	.7498	.7977	.8982
8	.5494	.6319	.7155	.7646	.8721
9	.5214	.6021	.6851	.7348	.8471
10	.4973	.5760	.6581	.7079	.8233
11	.4762	.5529	.6339	.6835	.8010
12	.4575	.5324	.6120	.6614	.7800
13	.4409	.5139	.5923	.6411	.7603
14	.4259	.4973	.5742	.6226	.7420
15	.4124	.4821	.5577	.6055	.7246
16	.4000	.4683	.5425	.5897	.7084
17	.3887	.4555	.5285	.5751	.6932
18	.3783	.4438	.5155	.5614	.6787
19	.3687	.4329	.5034	.5487	.6652
20	.3598	.4227	.4921	.5368	.6524
25	.3223	.3809	.4451	.4869	.5974
30	.2960	.3494	.4093	.4487	.5541
35	.2746	.3246	.3810	.4182	.5189
40	.2573	.3044	.3578	.3932	.4896
45	.2428	.2875	.3384	.3721	.4648
50	.2306	.2732	.3218	.3541	.4433
60	.2108	.2500	.2948	.3248	.4078
70	.1954	.2319	.2737	.3017	.3799
80	.1829	.2172	.2565	.2830	.3568
90	.1726	.2050	.2422	.2673	.3375
100	.1638	.1946	.2301	.2540	.3211

Source: Taken from Table VII of Fisher and Yates: *Statistical Tables for Biological, Agricultural and Medical Research* (6th Edition, 1974) published by Longman Group UK Ltd. London (previously published by Oliver and Boyd Ltd, Edinburgh) and is reprinted by permission of the authors and publishers.

TABLE B.3 Critical Values of Chi-Square

df	.99	.98	.95	.90	.80	.70	.50	.30	.20	.10	.05	.02	.01	.001
1	.0002	.0006	.0039	.016	.064	.15	.46	1.07	1.64	2.71	3.84	5.41	6.64	10.83
2	.02	.04	.10	.21	.45	.71	1.39	1.41	3.22	4.60	5.99	7.82	9.21	13.82
3	.12	.18	.35	.58	1.00	1.42	2.37	3.66	4.64	6.25	7.82	9.84	11.34	16.27
4	.30	.43	.71	1.06	1.65	2.20	3.36	4.88	5.99	7.78	9.49	11.67	13.28	18.47
5	.55	.75	1.14	1.61	2.34	3.00	4.35	6.06	7.29	9.24	11.07	13.39	15.09	20.52
6	.87	1.13	1.64	2.20	3.07	3.83	5.35	7.23	8.56	10.64	12.59	15.03	16.81	22.46
7	1.24	1.56	2.17	2.83	3.82	4.67	6.35	8.38	9.80	12.02	14.07	16.62	18.48	24.32
8	1.65	2.03	2.73	3.49	4.59	5.53	7.34	9.52	11.03	13.36	15.51	18.17	20.09	26.12
9	2.09	2.53	3.32	4.17	5.38	6.39	8.34	10.66	12.24	14.68	16.92	19.68	21.67	27.88
10	2.56	3.06	3.94	4.86	6.18	7.27	9.34	11.78	13.44	15.99	18.31	21.16	23.21	29.59
11	3.05	3.61	4.58	5.58	6.99	8.15	10.34	12.90	14.63	17.28	19.68	22.62	24.72	31.26
12	3.57	4.18	5.23	6.30	7.81	9.03	11.34	14.01	15.81	18.55	21.03	24.05	26.22	32.91
13	4.11	4.76	5.89	7.04	8.63	9.93	12.34	15.12	16.98	19.81	22.36	25.47	27.69	34.53
14	4.66	5.37	6.57	7.79	9.47	10.82	13.34	16.22	18.15	21.06	34.68	26.87	29.14	36.12
15	5.23	5.98	7.26	8.55	10.31	11.72	14.34	17.32	19.31	22.31	25.00	28.26	30.58	37.70
16	5.81	6.61	7.96	9.31	11.15	12.62	15.34	18.42	20.46	23.54	26.30	29.63	32.00	39.25
17	6.41	7.26	8.67	10.08	12.00	13.53	16.34	19.51	22.62	24.77	27.59	31.00	33.41	40.79
18	7.02	7.91	9.39	10.86	12.86	14.44	17.34	20.60	22.76	25.99	28.87	32.35	34.80	42.31
19	7.63	8.57	10.12	11.65	13.72	15.35	18.34	21.69	23.90	27.20	30.14	33.69	36.19	43.82
20	8.26	9.24	10.85	12.44	14.58	16.27	19.34	22.78	25.04	28.41	31.41	35.02	37.57	45.32
21	8.90	9.92	11.59	13.24	15.44	17.18	20.34	23.86	26.17	29.62	32.67	36.34	38.93	46.80
22	9.54	10.60	12.34	14.04	16.31	18.10	21.34	24.94	27.30	30.81	33.92	37.66	40.29	48.27
23	10.20	11.29	13.09	14.85	17.19	19.02	22.34	26.02	28.43	32.01	35.17	38.97	41.64	49.73
24	10.86	11.99	13.85	15.66	18.06	19.94	23.34	27.10	29.55	33.20	36.42	40.27	42.98	51.18
25	11.52	12.70	14.61	16.47	18.94	20.87	24.34	28.17	30.68	34.48	37.65	41.57	44.31	52.62
26	12.20	13.41	15.38	17.29	19.82	21.79	25.34	29.25	31.80	35.56	38.88	42.86	45.64	54.05
27	12.88	14.12	16.15	18.11	20.70	22.72	26.34	30.32	32.91	36.74	40.11	44.14	46.96	55.48
28	13.56	14.85	16.93	18.94	21.59	23.65	27.34	31.39	34.03	37.92	41.34	45.42	48.28	56.89
29	14.26	15.57	17.71	19.77	22.48	24.58	28.45	32.46	35.14	39.09	42.56	46.69	49.59	58.30
30	14.95	16.31	18.49	20.60	23.36	25.51	29.34	33.53	36.25	40.26	43.77	47.96	50.89	59.70

Source: Taken from Table IV of Fisher and Yates': *Statistical Tables for Biological, Agricultural and Medical Research* (6th Edition 1974) published by Longman Group UK Ltd. London (previously published by Oliver and Boyd Ltd, Edinburgh) and is reprinted by permission of the authors and publishers.

References

Altheide, D. L., & Johnson, J. M. (1998). Criteria for assessing interpretative validity in qualitative research. In N. K. Denzin & Y. S. Lincoln (Eds.) *Collecting and interpreting qualitative materials* (pp. 283–312). Thousand Oaks, CA: Sage.

American Educational Research Association. (1999). *Standards for educational and psychological tests*. Washington, DC: Author.

American Psychological Association. (1999). Statistical methods in psychology journals. *American Psychologist, 54(8)*, 594–604.

American Psychological Association. (2001). *Publication manual of the American Psychological Association* (5th ed.). Washington, DC: Author.

Audience Dialogue (2004, February 24). *Software for qualitative research* (pp. 1–8). Retrieved April 21, 2004 from http://www.audiencedialogue.org/soft-qual.html

Babbie, E. R. (1998). *The practice of social research*. (8th ed.). Belmont, CA: Wadsworth.

Bailey, J. S., & Burch, M. R. (2002). *Research methods in applied behavior analysis*. Thousand Oaks, CA: Sage.

Barlow, D. H., & Hersen, M. (1984). *Single case experimental designs: Strategies for studying behavior change*. New York: Pergamon.

Basit, T. (2003). Manual or electronic? The role of coding in qualitative data analysis. *Educational Research, 45*(2), 143–155.

Berg, B. L. (2004). *Qualitative research methods for the social sciences* (5th ed.). Thousand Oaks, CA: Sage.

Berliner, D. C. (2002). Educational research: The hardest science of all. *Educational Researcher, 31*(8), 18–20.

Best, S. J., & Krueger, B. S. (2004). *Internet data collection*. Thousand Oaks, CA: Sage.

Bogdan, R., & Biklen, S. K. (2003). *Qualitative research for education* (4th ed.). Boston: Allyn & Bacon.

Boraks, N., & Schumacher, S. (1981). *Ethnographic research on word recognition strategies of adult beginning readers: Technical Report*. Richmond: Virginia Commonwealth University, School of Education. (ERIC Document Reproduction Services No. ED207007)

Boruch, R. F., & Cecil, J. S. (1979). *Assuring the confidentiality of social research data*. Philadelphia: University of Pennsylvania Press.

Boston College. (2004, February 26). *Qualitative research software* (pp. 1–2). Retrieved April 21, 2004, from http://www.bc.edu/offices/ats/rits/research/software/descriptions/qualitative

Campbell, D. T., & Stanley, J. C. (1963). *Experimental and quasi-experimental designs for research*. Chicago: Rand, McNally.

Charmaz, K. (2000). Grounded theory: Objectivist and constructivist methods. In N. K. Denzin & Y.S. Lincoln (Eds.), *Handbook of qualitative research* (2nd ed., pp. 509–535). Thousand Oaks, CA: Sage.

Chicago manual of style (15th ed.). (2003). Chicago: The University of Chicago Press.

Christians, C. (2000). Ethics and politics in qualitative research. In N. K. Denzin & Y. S. Lincoln (Eds.), *Handbook of qualitative research* (2nd ed., pp. 133–155). Thousand Oaks, CA: Sage.

Clandinin, D. J., & Connelly, R. M. (2000). *Narrative inquiry: Experience and story in qualitative research*. San Francisco: Jossey-Bass.

Code of Federal Regulations for the Protection of Human Research Subjects. (2004). Office For Human Research Protections Code of Federal Regulations, Title 45: Public Welfare, Department of Health and Human Services, National Institutes of Health.

Cohen, J. (1988). *Statistical power analysis for the behavioral sciences*. Hillsdale, NJ: Erlbaum.

Comrey, A. L., Backer, T. E., & Glaser, E. M. (1973). *A sourcebook for mental health measures*. Los Angeles: Human Interaction Research Institute.

Connelly, F. M., & Clandinin, D. J. (1990). Stories of experience and narrative inquiry. *Educational Researcher, 19*(5), 2–14.

Conoley, J. C., & Kramer, J. J. (Eds.). (1989). *The tenth mental measurements yearbook*. Lincoln: University of Nebraska Press.

Cook, C., Heath, F., & Thompson, R. (2000). A meta-analysis of response rates in web or Internet-based surveys. *Educational and Psychological Measurement, 60*, 821–836.

Cook, T. D., & Campbell, D. T. (1979). *Quasi-experimentations: Design and analysis issues for field settings*. Chicago: Rand McNally.

Cooper, H. (1998). *Synthesizing research*. Beverly Hills: Sage.

Cousins, J. B., & Whitmore, E. (1998). Framing participatory evaluation. *New Directions for Evaluation, 80*, 5–23.

Creswell, J. W. (1998). *Qualitative inquiry and research design: Choosing among five traditions*. Thousand Oaks, CA: Sage.

Creswell, J. W. (2002). *Educational research: Planning, conducting, and evaluating quantitative and qualitative research*. Upper Saddle River, NJ: Merrill/Prentice-Hall.

Daniel, L. G. (1999). *A history of perceptions of the quality of educational research: issues and trends with implications for the teaching of educational research*. Paper presented at the annual meeting of the American Educational Research Association, San Diego, CA.

Denzin, N. K. (1997). *Interpretative ethnography: Ethnographic practices in the 21st century*. Thousand Oaks, CA: Sage.

Denzin, N. K., & Lincoln, Y. S., (Eds.) (2000). *Handbook of qualitative research* (2nd ed.). Thousand Oaks, CA: Sage.

Dexter, L. (1970). *Elite and specialized interviewing*. New York: Basic Books.

Dillman, D. (2000). *Mail and Internet surveys: The tailor-designed method* (2nd ed.). New York: Wiley.

Eisenhart, M., & Towne, L. (2003). Contestations and change in national policy on "Scientifically Based" educational research. *Educational Researcher, 32*(7), 31–38.

Erickson, F. (1973). What makes school ethnography "ethnographic?" *Anthropology and Education Quarterly, 9*, 58–69.

Erickson, F., & Gutierrez, K. (2002). Culture, rigor, and science in educational research. *Educational Researcher, 31*(8), 21–24.

Fabiano, E. (1989). *Index to tests used in educational dissertations*. Phoenix: Oryx Press.

Fetterman, D. M. (2000). *Foundations of empowerment evaluation: Step by step*. Thousand Oaks, CA: Sage.

Fine, M. (1998). Working the hyphens: Reinventing self and other in qualitative research. In N. Denzin & Y. Lincoln (Eds.), *The landscape of qualitative research* (pp. 130–155). Thousand Oaks, CA: Sage.

Finn, J. D., & Achilles, C. M. (1990). Answers and questions about class size: A statewide experiment. *American Educational Research Journal, 27*, 557–577.

Fitzpatrick, J. L., Sanders, J. R., & Worthen, B. R. (2004). *Program evaluation: Alternative approaches and practical guidelines* (3rd ed.). Boston: Allyn & Bacon.

Franklin, R. D., Allison, D. B., & Gorman, B. S. (1997). *Design and analysis of single case research*. Mahwah, NJ: Erlbaum.

Gall, M. D., Gall, J. P., & Borg, W. R. (2003). *Educational research: An introduction*. (7th ed.). Boston: Allyn & Bacon.

Gibbons, J. D. (1993). *Nonparametric statistics: An introduction*. Newbury Park, CA: Sage.

Giesne, C., & Peshkin, A. (1992). *Becoming qualitative researchers: An introduction*. New York: Longman.

Goldman, B., & Mitchell, D. (2002). *Directory of unpublished experimental mental measures*. (Vol. 8). Washington, DC: American Psychological Association.

Goodwin, W. L., & Driscoll, L. A. (1980). *Handbook for measurement and evaluation in early childhood education*. San Francisco: Jossey-Bass.

Gorden, R. (1981). *Interviewing: Strategies, techniques, and tactics*. Homewood, IL: Dorsey.

Green, J. C. (2000). Understanding social programs through evaluation. In N. K. Denzin & Y. S. Lincoln (Eds.), *Handbook of qualitative research* (2nd ed., pp. 981–999). Thousand Oaks, CA: Sage.

Greenberg, D., Meyer, R. H., & Wiseman, M. (1995). Multisite employment and training program evaluations: A tale of three studies. *Industrial and Labor Relations Review, 47*, 679–691.

Grele, R. J. (1996). Directions for oral history in the United States. In D. K. Dunway & W. K. Baum (Eds.), *Oral history: An interdisciplinary anthology* (pp. 60–75). Walnut Creek, CA: AltaMira.

Guba, E. G., & Lincoln, Y. S. (1989). Fourth generation evaluation. Beverly Hills, CA: Sage.

Halperin, S. (1978, March). *Teaching the limitations of the correlatin coefficient*. Paper presented at the annual meeting of the American Educational Research Association, Toronto.

Hersen, M., & Bellack, A. (1988). *Dictionary of behavioral assessment techniques*. New York: Pergamon.

Hopkins, K. D., & Gullickson, A. R. (1992). Response rates in survey research: A meta-analysis of the effects of monetary gratuities, *Journal of Experimental Education, 61*, 52–62.

House, E. R., & Howe, K. R. (2000, Spring). Deliberative democratic evaluation. In K. E. Ryan & L. DeStanfano (Eds.), *New directions for evaluation: Promoting inclusion, dialogue, and deliberation 85*(pp. 3–12). San Francisco: Jossey-Bass.

Hunter, J. E. (2004). *Methods of meta-analysis* (2nd ed.). Newbury Park: Sage.

Interviewer's manual. (1999). Ann Arbor: Survey Research Center, Institute for Social Research.

Johnson, O. G. (1976). *Tests and measurements in child development: Handbook II*. San Francisco: Jossey-Bass.

Joint Committee on Standards for Educational Evaluation (1994). *The program evaluation standards* (2nd ed.). Thousand Oaks, CA: Sage.

Kazdin, A. E. (1982). *Single case research designs: Methods for clinical and applied settings*. New York: Oxford University Press.

Kerlinger, F. N. (1979). *Behavioral research: A conceptual approach*. New York: Holt, Rinehart & Winston.

Kerlinger, F. N. (1986). *Foundations of behavioral research* (3rd ed.). New York: Holt, Rinehart & Winston.

Keyser, D. J., & Sweetland, R. C. (Eds.). (1984–94). *Test critiques*, (Vol. 1–10). Kansas City, MO: Test Corporation of America.

Kiecolt, K. J., & Natham, L. E. (1985). *Secondary analysis of survey data*. Beverly Hills, CA: Sage.

Kleinman, S., & Copp, M. A. (1993). *Emotions and fieldwork*. Newbury Park, CA: Sage.

Krueger, R. A., & Casey, M. A. (2000). *Focus group interviews: A practical guide for applied research* (3rd ed.). Thousand Oaks, CA: Sage.

Lather, P. (1991). *Getting smart: Feminist research and pedagogy with/in the postmodern*. New York: Routledge.

Lawrence, S., & Giles, C. L. (1999). Accessibility and distribution of information on the web. *Nature* 400(6740), 107–109.

LeCompte, M. D., & Preissle, J. (1993). *Ethnography and qualitative design in educational research*. (2nd ed.). San Diego: Academic Press.

Lincoln, Y. S. (1990). Toward a categorical imperative for qualitative research. In E. W. Eisner & A. Peshkin (Eds.), *Qualitative inquiry in education* (pp. 277–295). New York: Teachers College Press.

Lincoln, Y. S. (1995). *Emerging criteria for quality in qualitative and interpretive research*. Paper presented at the annual meeting of the American Education Research Association, San Francisco.

Lincoln, Y. S., & Guba, E. G. (1985). *Naturalistic inquiry*. Beverly Hills, CA: Sage.

MacBeth, D. (2001). On reflexivity in qualitative research. *Qualitative Inquiry, 7*(1), 35–68.

Maddox, J. (Ed.). (2003). *Tests: A comprehensive reference for assessments in psychology, education, and business* (10th ed.). Kansas City, MO: Test Corporation of America.

Malone, S. (2003). Ethics at home: Informed consent in your own backyard. *International Journal of Qualitative Studies in Education, 16*(6), 797–816.

Maltby, J., Lewis, C. A., & Hill, A. (Eds.). (2000). *Commissioned reviews of 250 psychological tests*. New York: E. Mellen.

Marascuilo, L. A., & McSweeney, M. (1977). *Nonparametric and distribution-free methods for the social sciences*. Monterey, CA: Brooks/Cole.

Marcus, G. E. (1998). What comes (just) after "post"?: The case of ethnography. In N. K. Denzin & Y. S. Lincoln (Eds.), *The landscape of qualitative research: Theories and issues*. (pp. 383–406). Thousand Oaks, CA: Sage.

Marshall, C., & Rossman, G. R. (1999). *Designing qualitative research* (3rd ed.). Newbury Park, CA: Sage.

Mason, J. (1996). *Qualitative researching*. Thousand Oaks, CA: Sage.

McMillan, J. H. (2000). *Educational research. Fundamentals for the consumer* (3rd ed.). New York: Longman.

McMillan, J. H. (2004, April). *Teachers' classroom assessment and grading practices decision making*. Paper presented at the Annual Meeting of the National Council of Measurement in Education, New Orleans.

Miller, D. C., & Salkind, N. J. (2002). *Handbook of research design and social measurement* (6th ed.). Newbury Park, CA: Sage.

Miller, J., McKenna, M., & McKenna, B. (1998). A comparison of alternatively and traditionally prepared teachers. *Journal of Teacher Education, 49*, 165–176.

Mills, G. E. (2003). *Action research: A guide for the teacher researcher* (2nd ed.). Upper Saddle River, NJ: Merrill/Prentice-Hall.

Moustakas, C. (1994). *Phenomenological research methods*. Thousand Oaks, CA: Sage.

Murphy, L. L., Plake, B. S., Impara, J. C., & Spies, R. A. (2002). *Tests in print VI*. Lincoln, NE: Buros Institute of Mental Measurements.

National Center for Educational Evaluation and Regional Assistance. (2004). *A new generation of rigorous evaluations* (pp. 1–4). Retrieved May 12, 2004, from http://www.ed.gov/print/rschstat/evid/resources/studyplans.html

National Commission on Excellence in Education. (1983). *A nation at risk: The imperative for educational reform*. Washington, DC: United States Department of Education.

National Research Council, Committee on Scientific Principles for Education Research. (2002). *Scientific research in education*. Washington, DC: National Academy Press.

Nord, D. P. (1998, September). Uses of memory: An introduction. *Journal of American History*, 409–410.

Oja, S. N., & Smulyan, L. (1989). *Collaborative action research: A developmental approach*. London, England: Falmer Press.

Osborn, J. W., & Overbay, A. (2004). The power of outliers (and why researchers should always check for them). *Practical Assessment, Research, and Evaluation*, 9(6). Retrieved June 5, 2004, from http://PAREonline.net/getvn.asp?v=9&n=6

Patton, M. Q. (1996). *Utilization-focuses evaluation* (3rd ed.). Thousand Oaks, CA: Sage.

Patton, M. Q. (2002). *Qualitative evaluation and evaluation methods* (3rd ed.). Thousand Oaks, CA: Sage.

Peshkin, A. (1993). The goodness of qualitative research. *Educational Researcher, 22*(2), 23–29.

Pillow, W. (2003). Confession, catharsis, or cure? Rethinking the uses of reflexivity as metholological power in qualitative research. *International Journal of Qualitative Studies in Education, 16*(2), 175–197.

Popham, W. J. (1981). *Modern educational measurement*. Englewood Cliffs, NJ: Prentice-Hall.

Punch, M. (1994). Politics and ethics in qualitative research. In N. K. Denzin & Y. S. Lincoln (Eds.), *Handbook of qualitative research* (pp. 83–97). Thousand Oaks, CA: Sage.

Reynolds, A. J., Temple, J. A., Robertson, D. L., & Mann, E. A. (2000). Age 21 cost-benefit analysis of the Title 1 Chicago child-parent centers. *Educational Evaluation and Policy Analysis, 24*(4), 267–303.

Richardson, L. (1998). Writing: A method of inquiry. In N. K. Denzin & Y. S. Lincoln (Eds.), *Collecting and interpreting qualitative research* (pp. 345–372). Thousand Oaks, CA: Sage.

Rist, R. C. (2000). Influencing a policy process with qualitative research. In N. K. Denzin & Y. S. Lincoln (Eds.), *Handbook of qualitative research* (2nd ed., pp. 1000–1017). Thousand Oaks, CA: Sage.

Rosenthal, R., & Jacobson, L. (1968). *Pygmalion in the classroom: Teacher expectation and pupil's intellectual development*. New York: Holt, Rinehart & Winston.

Rowntree, B. S. (1941). *Poverty and progress: A second social survey of York*. London: Longman, Green.

Rue, G., Dingley, C., & Bush. H. (2002). Inner strength in women. Metasynthesis of qualitative findings and theory development. *Journal of Theory Construction and Testing, 4* (2), 36–39.

Ryan, G. W., & Bernard, H. R. (2000). Data management and analysis methods. In N. K. Denzin & Y. S. Lincoln (Eds.), *Handbook of qualitative research: 2nd ed.*, (pp. 769–802). Thousand Oaks, CA: Sage

Schonlau, M., Fricker, Jr., R. D., & Elliot, M. N. (2002). *Conducting research surveys via e-mail and the web*. Santa Monica, CA: Rand.

Schumacher, S. (1984). *Evaluation of CoTEEP field-testing of workshop-seminar series and principles for summative evaluation*. Richmond: Virginia Commonwealth University, School of Education. (ERIC Document Reproduction Service No. ED252499)

Schumacher, S., & Esham, K. (1986). *Evaluation of a collaborative planning and development of school-based preservice and inservice education, Phase IV*. Richmond: Virginia Commonwealth University, School of Education. (ERIC Document Reproduction Services No. ED278659)

Schumacher, S., Esham, K., & Bauer, D. (1985). *Evaluation of a collaborative teacher education program: Planning, development and implementation, Phase III*. Richmond: Virginia Commonwealth University, School of Education. (ERIC Document Reproduction Service No. ED278659)

Schuman, H., & Presser, S. (1996). *Questions and answers: Experiments in the form, wording and context of survey questions*. Thousand Oaks, CA: Sage.

Schwandt, T. A. (2001). *Dictionary of qualitative inquiry* (2nd rev. ed.). Thousand Oaks, CA: Sage Publications.

Seidman, I. E. (1998). *Interviewing as qualitative research: A guide for researchers in education and the social sciences* (2nd ed.). New York: Teachers College Press.

Shadish, W. R., Cook, T. D., & Campbell, K. R. (2002). *Experimental and quasi-experimental designs for generalized causal inference*. Boston: Houghton Mifflin.

Shepard, L. A. (1993). Evaluating test validity. *Review of Research in Education, 19*, 405–450.

Siegel, S. (1956). *Nonparametric statistics for the behavioral sciences*. New York: McGraw-Hill.

Smith, J. K. (1993). *After the demise of empiricism: The problem of judging social and education inquiry*. Norwood, NJ: Ablex.

Smith, L. M. (1990). Ethics in qualitative field research: An individual perspective. In E. W. Eisner & A. Peshkin (Eds.), *Qualitative inquiry in education: The continuing debate* (pp. 258–276). New York: Teachers College Press.

Smith, M. L., & Shepard, L. A. (1988). Kindergarten readiness and retention: A qualitative study of teachers' beliefs and practices. *American Educational Research Journal, 25*(3), 298–325.

Spradley, J. P. (1979). *The ethnographic interview*. New York: Holt, Rinehart & Winston.

St. Pierre, E. A. (2002). "Science" rejects postmodernism. *Educational Researcher, 31*(8), 25–26.

Stake, R. E. (1975). *Program evaluation, particularly responsive evaluation*. Kalamazoo, MI, Evaluation Center, Western Michigan University. (Occasional Paper Series, No. 5.)

Stake, R. E. (1995). *The art of case study research*. Thousand Oaks, CA: Sage.

Stake, R. E. (2000). Case studies. In N. K. Denzin & Y. S. Lincoln (Eds.), *Handbook of qualitative research* (2nd ed., pp. 435–454). Thousand Oaks, CA: Sage.

Stinger, E. T. (1996). *Action research: A handbook for practitioners*. Thousand Oaks, CA: Sage.

Strauss, A., & Corbin, J. (1998). *Basics of qualitative research: Grounded theory procedures and techniques* (2nd ed.). Thousand Oaks, CA: Sage.

Stringer, E. (2004). *Action research in education*. Columbus, OH: Pearson Education.

Stufflebeam, D. L., Foley, W. J., Gepart, W. J., Guba, E. E., Hammond, R. L., Merriman, H. O., & Provus, M. (1971). *Educational evaluation and decision-making*. Itasca, IL: F. E. Peacock.

Stufflebeam, D. L., Madeus, G. F., & Kellaghan, T. (2000). *Evaluation models: Viewpoints on educational and human services evaluation*. (2nd ed.). Boston: Kluwer.

Tashakkori, A., & Teddlie, C. (1998). *Mixed methodology: Combining qualitative and quantitative approaches*. Thousand Oaks, CA: Sage. (Applied Social Research Methods Series No. 46)

Thompson, A. (1998, September). Fifty years on: An international perspective on oral history. *The Journal of American History*, 581–595.

Tobin, K., & LaMaster, S. U. (1995). Relationships between metaphors, beliefs, and actions in a context of science curriculum change, *Journal of Research in Science Teaching, 32*(3), 225–242.

Touliatos, J., Perlmutter, B. F., Straus, M. A., & Holden, G. W. (Eds.). (2000). *Handbook of family measurement techniques*. Newbury Park, CA: Sage.

Tuckman, G. (1998). Historical social science: Methodologies, methods, and meanings. In N. K. Denzin & Y. S. Lincoln (Eds.), *Strategies of qualitative inquiry* (pp. 225–260). Thousand Oakes, CA: Sage.

Van Manen, M. (1990). *Researching lived experience*. New York: State of New York Press.

Viadero, D. (1999, June 23), New priorities, focus sought for research. *Education Week, 18*(41), 1, 36–37.

Wainer, H., & Robinson, D. H. (2003). Shaping up the practice of null hypothesis significance testing. *Educational Researcher, 32*(7), 22–30.

Walker, D. K. (1973). *Sociomotional measures for preschool and kindergarten children*. San Francisco: Jossey-Bass.

Wax, R. H. (1971). *Doing fieldwork: Warnings and advice*. Chicago: University of Chicago Press.

Webb, E. J., Campbell, D. R., Schwartz, R. D., & Sechrest, L. (2000). *Unobtrusive measures* (rev. ed.). Thousand Oaks, CA: Sage.

Weiss, H. B., Mayer, E., Kreider, H., Vaughan, M., Dearing, E., Hencke, R., & Pinto, K. (2003). Making it work: Low-income working mothers' involvement in their children's education. *American Educational Research Journal, 40*(4), 879–901.

Weston, C., Gandell, T., Beauchamp, J., McAlpine, L., Wiseman, C., & Beauchamp, C. (2001). Analyzing Interview data: The development and evolution of a coding system. *Qualitative Sociology, 24*(3), 381–400.

Wijnberg, M. H., & Weinger, S. (1998). When dreams wither and resources fail: The social support systems of poor single mothers. *Journal of Contemporary Human Services, 79*(2), 212–223.

Wolcott, H. F. (1973). *The man in the principal's office: An ethnography*. New York: Holt, Rinehart & Winston.

Wolcott, H. F. (1995). *The art of fieldwork*. Walnut Creek, CA: AltaMira.

Wolcott, H. F. (1999). *Ethnography: A way of seeing*. Walnut Creek, CA: AltaMira.

World Health Organization (WHO). (2002). *Health behavior in school-aged children: 1997–1998 (United States)* [Computer file]. Calverton, MD: Macro International. (Distributed by Inter-University Consortium for Political and Social Research, University of Michigan, Ann Arbor)

Yin, R. K. (2004). *The case study anthology*. Thousand Oaks, CA: Sage Publications.

Name Index

Subject Index